Page 58: Para
    read Za(

Page 269: Paragraph 1, Line 3 Charuk should
    read **Zacharuk**

Page 153: Paragraph 3, Line 1- 1913 should
    read **1914**

Page 158: Paragraph 2, Line 7- 1913 should
    read **1914**

DREAM TO REALITY

Jerry,
Enjoy the read and the trip down memory lane.
George Tkachyk

―✦―

GEORGE TKACHYK

Order this book online at www.trafford.com
or email orders@trafford.com

Most Trafford titles are also available at major online book retailers.

© Copyright 2013 GEORGE TKACHYK.

All rights reserved. No part of this publication may be reproduced, stored in a retrieval system, or transmitted, in any form or by any means, electronic, mechanical, photocopying, recording, or otherwise, without the written prior permission of the author.

Printed in the United States of America.

ISBN: 978-1-4669-7383-1 (sc)
ISBN: 978-1-4669-7395-4 (e)

Trafford rev. 04/18/2013

 www.trafford.com

North America & international
toll-free: 1 888 232 4444 (USA & Canada)
phone: 250 383 6864 ♦ fax: 812 355 4082

CONTENTS

INTRODUCTION vii
ACKNOWLEDGEMENTS. xiii
DEDICATION xvii
UKRAINE. 1
YURI TKACZ. 6
ON TO A NEW WORLD 24
THE CANADIAN PACIFIC RAILWAY 55
BRINGING MARY HOME TO CANADA 72
THE GRONLID YEARS. 90
THE SONNINGDALE YEARS .122
THE KRYDOR YEARS 152
EDMONTON~THE RETIREMENT YEARS. 231
TO UKRAINE 245
TO CHERNIVTSI, KITSMAN AND UZHENETZ 252
THE GOLDEN YEARS. 262
EPILOGUE. 279
APPENDIX I   Initial Documents. 285
APPENDIX II Job Related Documents 297
BIBLIOGRAPHY 301

INTRODUCTION

Michael Tkaczyk was one of thousands of immigrants who came to Canada from a region that is today known as Ukraine. Ukraine's size and borders have changed many times over the centuries due to social and political changes in Eastern Europe. Historically, the people who emigrated to Canada from Western Ukraine were of Ukrainian origin but their country of origin was recorded differently at different times, due to political borders changing or occupation by foreign military powers. The ships' logs, personal passports and immigration documentation often listed Ukrainians' country of origin as Galicia, Ruthenia, Bukovina, Romania, Austria, Poland or Russia.

Michael's reason for coming to Canada was basically the same as everyone else's from that region. He wanted to make a better life for himself and his family. The reasons for leaving however, were as varied as the people themselves. They left their homeland for any or all of the following:

- for personal reasons;
- to escape oppression by military powers;

DREAM TO REALITY

That first wave of immigrants was enticed into coming to Canada by the Canadian Government's desire to settle the West. Immigrants were offered "Land Grants" under the Canadian Land Act of 1872 if the settlers stayed on the land for a period of 3 years, built a house and cleared and cultivated the prairie and parkland into crop producing farmlands. The Canadian Government succeeded in settling the West with this "homestead" policy, since with the production of a viable grain and cattle industry, the railroad network spread throughout the west to deliver the products to a North American and world market, and conversely to bring settlers west.

After the outbreak of the Great War in 1914 and including the inter-war period of the 1920's, immigration changed in that East Europeans were not readily allowed into Canada due to their potential allegiance to the Austro-Hungarian Empire. Sponsorship of immigrants was more strictly controlled for security reasons. This was the time period in which Michael came to Canada, thus it was more difficult to get established. One had to have more money to buy land in the settled areas and one had to get sponsored out of his/her country into Canada by a Canadian land owner who in effect was financially responsible for the immigrant. There were land grants available for immigrants who wanted to settle farther north in Manitoba, Saskatchewan and Alberta in areas such as the Peace River country.

Michael was fortunate to have planned out his personal affairs and acted on opportunities that became available to him. He eventually reached Canada to pursue his dream; a dream that was to become reality through hard work, perseverance and faith.

George Tkachyk

TRANSLITERATION

Transliteration is commonly referred to when words of one language are translated and transcribed into another language. This is particularly true of the Cyrillic alphabet since there are letters in the Cyrillic alphabet that have specific and distinct sounds and appearances. Translating those symbols and sounds into the English Language can be difficult. Names of people and place names are the most common examples of transliteration. In fact names of people can be a challenge to trace due to the changes in spelling.

In this biography the surname Tkaczyk is spelled in many different ways. The actual name is Tkach. In Romanian it is Tcaci, where the ci takes on the ch sound. In Polish the name is Tkacz, where the cz takes on the ch sound. The name can be Tkaczyk or Tkachyk to indicate the diminutive, or the name can be Tkaczuk or Tkachuk to indicate the superlative. Then again, it can be misspelled to Thachek, Thachuk, Thachyk, Tkatchyk, Tkatchuk, etc., as illustrated on documents in this biography.

> Note:
> The author, baptized and registered George Tkaczyk, used the name Tkachyk for convenience when writing

his grade twelve departmental exams in Saskatoon, and the name became common use after that. All of George's documents from universities and government agencies had been in use with the Tkachyk spelling. The official name change of Tkaczyk to Tkachyk occurred when a marriage license had to be applied for.

Cities often have their own transliteration problems. Kiev, Kiyev, Kyjiv, Kyiv are four spellings for the Capital City of Ukraine, taken from four different maps. (There are other spellings.)

Bukovina, Bukhovyna, Bukovyna today is a province of Ukraine. It was a region that was controlled by Austria, Romania, Russia and the Union of Soviet Socialist Republics, but was usually attached to Ukraine. Galicia or Halychyna was an area to the north of Bukovina that was controlled by Poland, Austria or Russia at different times in history.

In this writing most cases of using Ukrainian names and terms, a second word in parentheses is used to indicate transliteration for the first time.

ACKNOWLEDGEMENTS

The concept for this account of the life and times of my father, Michael Tkaczyk came about from family discussions about Dad's difficult and often traumatic times as a child in his native Ukraine. What started out as a request for the documentation of a few facts and photos, started to take on a life of its own, what with historical facts and accounts both written and verbal from family members. From that simple request for a few notes on my father's life, I started to accumulate larger amounts of information from family members such as documents, folders, history books, Dad's writings/notes, envelopes of photos, correspondence and various memorabilia that lay in filing cabinets, trunks, boxes and photo albums. Most of the items I remember seeing once, twice or several times and asking Dad about them as a child. We discussed the items in my adult years, and he related those accounts to me.

Dad/Dido in his humble, unassuming sort of way would have waved this project off as much ado about nothing. His claim would be that there were many others that came before him that experienced worse conditions, accomplished much more, and that he was only doing what had to be done for himself, and his family.

GEORGE TKACHYK

I have to thank my children Laurie, Dan and Rob who kept asking questions about Dido's past and were the impetus for starting this project.

Thanks to my sister Mary who lived and experienced a great deal of this biography. She shared with me, factual and first hand accounts of family life in Ukraine in the 1930's and her experiences in traveling to Canada and making a new start in a new country, adopting a new language, new customs, a new family and fulfilling part of Dad's dream. Her photos and frequent updates of information, before my memory banks as a child kicked in, were invaluable, as was her moral support for the project.

Thanks to brother-in-law Rev. Fr. Alex Hupka for proofreading and validating historical information.

Thanks to my sister Lessia, for her searching out of photos and documents from the vast collection that Dad and Mom accumulated and had in their possession, and for her collaboration on the many aspects of this document.

Thanks to niece Dorianne Slipchuk-Martyniuk who supplied the mini-biography that Dad wrote out for her in Ukrainian. It validated and clarified many of the accounts that he shared with Mary and me.

Thanks to nephew George Hupka who shared his filmed documentaries and verbal comments on his visits to Ukraine.

Last but not least, thanks to my wife Vera for her patience while I was glued to the computer for hours on end, searching for information, scanning photos and maps, or writing and formatting the document. This truly was an enjoyable experience for me, a labor of love, a trip down memory lane made even more memorable by the assistance and verbal and moral support from all of you.

George Tkachyk

DEDICATION

This book is dedicated to two people; Michael Tkaczyk and his daughter (my sister), Mary Tkaczyk who withstood hardships that most people only read about.

My father, Michael Tkaczyk grew up as a child at the end of the time period when feudal social structure was waning in what today is Ukraine. Class structure was still a determinant of one's place in society in the early 1900's. While the First World War raged and the Union Of Soviet Socialist Republics was developing, Soviet control of Bukovina was looming. Michael had to address delicate situations to allow himself a chance to get to Canada.

My sister Mary, at the age of five months, lost her birth mother to influenza. Michael had just arrived in Canada and was getting himself established. He couldn't immediately come back to Ukraine for Mary due to financial reasons and security reasons. Mary was looked after very well by her aunts and maternal grandmother in the interim, but Mary yearned for a parent. Michael in the meanwhile, was attaining his citizenship and trying to earn enough money to go back to Ukraine and bring Mary to Canada.

GEORGE TKACHYK

The interwar years in Bukovina were extremely trying with political posturing between Romania and Soviet Russia over who was to control Bukovina, and the Soviets orchestrating the 1932-33 Holodomor in Ukraine. However, at age 4 and 5, Mary was shielded from the horrors of the "Holodomor" (the orchestrated death by famine) by her relatives and the political stalemate between Romania and Russia over the political control of Bukovina. Mary, at age seven, in 1935, was brought to Canada by Michael, where she immediately became a Canadian citizen.

In Ukraine, Michael and Mary lived through horrendous times in history, yet when they arrived in Canada, they adjusted to a new country, new lifestyles and a new family. They made the best of their opportunities. But they could not have done it alone and without hard work.

They had supportive families in Ukraine—the Tkaczs or Tkaczyks, the Hryhirchuks, the Kotyks and the Klewchuks, many who are long ago deceased. A great thank you is due to them for their courage, strength, stamina, and faith in supporting Mary and Michael in their quest for a better life in Canada.

Then there was the support of the Canadian families. George, Nick and William Kotyk, Michael's brothers-in-law who assisted Michael in getting to Canada and helping him get started with jobs in the early years of 1928-1940.

In Canada, after Michael and Mary were settled, the Pohoreskis, Panchuks, Dobrowolskys, and Patricks provided the family support, acceptance, and camaraderie that was paramount in Michael's and Mary's success, and the fulfillment of Michael's dream.

1

UKRAINE: May 2, 1928

Tears welled up in his eyes as the train pulled out of the railway station. It was May 2, 1928, and Michael Tkaczyk, age 26, was leaving his home, his village of Uzhentsi (Uzhenetz) in Bukovina, Western Ukraine. But most of all, he was leaving his family, all be it for a short time, at least that was his initial intention. His family had gathered on the station platform in Chernivtsi to bid their good-byes and good wishes. Foremost among the large family gathering were his wife Parascheva (Paraska) and their firstborn child Maria (Mary), two months old.

It had been a difficult decision to temporarily leave his family, travel to a foreign land to start a new life, then return to bring his family back, but it had to be done. Leaving his wife and two month old daughter Maria (Mary), their first child, was not easy, but what other choice did Michael have? Timing was crucial. He may not get another chance at this new life and an opportunity for freedom, independence and prosperity. The offer of sponsorship to Canada was in place, as was financial assistance. His ticket had been pre-paid by his brother-in-law

Bill Kotyk who was already in Canada. The political situation in Eastern Europe, Ukraine in particular, was brittle at best. The time limit on the ticket was ten days and he just made the time line. Others from his village and surrounding communities had travelled to Canada before him, in fact, his father had been to Canada in 1898 and again in the early 1900's, and had come back to bring his family over to Canada but had been trapped in his native Ukraine upon his return, by the politics and the political turmoil of the time. His father couldn't get the proper documentation for himself and the rest of his family. The stories that Michael's father told him about the new land Canada, were just too intriguing and too enticing to Michael and now was the appropriate time to strike out on this new venture for himself and his family.

Michael had been corresponding with his brothers-in-law Nick and Bill (William) Kotyk who had immigrated to Canada several years earlier. Nick had been in Canada since 1914 and had his Canadian citizenship. Since he had not yet purchased land, and one had to be a land owner to sponsor immigrants, Nick would assist in locating sponsors for the new emegres. Nick had already maximized his sponsorship capabilities, since he had sponsored his sister Mafta to come to Canada in 1921. He sponsored his brother Bill who came in 1924, and was presently in the process of sponsoring his brother George to come to Canada. Therefore, Bill had arranged the transportation fares and the sponsorship to Canada for Michael. Bill had been working for the Canadian Pacific Railroad and was financially stable enough to lend Michael the money for ship passage, but he did not have his Canadian citizenship. In addition, Bill had to be a landowner to sponsor Michael so that he could guarantee employment to the new landed immigrant. Since Bill had not yet been able to purchase land, he sought out the assistance of a landowner by the name of Thomas

DREAM TO REALITY

Kuryliuk, who was a Canadian citizen, to sponsor Michael. Thomas Kuryliuk came from "Stavchany", the village from where the Kotyks came, and a neighboring village to the east of Uzhenetz. The Kuryliuks had a farm at Wroxton, a small farming community which was 42 kilometers east of Yorkton, Saskatchewan. The Kuryliuks could provide several months work during the spring planting, summer haying and autumn harvest. Michael would have a start financially and then be on his own to find work elsewhere. For many in politically and economically deprived Eastern Europe, this was the only way out of a desperate situation. Getting help financially and being sponsored was a great asset and Michael was not about to let it slip through his grasp. As mentioned previously, being sponsored as an immigrant to Canada at this time required a registered landowner to sponsor the immigrant so that he would have a place to stay and so that he would be employed by the landowner. While the Canadian Government wanted reliable immigrants to settle this country, they had not yet developed the social safety nets of today to support the newly landed immigrants. Agricultural enterprises required a great deal of manual labor, since mechanization as we know it today, was to make its appearance in the 1940's and later. Thus the need for manual labor was the logical sponsorship vehicle that would settle Canada's West. Ukrainians from the Bukovina region as well as other regions of Ukraine were most eager to get to Canada, since the first wave of immigration in the late 1890's and early 1900's were successful in setting up farms, small lumber mills and getting employed in various labor intensive ventures such as railroading and mining. However, in the 1920's and 1930's, immigrants required sponsorship by relatives or Canadian citizens, and this was not always easy to come by. Most Ukrainian Canadians were besieged for sponsorships, and by the mid 1930's the Canadian government had narrowed sponsorships down to immediate family only.

GEORGE TKACHYK

Michael had made the right moves strategically and politically within his region of Ukraine. He made sure that he would procure the appropriate documentation to get out of Bukovina. It was impossible to get the documentation from the Russian authorities, thus he had to work the system properly to obtain the documentation from the Romanian Government that was in control of Bukovina at the time. Other Ukrainians north of Uzhenetz had to get their documentation from Poland or in previous years from Austria. Russia was not a forward thinking country either under the Czars or under the communists. While they were bickering with neighboring states over control of the regions, the population was slowly leaving the country. The Czars were only interested in feudal control and riches for themselves and their inner circle. The communists were so self centered they tried to force the freedom loving population to accept their socialist ideas by force. People were trying to escape in droves and the West was the obvious choice of destination.

Michael's planning was not in vain. This was not a spur of the moment decision. He was going to carve out a new life for his family and himself in a land of promise. He had heard enough promising things about Canada from his father and others. With the political situation in flux and deteriorating by the day, this might be his only chance to leave Bukovina. All he needed was someone to sponsor him to Canada. As it turned out he made the right moves at the right time.

Michael had convinced his family that he would go to Canada, get employment, save enough money, obtain his Canadian citizenship and as a sponsor bring them all back to Canada

DREAM TO REALITY

for a more rewarding and stable life. Canadian citizenship was the key since political regimes in Eastern Europe could not then interfere with his residency or movements. He could then sponsor family members to Canada. Reluctantly, Paraska and the family gave Michael their blessing and he prepared to venture into a new world.

2

YURI TKACZ

Michael's father, Yuri (George), had been to Canada and back to Bukovina, twice in the years spanning 1898-1907, but the conditions for immigrants during this first wave of immigration were very primitive. Sod huts, not much better than caves and cold winters took their toll on human lives in the early years of settlement. The railway companies due to the opening of the West and the North of Canada employed many of the immigrants as laborers laying the branch railroad lines through the Prairie Provinces. Workers on the railroad were housed in bunkhouses on rails. The practice of cramming 40 to 50 men into a bunkhouse and eating in cookhouses on rails was common in early railroad construction. This was hardly a lifestyle for a family. Then there was the "Canada Land Act" or "Land Grants" where for a fee of $10.00, immigrants were allowed to take out a homestead (a quarter section of land, 160 acres of wooded prairie or northland). This quarter section of land was ½ mile square and was given to the homesteader with clear title if he lived on it for three years, cleared 30 acres or more and built a dwelling on the land. Ten dollars was a lot of money at the turn of the century, especially when a person's wages working for the railroad was anywhere up to five dollars a week, then you had to pay for food and lodging and your personal expenses. There were also the gamblers, con artists and other undesirables that were ready to take the hard earned pay from an unsuspecting newcomer. The Land Grant offering of 160 acres of land was just too enticing for the Ukrainian immigrant to pass up and an unheard of land holding for a peasant from Bukovina.

Yuri's hope was to earn enough money working as a laborer on the railroad to bring his family to Canada and then start up a homestead. Even with the harsh conditions that he endured, Yuri was prepared to bring his family to Canada. But when he returned to Ukraine in 1900, he found that getting the proper documentation such as passports, visas and financing for his family was near impossible due to the bureaucratic and economic nightmare that Ukraine was undergoing. In addition, the money that Yuri had sent back to his wife Maria was spent on acquiring additional land and paying off the back taxes on their inheritances of two hectares of land. In the meantime there were rumblings of discontent with the Czarist regime in neighboring Russia. The working people and the peasants were preparing to revolt against the Czarist regime of the Romanovs and this was spilling over into neighboring countries and thus affecting Ukraine. With the end of the feudal system in 1848, the serfs were technically free people but in reality they had gained little. They were not indentured to the Aristocrat or the land, but they still worked for the Aristocracy at subsistence wages or less, and were not making any social or economic progress. Uprisings of peasant workers were everywhere in Eastern Europe.

In addition, Yuri's family, immediate and extended, were not quite convinced that a wholesale move to Canada was in everybody's best interest. Some of Yuri's extended family owned a few hectares of land as did Yuri and Maria. Maria's side of the family planned to expand their meager land holdings. They convinced Yuri to put his plans on hold even though conditions were marginal and deteriorating in Bukovina. The family had hopes that conditions would improve. Besides living under the power of the Pahneh (Pahn, landlord), and the Czars of Russia was not all bad for some. Subsistence living was not new to the peasants of Eastern Europe and for some this lot in life was adequate and accepted. However, there was always that hope and vision that one day Bukovina would be free of its oppressors.

The feudal system, while it declined or disappeared altogether in many parts of Europe, still existed in some form in Eastern Europe. The western part of Ukraine was still in the grips of the feudal system and landownership was limited to the chosen or privileged few. Michael's parents were poor. His father Yuri was orphaned at age three from his mother and at age twelve by his father. Yuri was fortunate to have been taken in by an uncle on his mother's side, Dmytro Hnachuk (Hnatiuk). As a twelve year old boy, Yuri's only life skills were that of a sheepherder, a keeper of cattle and fowl. His only good fortune was that he had been left one hectare of land from his mother's inheritance (estate), and that his uncle Dmytro passed it on to him when Yuri got older. In the 1850's to the early 1900's land holdings were for the rich and privileged, so to own a meager one hectare of land was significant in itself. Yuri was fortunate that his benevolent uncle helped look after him and protected the land holding until he was at the age of majority.

> Note: A hectare of land is approximately the size of two football fields goal line to goal line—100m x 100m.

DREAM TO REALITY

Over the next ten years Yuri grew up working for his uncle herding the few animals his uncle owned, plus gardening on his personal one hectare of land. It was difficult to accumulate any wealth to purchase more land since the one hectare produced only enough food for subsistence. When Yuri married Maria Hryhirchuk, Maria was given one hectare of land as a dowry, but even with two hectares of land Yuri had to work for other landowners to earn extra money to survive. Living off two hectares of land was barely subsistence level living. They could not accumulate enough wealth to purchase more land or more livestock at this rate, and that is what the feudal system was all about—a rigid class, social and economic structure.

When Yuri went to Canada in the late 1890's to earn some money building the railroads in The North West Territories (Saskatchewan and Alberta), that was the only real surplus income Maria and Yuri had. Yuri sent money to Maria with regularity. Maria in the meantime was using the money to buy additional hectares of land. Soon they had about seven hectares of land and this became sufficient to provide all the food that was required for the family—fruit, vegetables, livestock, chickens, ducks and geese. Any extra money to be made was at the mercy of the Pahneh when they needed farm labor. Life was harsh and simple, but the basic human needs were met. Families lived in one or two room log homes or huts with mud and straw mixed together to plaster the spaces between the logs and boards. Roofs were grass or straw thatched into bundles and woven through thin wood stringers. The interior and exterior walls were whitewashed with lime to make a bright white interior and exterior. Farm animals and fowl lived in an attached lean-to structure.

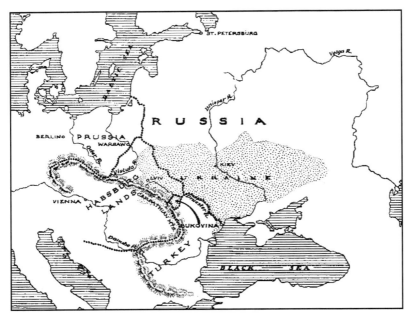

Ukrainian Lands in the Eighteenth Century after the
Polish Partitions (1795) Showing Boundaries between Russia,
Prussia, Habsburg Lands (Austria) and Turkey.
Source: Simpson: UKRAINE, An Atlas of Its History and Geography.

Conditions were primitive to say the least. A large built-in clay oven (a peech or pyetz) was the stove, oven and heating system for the house. Since bread was the major food item, a baking device such as the pyetz was preferred to a flat topped stove. The oven would be used to heat or bake other foods as well as bread, thus it was a more functional "appliance", plus it was made of clay, an inexpensive and readily available commodity. Michael and his siblings slept on the warm flat top of the pyetz on straw or hay filled ticks during cool or cold nights, since the pyetz retained heat from the days baking and cooking. Village Life centered on the local Church and school with folk songs, folk dancing, liturgical and Church commitments being the main focus of activity. The local priest (Paroch) was instrumental in teaching the families to read and write

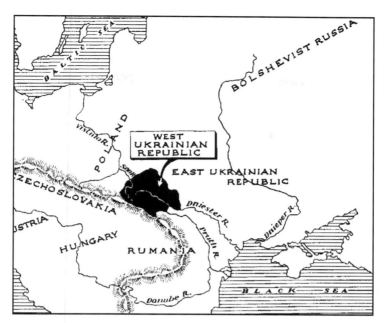

The West Ukrainian National Republic as Established by the Ukrainian National Council in Galicia, November 1, 1918
Source: Simpson, UKRAINE, an Atlas of Its History and Geography

through religious instruction and church services at the local church. Formal schools were private institutions for the most part. Public schools were in their primitive stage of development.

Little did Yuri know that the growing unrest in the early 1900's in neighboring Russia was going to explode into a full scale revolution that would affect Ukraine directly, and his plans to take his family to Canada. The Bolsheviks were gaining popularity in Russia, and the Czarist Regime would come crashing down in 1905 with the overthrow and execution of Czar Nicholas and his family. The years following the Czarist overthrow were thirteen years of internal strife and civil war with the Bolsheviks eventually gaining control in 1918. The Bolshevik promise of a great new political structure was that all commoners would gain from the fall of the Czarist regime and aristocratic control would cease to exist. Land ownership would be available to all who wanted it. This was too good to be true to the Russian and Ukrainian peasantry. This revolution within the borders of Russia affected the neighboring countries. The Ukrainian people could see an opportunity to enjoy their own independent state, if they could take advantage of the political turmoil of a revolution in Czarist Russia, and create their own government and not be under the yoke of an oppressive ruler.

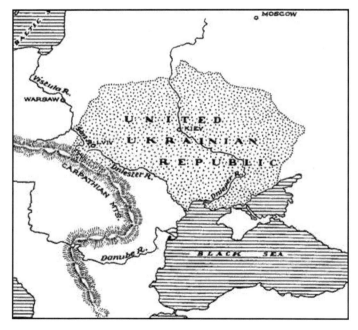

United Ukrainian Republic as Proclaimed January 22, 1919.
Source: Simpson, UKRAINE, an Atlas of Its History and Geography

The years between 1918 and 1938 were ones of constant turmoil with Ukraine setting up a provisional government and the Bolsheviks/Communists supporting certain factions that were socialist leaning. Eventually Ukraine was overthrown and became a state within the Union of Soviet Socialist Republics. An independent Ukraine did not materialize.

Landlords loyal to the Czarist regime and a fractured leadership among the various regions of Ukraine could not form a common and united front. The Bolsheviks were intent on spreading their propaganda throughout Ukraine and were successful in convincing many regions to support their cause. Many uneducated peasants, hungry for freedom and land saw this opportunity to rid themselves of the Czarist regime and any vestiges of feudalism. However, they never really achieved that freedom and personal independence since Bolshevism gave way to Soviet style Communism that eventually devastated Ukraine economically, socially and politically, eventually killing more than 10 million people in the "Holodomor" or Great Famine. While Lenin had offered the Ukrainian People a form of land ownership but under a socialistic state, Stalin in his ruthless method of taking absolute control and putting down any form of Ukrainian Nationalism, instituted collectivization of all farms and farm products and at all cost to human life. Bukovina being at the southwestern edge of Ukraine was the buffer zone between Romania, Czechoslovakia, Austria, Poland and Russia. The Poles and the Romanians for the next two decades would fiercely defend their borders from the Bolsheviks and the Soviets, but they too would eventually succumb to the Soviets. Romania would administer Bukovina to 1940 when the Soviets brutally evicted them through massacres and forced evacuation. The Soviets were masters at ethnic cleansing, eradicating any and all opposition through mass murder and famine. The three preceding maps indicate the political posturing, turmoil and takeovers with the redrawing of political boundaries in Eastern

Europe and Ukraine during the 18th century, 19th century and the early 20th century.

In 1902, in the village of Uzhenetz, province of Bukovina, Michael Tkacz was the first born to Yuri (or as the Romanians called him Gheorge, George in English) and Maria (nee: Hryhirchuk) Tkacz (Tkaczyk, Tkachyk). Michael was the eldest of four children—Maria, Ivan (Eevahn) and youngest sister Zoya. Michael had two additional younger sisters; however they succumbed along with their mother Maria, to an influenza outbreak in the years 1918-1921. The death rates in these poorer regions of Eastern Europe were high with little or no medical attention available to the common people. Immunization was a relatively new medical development at the time and influenza outbreaks were common, and when they struck, they stuck with a vengeance.

The name Tkacz and its various derivatives was a common name in Bukovina and Western Ukraine. The word tkach means weaver. By adding the "yk" ending, Tkaczyk takes on the diminutive form and with the "uk" ending the name Tkaczuk takes on the superlative form. Thus Tkaczyk becomes a weaver on a small scale and a Tkaczuk becomes a weaver on a large scale. The diminutive or superlative could refer to a physically small or a physically large person as well. According to Michael's recollection, weaving was of a utilitarian nature and there were no large scale commercial weavers in his family. Neither Michael nor any of his family members were physically huge people, thus Tkaczyk seemed an appropriate name. There were various spellings of the name as well, depending on the region you came from. The

Romanians spelled the name as Tcaci, the poles used a "cz" for the ch, and thus the name became Tkaczyk. Throughout this biography the name will be spelled in various ways. Documents, be they citizenship papers, passports, ship manifests, or employment documents will portray the name with its various spellings.

Yuri returned to Canada in March of 1903, five months after the birth of Michael. He was determined to continue his quest for a better life for his family. He worked for the Canadian Pacific Railway in Saskatchewan along with many of his countrymen with same hopes and dreams of building a better future for their families. Due to the Bolshevik Revolution in October, 1905, and the subsequent military upheaval in his home country, he decided to return to Bukovina to be with his family and protect his family and meager land holdings. He came back to Bukovina in 1907 with hopes of taking his family out of Ukraine and back to Canada. The military activity of the Russian Imperial Army, the Bolshevik revolutionaries, the Austrians, Poles and Romanians was constant in the area around Chernivtsi and north to Lviv. Control of the rail lines was crucial and the two major cities were key centers of control. The Bolsheviks were intent on trying to gain as much power and land as they could. Yuri's family was in constant danger since they were 20 kilometers from Chernivtsi and on the floodplain between the Dniester and Pruth Rivers. The Russians would raid the peasants for food and draft animals and severely abuse the citizenry in the process.

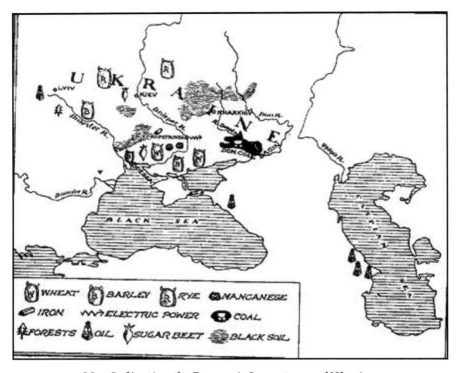

Map Indicating the Economic Importance of Ukraine.
Source: Simpson, UKRAINE, an Atlas of Its History and Geography

When Yuri returned he was a virtual stranger to Michael, age five. He left when Michael was a baby and hadn't written to them while he was away. Michael had a difficult time adjusting to this "new" male in the household. Michael literally grew up with his mother, grandfather Hryhirchuk and aunts who lived nearby. Being raised without a father in the household during the five years of his young life along with the trauma that the family faced with the marauding Russians plundering, raping and killing villagers, Michael took a few years to warm up to a father that he really didn't know.

DREAM TO REALITY

Yuri delayed his return to Canada, but after 1907 it was too late. He had not stayed in Canada long enough in consecutive years to become a Canadian citizen, therefore he had to depend on his Ukrainian citizenship. He could not get Ukrainian passports, visas or any appropriate documentation for his family since the Bolshevik military and political upheaval drove the bureaucratic system to a halt. Demographic records were either lost or destroyed. Bickering and indecision over who had the records, or who had authority to approve and grant records was constant. Birth, death and marriage records were not always available. Civic law was in a shambles, thus occupying forces would have to create citizenship records from local priests or village elders. During the Bolshevik Revolution and subsequent rule, emigration was at a virtual standstill unless one took it upon one's self to escape under cover of darkness to neighboring countries such as Romania or Poland and ask for political asylum; or you had to hold some form of document legitimizing your relation to another country such as Poland or Romania. Russian citizenship was out of the question. Borders were closely watched. The Bolsheviks did not want people leaving since they needed a labor force or they wanted to conscript males into their military. If you made it known that you wanted to leave, the Bolsheviks treated you as a traitor and you were taken to a forced labor camp or executed. On the other hand, the bordering countries did not want refugees because they became a burden on the government.

Yuri's hopes of starting a new life in Canada for his family were dashed.

Life in Ukraine from 1905 onward was chaotic at best. The Bolsheviks were attempting to take over all of Ukraine and were expanding into Poland and Romania. They already had taken over Lithuania, Estonia, Latvia and Byelorussia to the north of Ukraine. The Bolsheviks next attempted conquest was Poland, Ukraine and Romania for the rich farmlands and forested regions to the west, and rich mineral and petroleum laden areas to the south and east. As well, the Bolsheviks wanted to control the strategic Dniester, Dnieper, Donets and Volga River basins, as well as Black Sea access. Russia did not have a convenient year-round port except for St. Petersburg on the Baltic Sea. Murmansk on the Arctic Ocean had severe weather limitations and then there was Vladivostok on the Pacific Ocean. It was a port that was ice free all year, but there was a distance and geographic problem. Building a railroad to sustain travel through a barren wasteland of Siberian tundra, muskeg, swamp, forest, desert and mountain was a monumental task yet to be completed. Ukraine was to become Russia's strategic conquest. The Austrians, Romanians and Poles did not want to see Russia as their neighbor and were desperate to keep Ukraine as a buffer state between themselves and Russia. The Poles and Romanians were consistent in their efforts to drive the Russians back from their frontiers. Consequently, Romanian military forces were a common sight in the Bukovina region as they attempted to drive the Russian invaders back to the northern border of Ukraine. In fact the Romanians conducted much of the administrative work in Bukovina in the early 1920's carrying

DREAM TO REALITY

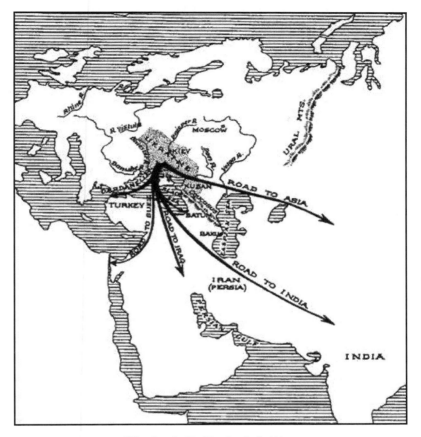

Ukraine in its Strategic Setting.

Source: Simpson, UKRAINE, An Atlas of Its History and Geography

out census taking, administering civil law and constructing roads and bridges where it was conducive to trade, transport and military needs.

In the years leading up to 1928, Ukraine did not hold many possibilities for the future of its young people. The Soviet Union was becoming established. Ukraine was slated to become a state of the Union of Soviet Socialist Republics, and as such emigration would be effectively non-existent with the dread "Iron Curtain" in place. While the communists touted their classless society, where everyone would be equal and benefit from the state collectivization of farms and with state controlling all economics, education, health, politics and civic affairs of the country, it was everything but a classless society. The bureaucratic structure became the new class system with graft, corruption, patronizing and favoritism ruling. Religion was outlawed. Religion had no place in communist society. Severe limitations were placed on the Russian Orthodox Church except for one power move. The Russian patriarchy had control of the Ukrainian Orthodox Church since the mid 1600's. The Soviets were so concerned that within a Ukrainian Patriarchy, a Ukrainian nationalistic revival might occur, that they outlawed the Ukrainian Orthodox Church hierarchical structure, many of whom were executed. The Ukrainian Catholic or Uniate Church still existed in Western Ukraine in the Lviv area and on to the Polish border. The Soviets knew that the religious faith of the Ukrainian people played a critical role in their existence, and in order to exercise greater control over the faithful masses the Soviets placed "puppet" Russian hierarchs to control the Ukrainian Orthodox Church. Since the Orthodox Church played a critically important role in the social and religious aspects of Ukrainian life, the entire fabric of society was altered under the Soviet take-over. Michael and others like him could see no future in the oppressive, monolithic Soviet political system.

Central Europe in the Interwar years, 1923-1938 Showing the Boundaries between The Soviet Union, Romania, Poland, and Czechoslovakia, and Indicating the Ukrainian Areas in Each of These Countries. Source: Simpson, UKRAINE, An Atlas of Its History and Geography.

Ukrainians throughout history have loved their freedom and fought for it through military, diplomatic, intellectual, literary and peaceful means. The yoke of communism was all too evident to Michael and with world politics as they were following the Great war of 1914-1918, Western Europe was more concerned with its own affairs and the rise of fascism. Conditions in Ukraine would not change for the better, in fact they were to deteriorate very quickly under communist rule.

Areas in Eastern Europe Seized by The Soviet Union September, 1939 to July, 1940. Source: Simpson, *UKRAINE, An Atlas of its History and Geography.*

Michael could see that the future was not about to provide a bounty of opportunities to a young family. There was not much land to sub-divide among himself and his three younger siblings, Maria, Ivan and Zoya. While in a male dominated society, the land would be divided between his brother Ivan and himself, with small portions reserved for the two sisters' dowries. His sisters would basically have to depend on their future husbands' inheritances. Buying land at this time was near impossible. Land to purchase was scarce and money more so. The Tkacz's land holdings of eight hectares were barely enough to feed the family, let alone provide produce and goods to sell on the open market to accumulate any wealth. At best the majority of people in Ukraine were subject to a subsistence economy. Education beyond the elementary school years was available only to the rich and privileged, the families of the Pahneh. Industrialization had not yet reached the farmlands of Western Ukraine, thus agriculture was still in a primitive state. Horses and other draft animals or humans pulled ploughs. Crops were hand seeded, hand harvested and hand milled. There were only a few millers associated with the large land owners who operated wind, water or animal driven mills. Families were still subject to a ruling class, but the ruling class was changing. It was changing to a brutal self serving Bolshevik, soon to be a Soviet Communist government.

The future for Ukraine looked bleak and the stories of the new world seemed so promising.

3

ON TO A NEW WORLD

Michael was fortunate to go school as a young child and loved his formal schooling. By age 12, in 1914 the Great War had broken out and young Michael's schooling came to an abrupt end. He had completed the fifth class in Ukrainian and the fourth class in German, since Austria was an occupying force and an adjoining country. He also learned other languages informally—Russian, Romanian, Hungarian, and Polish; all these languages were necessary due to military occupation or border proximity.

The years of 1912-1918 were disastrous for Michael and his family. The Bolshevik Revolution was in high gear. The Great War broke out in 1914, gradually involving all of the European countries and Asia Minor, and extended through to 1918. Military activity in Bukovina was at its highest ebb at this time. During the four years of the Great War, the Russian Front moved through the Bukovina region to the Carpathian Mountains and back again three times, while trying to push the Austrians and Hungarians out. The land on which Michael's family lived was on a flood plain of fruitful fields of grain, orchards and ponds between the Dniester and Pruth Rivers. During those years of the war the land was devastated—crops and orchards ruined, buildings destroyed, property stolen and the Ukrainian people brutally treated and abused by the Russians. The Russians employed a war tactic called "The Scorched Earth Policy" that prevented their pursuers from gaining any advantage through food or wealth accumulation. The Russian train of thought was, "If we can't have it, no one will have it", and they laid waste throughout the Bukovinan countryside. The Russians were very good at this tactic. They were certainly short on diplomacy, but strong on destruction and brutality. The Austrians, on the other hand, true to the Habsburg tradition, were strong on diplomacy and won the favor and the hearts of the Ukrainians by actually helping the villagers procure food, rebuild homes, farms and roads.

During the war years, well into 1916, Michael by the age of 14 had been used along with the family horses and wagon to deliver goods and supplies to the Russian soldiers at the Russian front lines of battle. Before long the Russians stole the horses from Michael and set him to dig trenches for the Russian troops on the front lines. Children aged 10 and up were forced to dig trenches and fox holes while artillery and rifle fire exploded around them. The Russians were risking children's lives to protect their own. Michael never forgot those dreadful years or the ruthless Russian oppressors who abused the population, caused death, misery and hardship to all.

The face of Europe and Asia Minor changed drastically in the years leading up to the Great War, during the war years and following the war years. By 1917, not only was Russia involved in the Great War, but the revolution within Russia was raging with the Bolsheviks attempting and succeeding in the takeovers from aristocratic gentry in all regions of the Russian sphere of influence. Civil war was also brewing in Austria, Hungary, and Germany and within the Ottoman Empire in Turkey, the Balkans and the Middle east. The four large Imperial Powers, Russia, Austria, Germany and Turkey were crumbling from within as well as being attacked from outside their borders. Out of four large Imperial Nations, there was a myriad of countries trying to establish or re-establish themselves and were waging war on one another, or trying to formulate alliances to gain control of their regions. It was chaotic at best. In 1918 Ukraine formed one of several provisional governments under Simon Petlura, however that did not last long. Soon Michael's Ukraine was divided up among neighboring states with Romania annexing Bukovina in 1920.

Other tragedies struck Michael's family on three different occasions. First, Michael's two youngest sisters died during an influenza epidemic in 1918-1921. Then his mother, Maria succumbed to the wave of Spanish Influenza that hit Eastern Europe in late 1918. Thus at age 16, Michael, being the eldest child was instrumental in raising his three younger siblings, Maria, Ivan and Zoya, and helping his father support the family. Michael farmed the small land holding with his father following the war in 1918. Western Ukraine had been split up among neighboring countries. When Simon Petlura's attempt at forming a national Ukrainian government failed in 1918, Ukraine was divided up with border states being ceded to Russian friendly countries with central and Eastern Ukraine under the firm grip of the Russian Bolsheviks. Poland occupied the northwestern portion of Ukraine from Belarus south to Lviv and all of Galicia. Romania controlled the south western portion, primarily Bukovina. When Michael turned 22, he was drafted into the Romanian Army to assist the Engineering Corps in rebuilding roads, bridges and railway lines that had been destroyed during the Great War. He served in the

Romanian Military for two years. This was negative in that he worked for little or no pay. It was primarily subsistence pay or its equivalent—food and lodging. However, on the positive side, being in the army entitled Michael to become a Romanian National, that is he could apply for and receive Romanian citizenship, and receive a Romanian passport. This would allow him the freedom to leave the country. He had been planning a Romanian passport acquisition, but his Romanian military status would speed the process up. Had Bukovina been under Russian occupation, Michael's passport acquisition would have been out of the question entirely. There were signs that Russia was planning a takeover of Bukovina, thus time was of the essence for Michael to procure Romanian documentation.

During Michael's service in the Romanian Military, the Russians under their new leader Josef Stalin, initiated the collectivization of all farms. This forced takeover of all agricultural lands in Ukraine led to three catastrophic orchestrated famines. The first of these famines occurred in 1921-22, the second and most devastating in 1932-33, and a third in 1946-47. The first and second famine didn't affect Bukovina as severely as it did Central and Eastern Ukraine, since Romania controlled Bukovina. The Russian Soviet government confiscated/stole farm products from starving Ukrainians under the guise of centralizing food stores. In actual fact, they were selling the farm products on the international market, and denied that there existed a food shortage. Meanwhile, millions were starving to death. An estimated 10 million deaths (1/3 of the existing population) would be attributed to this "Holodomor" (death by starvation) or artificial famine under the rule of Josef Stalin. Michael's family was most fortunate to escape the brunt of the first two famines with minimal family casualities.

On the positive side, Michael was discharged from the Romanian Army in 1926. His younger sisters were grown young ladies of 13 and 15 years of age. With his sisters approaching the ages where they wanted their independence, Michael decided to get married. At the age of 24, Michael took the hand of Parascheva (Paraska) Kotyk in marriage. Paraska was the daughter of Yakiv and Maria Kotyk from the neighboring village of "Stavchany". Paraska came from a family of five siblings. Two of her three older brothers had already immigrated to Canada through sponsorship of family or acquaintances, as had many young men from Bukovina and surrounding areas. Michael and Paraska were about to make the same move, but Michael was still completing his preparation for his Romanian citizenship, so that his documentation would be in order to prevent the Russians from interfering with his movements.

Michael Tkaczyk, centre with wife Paraska and brother-in-law George Kotyk, 1927, Uzhenetz, Bukovina.

In March of 1928, Michael and Paraska were blessed with the birth of a baby girl, Maria (Mary). While this was an extremely joyous occasion, Michael was concerned because he could not take his wife and newborn daughter to Canada with him due to a sudden and unexpected lack of sponsorship and finances.

DREAM TO REALITY

All of Europe was recovering from the war to end all wars, the Great War of 1914-1918. Among all the European countries, there was political negotiation and healing; economic restructuring; borders were changing; sovereignty of nations collapsed; others emerged; some blended, and in some cases sovereignty disappeared altogether. Eastern Europe was taking on a Communist cloak in Bulgaria, Hungary, Czechoslovakia, Yugoslavia and Romania itself, but the resistance to communism and Russian control made it difficult for the Russians to apply sanctions or military power on the states that were farther removed geographically, from the epicenter of communism. Fascism was in its infancy in parts of Europe and that would have a further effect on emigration from Ukraine, Poland and Romania. In Central Europe the 1920's and the 1930's, were not the most stable years to be sure, and with all this in his mind, Michael was sure that it was the right time to emigrate to Canada and start a new life for his wife and daughter Maria (Mary). His greatest regret was that he could not take his wife and daughter with him immediately due to lack of additional sponsorship and finances, plus the bureaucratic inconsistencies for civilians that were occurring in Bukovina. Michael, being a Romanian national had applied for his Romanian passport in February of 1928 and received it on April 7, 1928.

Bill Kotyk, Paraska's brother had fulfilled his two years in the Romanian Army and was sponsored to Canada in 1924 by his older brother Nick. Michael had been in correspondence with Bill in Canada for quite some time. Bill had set up sponsors and a pre-paid ticket to Canada for Michael. In late April Michael received notification from a travel office in Chernivtsi, that a prepaid ticket to Canada was waiting for him and that he had ten days to claim and activate the ticket before it became invalid. When he explained to Paraska, that he had to leave for Canada within ten days, she broke down in tears since she would be left alone with two month old Maria. Paraska knew that this was to happen, but the timing was just too abrupt. In addition she was concerned with the political instability in Bukovina, and the general fears for Michael's safety, travelling half way around the world to a new country and the relative unknown. Then there was concern for their own safety in a land where political stability was a stranger. After discussing the matter at length they agreed that this was an opportunity of a lifetime for them all. They baptized Mary and a few days later Michael got his documents together and was ready to set off for Canada and to prepare for bringing his wife Paraska and daughter Mary to Canada at a later date.

As the train moved slowly out of the station and towards the outskirts of the city of Chernivtsi, Michael's mixed emotions of sadness, loneliness, and anticipation of a new life, churned inside him. Soon they were out of the city and into the rolling green hills of the countryside of Bukovina, Michael watched the landscape move past him. It was early May and the countryside was a beehive of activity. The trees were taking on their infinitesimal shades of green. The orchards with their various fruit trees were breaking out into a beautiful palette of colors. Farmers were out in their fields tilling the dark podzolic (grey/black) soils that made up the steppes of Ukraine, famous for its grain production; The "Breadbasket of Europe", it was called. In fact the sturdy grain that was brought over from Ukraine, as seed grain in the late 1800's was the base for the development of the "Marquis" strain of wheat and was the standard grain grown on the Canadian Prairies until the "Durham" strain was developed. The scene that was moving past Michael's train window would today

Rolling hills and fertile farmland near Uzhenetz, Bukovina, May, 2006

look idyllic. There were cattle and sheep in the meadows. Children were herding sheep, ducks and geese. There were rolling hills, streams and villages with churches with their hallmark onion-shaped domes glistening in the sunshine. He was leaving a beautiful land, but one that was about to endure a severe and austere future under the iron fist of communism. Michael was determined to make sure he would get his family out of the grasp of the Soviets, and into a country that had freedoms and a future. From time to time his memories would return to a more troubled and sometimes tragic childhood. He remembered a time when Russian soldiers, in their attempt to annex Bukovina would sweep through the villages when men would be in the fields working. The Russians would take what they could, rape women and children, pillage, and if the villagers issued any resistance, the Russians would burn down houses and set fields of grain on fire, or even kill people if they resisted. He remembered when he was four years of age, his mother grabbing him and his siblings and running from the Russian soldiers and hiding in the cold, frigid, muddy waters of the wooded swamps and lowlands for the day, while the soldiers burned farm buildings. Michael's father was in Canada at this time trying to earn enough money to bring his family to Canada. This was little solace to a four year old being terrorized by marauding Russians. Michael's mother, years later, her joints wracked with arthritic pain brought on by the freezing waters, succumbed to pneumonia and influenza, her body weakened by the side effects of the brutal treatment of the Russian military and the difficult life under the Czarist regime. Michael, being the eldest, was by the age of sixteen years, charged with helping raise his younger siblings. Throughout his life and into his golden years, Michael had nothing but contempt for the Russian Czarists, Bolsheviks and Communists. The Russians have been known throughout history in Eastern Europe as brutal and uncaring landlords and rulers. The disdain by the Western Ukrainians for the Russians still exists today as witnessed by Perestroika in the 1980's that led to the downfall of the Soviet Union and an independent Ukraine. The most recent evidence of the Western Ukrainians rebuke of the Russian influence on Ukraine was the Orange Revolution of 2005 that saw the Russian influenced and tainted government of Ukraine peacefully overturned, and democratic elections held under the watchful eyes of western observers. Today Eastern Ukraine is more sympathetic to Russia than Western Ukraine since they were "Russified" generations ago while Western Ukraine was, and still is more resistant to Russification.

While enduring the atrocities and inhumane treatment by the Russians, Ukrainians found the Romanians and Austro-

Hungarian military to be the exact opposite from the Russians. They were much more humane and kinder to the population. Keep in mind, no occupying force was pleasant to deal with or live under, but when the Romanians or the Austro-Hungarians would beat back the Russians they would feed the villagers and not steal from them; they would help the villagers re-build their villages and farms; and in return the Ukrainians offered their co-operation to the Romanian and Austro-Hungarian military forces. The Romanian and Austrian military would often recruit/conscript young men from the villages for civic or military duty. The military front moved back and forth through the Bukovina region throughout the Great War. As a result, when Michael got older, he was conscripted into the Romanian Military Engineers and helped re-build the roads and railroads the Russians were bent on destroying. His pay was meager, if he got paid at all, but at least he got fed and housed and was working with friendlier occupying forces and not submitting to the Russians. By joining the Romanian military he knew he could apply for and receive Romanian citizenship, which would later allow him to obtain a Romanian passport and visa to get to Canada.

By 1926, Michael was laying his plans for coming to Canada. In 1928, the Russians could not stop him from leaving Ukraine, as they had stopped his father. He was coming to Canada as a Romanian citizen. The Russians had no claim on him. Although Michael only had a grade four-five level of schooling, he, through all his experiences with the various occupying military forces and being in the Romanian Army, had learned to speak, read and write six languages-Ukrainian, Austrian (German), Romanian, Polish, Russian, Hungarian, and the seventh language would be English when he landed in Canada. Michael was not a linguist by any stretch of the imagination, but he could function comfortably in any one of the East

European languages. With the versatility Michael developed in the Romanian Army building roads, railways and bridges, and his fluency in languages, he would have little difficulty travelling and communicating his way through Europe, and later obtaining work in Canada, which was populated by immigrants from all over Europe.

As the train headed north to Lviv and on to Krakow (Poland), Michael recalled his childhood memories. His mind flashed back to the times he tended ducks and geese as a child; when he helped plant the garden, weed it, water the plants and pick apples, pears, plums and walnuts. It seemed like yesterday. Thoughts began to flood through his mind about his childhood, his youth, and the school he attended to grade four/five. Limited schooling was done at home by parents or perhaps none at all. Literacy was not that common in the early 1900's in Ukraine. Only the children of the privileged and wealthy were allowed to attend schools and pursue higher learning.

Then he reflected about the stories he had heard about Canada: There Were Vast Areas Of Arable Land Available. There Were Opportunities For Work. All Children Got to Go to School. There Was Freedom Of Speech. There Was Freedom Of Religion. There Was Freedom Of Movement. There Was Freedom To Own Land. There Was Freedom to Elect Your Government. There Was Freedom Of Opportunity. Freedom! Freedom! Freedom!

Those freedoms were unheard of in a Russia controlled Ukraine. There had always been a military, a corrupt leader, a Czar, a revolution or a political upheaval that threatened one's freedoms. Ukraine had been fighting for freedom and democracy for as long as Michael knew, but the oppressive hand of Russia refused to let go. Canada seemed to offer limitless opportunities as to what one could do with one's life. The Canadian government wanted immigrants; they wanted hard working people to till the soil, to work in the factories, to build the railroad and to build the West. Canada needed hard working, determined settlers with a vision of what could be. All Michael had to do was to get to Hamburg by train, cross the Atlantic by steamship, then travel across most of Canada to the Prairies by train to meet up with his countrymen who would help him learn English so that he could find a job and pursue his dream.

While all this was very exciting to think about, it was also bittersweet. He was leaving a land in which he was born, in which grew up, a land steeped in history, a land with rich fertile lands, a land blessed with a temperate climate to enable the population to harvest the fruits of the land. Yet with the political events that were taking place, he had to look for a brighter future. He was leaving his family, his wife and his two month old child. He was leaving a country that he and his countrymen always dreamed of being free; free from occupation; an independent Ukraine. He was going to temporarily leave all this uncertainty and look to build a brighter future. Perhaps there might come a day for a free and independent Ukraine.

As the sun set and darkness crept on, his mind wandered back to the land he was leaving and the stories that he had been told time and time again by his parents, grandparents and elders in the village.

He reflected on the stories that were told to him over and over as a child about the ancient and little known peoples, the

Scythians, who occupied the steppes and the Black Sea shores, and whose burial mounds were accidentally uncovered from time to time with human remains and their gold jewelry and breastplates adorning them into the afterlife.

Then came the memories of the lessons taught to him by the "paroch" (parish priest) about St. Andrew, the First called; the Apostle who came to Ukraine to convert the pagans to Christianity, and St. Andrew's martyrdom in Greece, by the Romans years later.

He reflected on the stories of the Norse Vikings coming down the Dniester and Dnieper Rivers in the sixth to ninth centuries in their longboats, on the way to sack the Byzantine capital of Constantinople. The Vikings were so taken by the beauty of the Byzantine Cathedrals, the architecture and the rite of Christianity, that they never did sack the city. They ended up as mercenaries, protecting it from invaders. Rurik, one of the Norse leaders decided to stay in Ukraine and founded a settlement that later became the capital city of Kiev on the Dnieper River. This was the same site that St. Andrew had visited 800 years earlier. Olha, of the Rurik dynasty, was so impressed with the Orthodox Christian rite that she adopted it and became a Christian. It was left to her grandson Vladimir the Great, who later became the ruler of Ukraine, to accept Christianity as the national religion of Ukraine in 988. After their deaths, Vladimir, the Great and Olha would achieve sainthood for converting Ukraine to Christianity and for all their positive deeds during their lifetimes.

Then came the accounts of the Mongol hordes (Tatars) that were led by the famous Genghis Khan. In his mind Michael could visualize the Tatars, on their horses, galloping through the steppes on their way through Ukraine to conquer European

Kingdoms during the 1200's. The legacy that Genghis Khan left the Ukrainian people was the fearless freedom fighting spirit and horsemanship of the Cossacks.

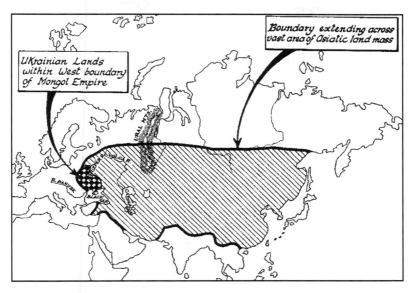

Genghis Khan's Empire, Showing Ukrainian Lands within the Empire
Source: Simpson, UKRAINE, An Atlas of Its History and Geography.

He reflected on the stories about the famous Cossacks, their exploits on the field of battle, their fearlessness and the Hetmans, the leaders of the famous Cossacks that fought for Ukraine's freedom during the 15th, 16th, and 17th centuries.

Michael reflected on the stories about Ukraine and its famous poets that his parents read to him and that were the foundation of his primary school learning; Taras Shevchenko, Ivan Franko, and Lesia Ukrainka and their visions of a free Ukraine and an enlightened society.

The stories, the thoughts, the memories of the folk dances and folk songs that told the stories of all the heroes and heroines kept coming back. Would all that be washed away in the new land? With all the thoughts running through his head he finally fell asleep to the sound of the wheels of the train on the railway track. Hamburg was still a few days away. Before him lay the cities of Lviv (Ukraine), Krakow (Poland), Frankfurt (Germany) and then finally Hamburg on the German coast.

Hamburg, Germany was a busy port city, a terminus for travelers entering Europe and an embarkation point for emegres leaving Europe and sailing to Great Britain, the Americas and the rest of the world. Hamburg was also a European terminus for Canadian Steamship Lines for travelers voyaging to the South Pacific via Canada. From the 1850's, Europeans heading for the United States of America used Hamburg as one of the points of departure. Some of the

Michael Tkaczyk's Document Folder—Exterior

immigrants were heading to New York, Boston, Quebec City or Halifax, since both the United States and Canada were offering incentives to immigrants to populate their respective western regions. These ports would be the immigrants' first experience in the new land. The Land of Opportunity was across the Atlantic with freedoms that people from Eastern Europe could only dream about. Countries in Western Europe were moving to more democratic systems of government, but the class system of society was still entrenched in many countries. This of course was about to change, but it would take time.

Michael Tkaczyk's Document Folder — Interior

Time was not on Michael's side. The feudal czarist regime was overthrown in his country, but he could see more sinister political developments about to swallow up his country and his countrymen. That political development was communism. His fear for the safety of his family was paramount, since the new Bolshevik regime, which was about to become the Soviet Union, had developed a strengthened military, a feared secret police known as the KGB, and a ruthless set of leaders and bureaucrats. Karl Marx and Lenin had planted the seeds of a socialistic regime that was to create a society where class structure was eliminated and wealth distributed to everyone, so that everyone would be equal. Marx and Lenin never saw their philosophy come true. During Lenin's "reign" there became a new class structure of bureaucrats and masters over the general population. The Bolsheviks became the powerful and controling group. Soon power and corruption crept into the organization and the powerful few at the top of the organization were abusing their power. Bolshevism became more brutal than the czars had been. Josef Stalin was planning his ascent to power as Lenin's health was failing. He soon took power and became all-powerful. His brutality and his five year plans were orchestrated to destabilize Ukrainian insurgency. He did this by initiating purges of the Ukrainian Orthodox Church and purging dissident intellectuals. His collectivization of the farms was intended to eliminate the "Kurkuli" as a class (Kurkul means rich peasant). The Kurkuli or Kulaks were the target when Stalin implemented The Great Famine of Ukraine, or the "Holodomor" (Death by Starvation), which would kill in excess of 10 million Ukrainians. At least with the Czars you knew where you stood, socially speaking, and you never got out of the niche. With the Stalinist regime you never knew where you stood—You became a communist, toed the party line and survived, perhaps. The communist system encouraged spying on your neighbors and turning them in to the authorities. One was constantly looking over one's shoulder for fear of being turned in to the authorities (KGB) and fear of prosecution. If you didn't obey the KGB, you ran the risk of starvation, being loaded into railway boxcars to be sent to concentration or labor camps in Siberia or you were shot. Few people ever returned from the labor camps.

DREAM TO REALITY

Collaboration with the communist movement meant that you had to join the Communist Party and convert to their socialistic beliefs and philosophy. You then became a small cog in the communist machine. It was a militaristic, lock step system that gave you no freedom, perhaps some privileges, if you abided by their orders, but no freedom. You had to give up your religion, sometimes give up family and friends and even your personal freedoms, such as they had become, and convert to the Communist Manifesto. You were constantly watched. The secret police or the KGB was all powerful and most unforgiving. Violate the manifesto and you were dismissed from the party, publicly humiliated and sent off to a labor camp or terminated. Some of Michael's family suffered this fate during the infamous Stalinist Purges of the 1940's and 1950's. This was not Michael's vision of a better life.

Michael cleared Canadian customs, health and civil inspections in Hamburg on May 7 to May 11, 1928. He boarded the steamship, MONTROYAL (a small ship by today's ocean going standards) on May 12, 1928. The MONTROYAL would take him through the English Channel and then across the Atlantic Ocean to the Port of Quebec City in Canada. For Michael, just boarding this giant of the seas was memorable. There were dockworkers loading the ship with luggage and other commodities, while passengers from all over Europe were moving through stations of immigration officials and ship personnel checking manifests and passenger documentation. One could hear languages of all types being spoken, translated and transcribed onto manifests. At least Michael had command of various languages so that he could communicate in German with immigration officials and other languages with passengers and dock workers. The only problem was that the working language of the ships and in Canada was English and he had not yet mastered it.

Michailo Tkaczyk Arrived In Quebec City, Province Of Quebec, Canada Aboard The MONTROYAL, Canadian Pacific Steamship Lines on May 23, 1928 Source: Pier 21 Historical Society, Halifax. Archives Canada

Canadian Steamship Lines operated a fleet of steamships that transported people and cargo from Antwerp, Belgium; Hamburg, Germany; LeHavre, France; and Liverpool, England to Canada. Halifax, Quebec City and Montreal were the ports of destination in Canada. Canadain Pacific Steamship Lines would travel to other international ports in the United States, South America, the South Pacific Ports in New Zealand and Australia, Polynesia, the Orient, India and South Africa. Canadian Steamship Lines was later bought out by P&O Orient Steamship Lines. Later the Steamship Line was bought by Cunard Steamship Lines, owned by Samuel Cunard and based in Nova Scotia.

DREAM TO REALITY

The MONTROYAL was not your typical cruise ship that we think of today. The MONTROYAL was commisioned by P&O Orient Steamship Lines of Great Britain, and built in 1906 as a coal burning steamship, in Glasgow, Scotland by the Fairfield Shipbuilding and Engineering Company. It was originally christened the EMPRESS OF BRITAIN. The EMPRESS OF BRITAIN sailed the world serving the British in looking after their empire. The British Empire included colonies throughout Southeast Asia, India, Australia, NewZealand, Canada and many islands throughout the Seven Seas. In 1924 Canadian Pacific Steamship Lines purchased the EMPRESS OF BRITAIN, re-named her THE MONTROYAL and converted her to an oil burner, a gigantic technological leap in the days of steampowered ships. As a result, in June of 1924, she steamed from Southampton, England to Quebec City in a record time of 4 days, 8 hours and 51 minutes at an average speed of 20.49 knots. The average crossing of the Atlantic with a coal fired steamship took any where from 7 to 9 days. In addition, the MONTROYAL as an oil burner, was a much "cleaner" ship both physically and environmentally. A "stout" ship in its day, THE MONTROYAL was 548 feet (173 meters) long and 65 feet (22meters) wide, weighed 15,656 tons and had two funnels (smoke stacks) and two masts. Today's cruise ships are two and three times that size and carry 2500 to 4000 passengers. The steam engines were originally powered by coal providing the heat to create steam pressure in boilers, to drive the turbines and the twin screw propellers that would give the ship a top speed of approximately 22 knots. Maintaining that speed with humans feeding coal by shovel into a furnace to maintain boiler pressure, was no mean feat. Most cruise ships of the day would cruise at 15 to 18 knots or slower if the North Atlantic was particularly rough. Conversion to oil burners was a more economical, clean and efficient upgrade. The MONTROYAL sailed on the Liverpool-Quebec, Hamburg-Quebec, Montreal-

Antwerp, Cherbourg, France-Montreal and Southampton–Quebec run, ferrying tens of thousands of immigrants from Europe to Canada. It was used during the Great War as a troop and supply carrier and later re-fitted for use as a steamer to transport goods and people at an economical cost. In June of 1930, the MONTROYAL was taken out of service, decomisioned and sold to Stavanger Shipbreakers of Norway and salvaged for scrap metal.

Frills were non-existent on ships of this era, except for first class cabin passengers. Lower class cabin passengers were not allowed to mix with first class passengers. The decks were separate and maintained so by the ship's crew. Sailing on this huge steamship was a new experience to Michael. He had seen steam locomotives on railroads, and had just experienced several thousand kilometers of a crowded train ride, but a steam powered ship was a sight to behold. The steamship was gigantic to him, but by today's standards it was a small ship. The MONTROYAL was fitted to accommodate 600 First class cabin passengers, and about 800 Third class passengers. The second class passenger cabins were converted for third class passenger use. The third class passengers were passengers from Eastern and Central Europe and were confined to a lesser quality of service. Quarters were cramped. There were no staterooms for basic immigrant fare. One slept in a bunk in a large open area; no third class stateroom. There were only communal bathrooms and deck space was limited since third class passengers could not mingle or mix with first class passengers. The voyage was rough due to heavy seas. The Atlantic was not hospitable at the best of times. Sea sickness was prevalent, however Michael was fortunate in that he did not get sick, but the disembarkation point of Quebec City couldn't come soon enough. It took nine days to cross the Atlantic. Conditions on the MONTROYAL were spartan to say the least. Crossing the Atlantic was a cold, and often wet proposition. On these immigrant steamers it was more pleasant to stay outside on deck in the cold during the daylight hours, if for nothing else, but the fresh air. It was always cold, damp and sometimes downright wet on deck but at least the air was fresh.

The shoreline at long last appeared on the horizon. Steaming past Newfoundland and the French Islands of St. Pierre and Miquelon and into the St. Lawrence Estuary, the anticipation was growing. It seemed forever as the MONTROYAL kept working her way up the St. Lawrence. On past Anticosti Island and along the wooded and rocky shoreline of the St. Lawrence they steamed. Then into the narrower section of the river where you could actually see both shores. There were settlements along the shore, fishermen out in their dories pulling in nets with their catch for the day. Excitement was starting to build since soon he would be boarding a train to cross the country to get to his sponsor. The countryside looked very interesting to Michael. It was a very different kind of entry than he expected. Rivers tumbled out of the forested rocky hillsides; huge rivers rushing and tumbling from the Laurentian Highlands into the St. Lawrence. These were not like the calmer rivers of Western Ukraine. These rivers looked more like the ones he had seen as he crossed the Carpathian Mountains in the far Western region of Ukraine. Soon from the deck Michael could see the skyline of a city. The ramparts of what looked like a castle. That was the citadel of Quebec City, standing guard on the height of land. As the tugboats guided the steamer into its berth, Michael could see the docks teeming with dockworkers waiting to unload the ship. Gangplanks were being readied to disembark the passengers and queues were being set up to move the immigrants through to "Immigration Hall". Every port of entry had an Immigration Hall to process the newcomers. Rows and rows of customs and immigration officials were waiting to process the absolute newcomers while other customs officials would process Canadian citizens who had been abroad for business or personal reasons. After the nine day Atlantic crossing, Michael was most eager to gather his belongings and ready himself for the queues for the immigrants, and his new adventure.

Twenty one days from the date he left home, on May 23, 1928 Michael Tkaczyk (Tkaczuk)(Tkachyk) set foot on Canadian soil. He breathed deeply as he walked on the soil that soon was to become his country, his home.

The ship's manifest listed "Michailo Tkaczuk" of Romanian Nationality; of Ukrainian Race/Origin; passage paid by William Kotyk; sponsored by Thomas Kuryliuk; and place of residence, Wroxton, Saskatchewan. It also listed his wife Paraska in Romania and his occupation/profession as that of "farmer". Michael entered Canada on that day with $10.00 in his possesion. The most important entry on the manifest was at the end of line 23 with a stamp of "LANDED IMMIGRANT" and initialled by the immigration officer. This signified that Michael complied with all the regulations governing immigrants; regulations such as health, security and valid documentation from his home country and point of origin, "Romania". This signified that Michael was on Canadian soil and could remain so until he applied for his citizenship. Others from the MONTROYAL were not so fortunate. Some failed to comply with one or more of the regulations and were refused entry to Canada and were taken into custody and returned on the next ship to Europe. Mixed emotions ran high in Immigration Hall due to the acceptance or rejection of immigration applicants by Canadian officials. Along with his Romanian passport, Michael had to carry with him, his Canadian Pacific Railway prepaid train ticket and his sponsor's identification card that was issued by the Department of Colonization and Development. It indicated his nominee (sponsor) and Michael's, name. The Government of Canada used this card as a tracking device to ensure that the immigrant actually got to his sponsor.

The second leg of his journey was complete. Now the final section of his journey was to be completed, but first he had to clear Immigration and Customs. As Michael entered Immigration Hall he organized his documents and papers for presentation to the immigration officials. Michael's documents were of Romanian origin, indicating Romanian citizenship thus Michael was registered as of Romanian origin. Immigration officials made little difference between the countries, regions or even municipalities of Eastern Europe. Borders of Eastern Europe changed frequently, and communications travelled so slowly that often the country of origin was incorrect. Ukrainians besides being called Ukrainians were often referred to as Galicians, Ruthenians, Romanians, Poles, Bukovinians, Slovenians, Russians, Magyars (Hungarians), White Russians (Byelorussians) or they were associated with any ethnic group in the East European Region. In fact, in Canada during the Great War, many Ukrainians were imprisoned, property confiscated and they were charged as "unfriendly aliens" who might aid and abet the Kaiser's German forces or the Austrian military since in their homeland, Western Slavs were often under the political sphere of the Austrians in the late 1700's to the early 1900's. Going back to 1795 the Habsburgs of Austria controlled much of Bukovina, Eastern Poland, Galicia and Ukraine. The Habsburgs of Austria were generally liked and respected by the Poles, and Ukrainians. The Austrians treated people humanely, let them practise their religion, speak their language and practise their customs.

In Canada's early history, immigrants were not always trusted since they could be sympathetic to their homeland and in this case, Kaiser Wilhelm of Germany and Austria. Thousands of Ukrainians were incarcerated as political prisoners in prison camps in Northern Ontario and in the area around Banff. Much of Banff National Park (roads, bridges, buildings, trails) was built with this forced labor. Checking ships' manifests going back to the 1890's to 1918, listed immigrants from Bukovina, Galicia and Eastern Poland as Austrian. The Canadian Government has since then apologized for the error, and cairns have been erected in Banff National Park acknowledging the accomplishments of the so called "prisoners of war".

The majority of the immigrants on Michael's ship, the MONTROYAL were from Poland thus immigration officials used the Polish spelling to register names. Michael not being able to speak English yet, except for basic words and phrases, could not make himself understood when they were registering his name and Tkachyk came out as Tkaczuk due to the Polish spelling and pronunciation. Later Michael's name would take many forms and spellings such as Tkaczyk, Thaczuk on payroll slips and on his citizenship application and subsequent citizenship papers. The customs officials phonetically translated his Christian name as Michailo. Later he used Michael or Mike as the anglicized version. Besides, Michael wouldn't dream of questioning or correcting a uniformed figure of authority in the new land he was wishing to adopt as home. Coming from Eastern Europe, you did not question a uniformed person. Questioning or correcting the immigration officials, in Michael's mind was not a prudent move, since he did not want to jeopardize his entry into Canada. Michael saw other people being rejected by immigration officials. He did not know the reasons for their rejection, but he figured complying with the immigration officials was the easiest and most effective way to complete his entry into Canada. He was not about to take chances. So what if they misspelled his name or mistook his country of origin. Perhaps he could correct it later. He felt he was at their mercy. And perhaps he was. The immigration officials, on the other hand were dealing with large masses of people. Few if any immigrants could speak English. The immigration officials working through interpreters were at their wits end at times as well. Just getting through immigration and receiving documentation indicating, "Landed Immigrant Status" was an accomplishment. It was the proverbial foot in the door that would lead to bigger and better things. Besides, words and names got modified and twisted as to the user, speaker or writer throughout history. These were minor occurrances in the larger picture of Michael establishing himself in a new land. After receiving his landed immigrant status, it was on to the Department of Colonization and Development queue to receive his instructions as to which train Michael was to take and where he was to get the tracking booklet checked. This tracking device was to ensure that the immigrant got to his destination and his sponsor. The Government of Canada did not want immigrants becoming vagrants and a drain on society. They wanted the immigrant to get to his sponsor and become a productive citizen. At last Michael got out of Immigration Hall, breathed a sigh of relief as the immigration officials directed him to the train station where he would board a train and start his long trek West to the Province of Saskatchewan and his sponsor Thomas Kuryliuk and brother-in-law Bill Kotyk who were awaiting his arrival in Yorkton, Saskatchewan. Not having a map of Canada, Michael did not realize the breadth of the country, the length of the train ride, the many stops he would be making and the country side he was about to see. The Canadian Pacific Railway joined Canada from sea to sea and he would actually travel through the bulk of the country he was about to call home. He boarded the railway passenger car, presenting his railway ticket that Bill Kotyk had sent him and the identification card that the Department of Colonization and Development had provided. He was to provide this card before he boarded a train anywhere in Canada until he reached destination. The railway pass would get him to Yorkton, Saskatchewan where he was to start his new life. Little did Michael know at this time that the Canadian Pacific Railway would play a significant role in his future life.

The train travelled west from Quebec City to Montreal and on to Toronto. In Toronto he changed trains to the transcontinental train that would take him directly to Winnipeg. Then it was off from Union Station in Toronto to Sault St. Marie, through the vast northern forests of Ontario's portion of the Great Canadian Shield, past the Great Lakes and on to Thunder Bay (then called Fort William and Port Arthur) with its grain terminals. Finally the train emerged from the forests and lakes of Northern Ontario and out onto the flat prairies approaching Winnipeg. This country that Michael was passing through was vast and empty, not like Europe, where the train passed through large cities and past cultivated fields and villages continuously. As the train steamed onto the Prairies and closer to Winnipeg, Michael was aware that his journey was quickly coming to an end. From the letters that Bill Kotyk would write, Michael knew that as soon as they reached the open prairies, he would be nearing his destination. It seemed like a very long time of train travel, since the steam engines of the day had to refuel with coal and fill up their boilers with water frequently. A transcontinental train while travelling at 40 to 50 miles per hour (60 to 80 kilometers per hour), had to stop every 150 kilometers or so for "re-fuelling". Three and a half days since landing in Quebec City, Michael was finally in Winnipeg, where he had to change trains for the trip northwest to Yorkton and eventually on to Wroxton, Saskatchewan. The Winnipeg stopover was interesting to Michael since he heard his native tongue, Ukrainian used at will. There were railway workers, station platform attendants and others who were speaking Ukrainian everywhere. He found himself communicating and getting information from station platform employees who were Canadians of Ukrainian origin, regarding the train schedules and finding places to eat. The homesickness he felt several times during the trip and his longing for his homeland began to subside when he heard the positive stories from these recent Canadians, and the realization that his destination was but an overnight train ride from Winnipeg to Yorkton, Saskatchewan.

Boarding the train in Winnipeg bound for Yorkton was a simple task since for the first time in two weeks he did not have to go through a long drawn out documentation process. He just had to produce his train ticket and his identification card from the Department of Colonization and Development and he was on the last leg of his journey. The train travelled West through the glaciated lakebed of ancient Lake Aggizzi, just outside of Winnipeg then swung North at Portage La Prairie up onto the escarpment that was the shoreline of Ancient Lake Aggizzi and into the hills around Neepawa Manitoba. Finally the train headed onto the prairies leaving Manitoba and onto Yorkton, Saskatchewan.

As the train pulled into the Yorkton station, Michael caught a glimpse of brother-in-law Bill Kotyk, on the station platform waiting to greet him. After a long hug and exchanging a bit of family news, that afternoon Michael and Bill boarded the next train eastbound to Wroxton, Saskatchewan, home of the Kuryliuks. An hour later they were disembarking at the

Wroxton railway station and meeting up with the Kuryliuks, placing the luggage in the horse drawn wagon and heading off to the farm where Michael would call home for next few months. The rule set out by the immigration authorities was that Michael had to report to the official sponsor, and that his mailing address was that of the official sponsor. Michael could however, find employment elsewhere so long as he could be traced back to the sponsor. Spring seeding was almost completed. Late May and Early June were slow times

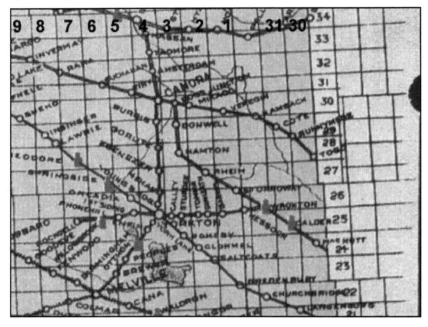

Map showing Railway Lines, locations of Post Offices and Saskatchewan Wheat Pool Elevator locations. Wroxton, Michael's destination East of Yorkton had a Saskatchewan Wheat Pool Elevator. Source: Saskatchewan Wheat Pool Archives.

on the farm so Bill Kotyk advised Michael that it might be a good time to come to Wynyard where Michael's brothers-in-law George and Nick were working for the Canadian Pacific Railways (C.P.R.), and that Michael might be able to pick up some spare work in the Wynyard-Foam Lake area. The next day they boarded the train for Yorkton and then on to Wynyard with the understanding that Michael would come back to the Kuryliuks for the harvest season in late August and September.

Arriving in Wynyard the next day, Michael was introduced to the railway workers who were primarily Ukrainian. Soon word spread in the community that a new person arrived from Ukraine and was looking for work. Between odd jobs on local farms tending to cattle, cutting hay, clearing brush, picking roots and being a spare laborer for the railway section crew maintaining the railway right-of-way, Michael got the first taste of the abundance of work available. The work was low paying, however he had nothing but time on his hands so he crammed as much work as he could into one day in an effort to make as much money as possible. The basic low pay was enough for room and board and a few dollars a week to spare. It was during this time that Michael quickly learned that hard work got you well known by employers and word soon spread that he was an able and willing worker getting his tasks done well. Ukrainian immigrants heavily settled in the communities such as Wynyard, Foam Lake, Sheho, Canora, Yorkton and smaller villages in between. The Ukrainian language, culture, and churches were available and this made Michael quite at home. He lived with Bill and Nick Kotyk for several months and prepared to go back to the Kuryliuks for the harvest season.

August and September came and harvest was in full swing on the Canadian Prairies. Michael was soon earning enough money to actually put in his pocket. It wasn't much by today's standards but two or three dollars in his pocket at the end of the week was ten times what he would have earned back in Bukovina at the time. Soon he was saving money to pay back

Bill Kotyk for his ship and train passage. Threshing crews were needed in the area thus he was working seven days a week during the harvesting season for the Kuryliuks, weather permitting and for other farmers in the area that required help. Threshing crews moved from farm to farm since most farmers didn't have the money to buy a threshing outfit, which consisted of a steam engine or tractor to power a threshing machine and the threshing machine itself. The farmer had to supply the teams of horses, hay racks to bring in the sheaves of wheat, and horse drawn wagons to carry the wheat to the granaries or the grain elevator. There were few if any grain augers to lift grain into granaries, thus the grain was shoveled by hand into the granaries. It was all manual work, and with all the manual help needed, threshing became a community effort—farmers helping farmers, some for pay, some for reciprocal work. The threshing machine and steam engine/tractor were stationary with the horse drawn hayracks bringing in the sheaves of wheat from the fields and men feeding the sheaves into the thresher which separated the wheat from the straw and chaff. The threshing machine was essentially a stationary grain combine, thus very labor intensive. In today's world the one person operated grain combine travels through the fields threshing the grain on the move, with trucks following the combine to off-load the grain when the combine's grain hopper gets full; basically a three person operation compared to a threshing crew of perhaps up to fifteen people.

When the harvesting in 1928 was completed and the huge gardens were taken in and stored for the winter, Michael left the Kuryliuks and began looking for railroad work again in the Wynyard area.

4

THE CANADIAN PACIFIC RAILWAY

Just as the Chinese immigrants had been instrumental in building the mountain section of the Canadian Pacific Railway, East Europeans, primarily the Ukrainians and Poles had been instrumental in building and maintaining the railway lines on the prairies. The seniority lists in the 1930's and 1940's of the Canadian Pacific Railway Brotherhood of Maintenance of Way Employees consistently show 60 percent to 80 percent of the employees were of Slavic origin. There were the main railway lines, the trunk railway lines and a myriad of branch railway lines connecting the smaller communities with grain elevators. Grain elevators dotted the prairie landscape every few miles and these giant storehouses of the Saskatchewan Wheat Pool, Home, Searle, McCabe, Pioneer and other grain buying companies had to be linked to the grain terminals at the port cities of Port Arthur and Fort William (Thunder Bay), Ontario on Lake Superior and the Port of Churchill, Manitoba on Hudson Bay. The railway was instrumental in getting the grain product to the consumer worldwide.

GEORGE TKACHYK

Agriculture was the lifeblood of the prairies producing the necessary grains to feed the world. From the money earned as railway laborers, and the remuneration was meager, many Ukrainians bought farmland since their forefathers had been agriculturalists for centuries and they naturally took up the same life. They loved the land, worked the land sensibly and became successful farmers throughout the Prairie Provinces. The railroad always needed spare or extra workers to provide the infrastructure or to provide the actual transportation for the people. Automobiles, trucks and highway systems were not common in the early part of the twentieth century, thus the railway lines provided a transportation system to bring bountiful grain harvests to the lake head grain terminals at Fort William/Port Arthur (Thunder Bay) and to the grain terminals at Port Churchill on Hudson Bay. As well, trains transported cattle to the meat packing plants, other food stuffs to the cities and manufactured goods back to the rural areas. As well, there was the transportation of people. This early form of public transit was most critical in transporting people around the country. Europe and the rest of the world were in dire need of large grain stocks, since Europe was rebuilding after the Great War. Canada and primarily Canada's West was providing the precious cargo of grain by the shipload. Manitoba, Saskatchewan and Alberta were literally covered with grain elevators every five to ten miles and railway lines had to link these elevators to bring the agricultural product to market. Trucks in the 1920's and 1930's were rare. There was no highway system. The dirt country roads were suited to horse drawn wagons, thus roads were rutted, rough and narrow. The railway system was expanding in leaps and bounds as the major mode of transportation.

Michael worked for Canadian Pacific Railways during the summer of 1928 making enough money to pay back the prepaid ticket that Bill Kotyk had sent him. He also sent money back to Paraska and Mary. He then worked sporadically as the railway needed him through the winter of 1928-1929, supplemented with farm odd jobs until the spring of 1929. In March and April of 1929 Michael was busy with the Kuryliuk farm operation with calving time on the farm, tending to cattle, helping with the spring seeding and garden planting. By the middle of May, Michael was back in Wynyard, Foam Lake and Hatfield working on the railway. That spring, George Kotyk, Michael's younger brother-in-law, unexpectedly arrived from Ukraine. He had a serious disagreement with his father and left the family farm. George's wife took out a loan against her inheritance of one hectare of land and bought George a ticket to Canada so that he could earn some money. Their land was now mortgaged and subject to foreclosure by the moneylender in Ukraine. Bill Kotyk who had been the financier to bring family and friends to Canada offered to assist his brother George by contributing one hundred dollars and Michael added eighty dollars to pay off the mortgage on George's wife's hectare of land in Ukraine. Then Michael and Bill arranged for employment for George so that he could pay them back and start earning money for himself.

Michael had been in Canada for one year and was beginning to become familiar with the geography of the land, the workings of the railroad, the workings of the labor force and the freedoms that were accorded to him by virtue of his landed immigrant status. He was also in communication with his wife Paraska writing letters and sending money to her and Mary. He was counting the time—four more years to get his "Naturalization Papers" (Canadian Citizenship) and Canadian Passport, so that he could go back to Bukovina as a Canadian Citizen and bring his wife and daughter back to Canada without fear of Soviet interference.

The Road Master in the railway system was the person in charge of the maintenance of a railway line or set of railway lines in a region, and responsible for the work crews in his region. The Road Master for the Yorkton region happened to be from Stavchany, the Kotyk's home town in Bukovina. This Road Master was partial to hiring East European immigrants to build and maintain the railway lines in the Yorkton, Canora, Foam Lake, Wynyard and Saskatoon areas. This was hard, backbreaking work and the Road Master knew that immigrant workers were hungry for work, were reliable and diligent. Michael was fortunate to be the recipient of spare or relieving job offers so that he could work on the "extra gangs" or "the gynnyk"(a Ukrainian-English colloquialism for the word—extra gang) as Michael called it. Michael worked on the "extra gangs" and for the farmers during his first year while he was establishing himself in this new land. Not only was this hard work and "multi-tasking" paying monetarily, but Michael's reliability was getting him known to the Road Master, a gentleman by the name of Charuk. Michael was successful in applying for and getting the volume of hours to pay off his debts of ship and train passage, sending money back to his wife and child and start saving money to bring his wife and daughter to this new land. As a sidelight, this Road Master's family would have an involvement in Michael's family's life in the 1980's.

But just as everything seemed to be falling into place, Michael's life and his plans were to take another dramatic turn.

DREAM TO REALITY

Tragedy struck Michael's family that summer of 1929. Shortly after Michael, George Kotyk and Nick Kotyk sent the money packet to George Kotyk's wife to pay off the mortgage on her inherited land, Michael received a letter from Paraska stating that she had come down with a severe cold and that she was very sick. In July of 1929 Michael received a letter from his sisters Maria and Zoya indicating that Paraska was gravely ill and that Paraska asked them to remind Michael not to forget about Mary. Paraska indicated that she may soon leave Mary, but that Michael must help Mary. In August, 1929, Michael received a letter from his sisters stating that Paraska had passed away from influenza. Michael was devastated. What was he to do? Not only did he lose his wife, but his 14 month old daughter was stranded half a world away. Does he return to Bukovina to look after 14 month old Mary? Does he go back for Paraska's funeral? Would the Soviets let him come back? Would they let him return to Canada with his infant daughter? The political turmoil was too unpredictable. Would he be trapped, unable to return to Canada? These questions raced over and over in his mind. Time, citizenship and passport documentation were the issues that would prevent him from returning to Bukovina at the present time. Would his Romanian citizenship be valid? The Soviets under Stalin were threatening the Romanians and were on the verge of taking over Bukovina. Transportation being what it was in the 1920's and being in a land half a world away from his homeland, Michael had difficult decisions to make. Discussing the matter over with his brothers-in-law, Nick, Bill and George Kotyk, and communicating with his family, his mother-in-law and sister-in-law Kateryna (George Kotyk's wife), Michael made the decision to have Paraska's mother and his sister-in-law Kateryna Kotyk be Mary's caregivers. Michael would provide the financial assistance from Canada until he could come for Mary. Since it couldn't be guaranteed that his Romanian citizenship would be valid to bring Mary back to

Canada and to guarantee him safe passage, Michael decided to wait the additional years to get his Canadian citizenship to guarantee his safe passage. He did not want to be trapped in a chaotic political situation. His plan now was to go back to Bukovina when the time was right and bring as many of his family back to Canada as he could. Josef Stalin's communism was strangling Ukraine. Borders were being shut down to emigration from East European countries. The borders were changing daily with the political unrest and revolutionary turmoil that was occurring. Michael's only recourse was to get as much work as possible, save as much money as possible and plan for a future for his daughter and himself in this new and promising land. He made up his mind that he had to stay in Canada for now. Michael had begun to appreciate, love and respect the democracy, freedoms and opportunities to advance in schools and vocations within Canada. Those freedoms were but a dream for citizens in Eastern Europe and Ukraine in particular. This country, Canada, would be an ideal place to bring up a child. Getting his Canadian Citizenship was paramount. This had cemented his resolve and determination to carve out a future in Canada for his daughter and himself. Now he had to lay the framework for bringing Mary to Canada.

The years of 1929 through to 1933 saw Michael getting himself established with the Canadian Pacific Railway (C.P.R.). His first good opportunity at landing a permanent job with the C.P.R. came when he was hired for relieving work for section men who maintained the railway lines in the East Central area of Saskatchewan between Yorkton and Saskatoon, in small farming communities with populations of 2 to 1500 people. He would be assigned to work as a section man (laborer) relieving a regular permanent worker while the worker was on medical leave or on holidays. This meant moving frequently since these relieving jobs lasted a week or two at a time. This was not a great problem for Michael since he had no immediate family present and for him it was pack a suitcase and move. Michael got to work in many communities in the Wynyard area. This enabled him to learn English as well as maintaining his cultural roots. Michael liked the Wynyard area where churches and Ukrainian cultural activities were taking hold. In addition he heard that in nearby Saskatoon there was the Peter Mohyla Institute (later to be renamed The St. Petro Mohyla Institute) where young rural Ukrainians were being given a chance to advance their education and maintain their cultural and social standing in the community. Michael who only completed his grade 4-5 in Bukovina due to the outbreak of the Great War, treasured education, but the social structure at the time, lack of facilities, money and political unrest prevented the majority of Ukrainians from obtaining a higher education. Michael was determined to give his daughter Mary every opportunity to complete her schooling when he brought her to Canada. The motivation of Saskatoon lawyer and Ukrainian cultural activist Julian Stechishin and others at the Peter Mohyla Institute encouraged Michael to read the Ukrainian Voice (whose editor was Myroslaw Stechishin, Julian's brother) to be kept abreast of Canadian current events and the latest news from his homeland. By reading this and other newspapers, Michael kept current with political, social, educational and religious affairs abroad and in Canada.

If there was a grain elevator standing on the prairies, there was usually a post office and a store within fifty meters of the elevator. Sometimes the grain elevator operator was also the postmaster, storekeeper and service station (gas bar) all in one. It was basically a grain elevator and any other services the local farmers would need. Wynyard and Foam Lake were communities with populations of 100 to 300 people. These were the largest centers of population outside of Yorkton and Saskatoon. Michael worked in communities such as Lanigan, Sinnett, Hatfield, Goodeve, Nokomis, Sheho, Theodore and Insinger or wherever relieving duties would take him. Today some of those communities no longer exist. The grain elevators are gone, water towers and coal docks dismantled, railway lines removed, railway stations and platforms gone, loading docks gone, telegraph lines gone, tool sheds gone, railway bunkhouses and section houses for railway workers moved; perhaps a few concrete foundations were left where grain elevators used to stand and raised railway beds where the railway tracks used to run. These small communities or "sidings" as they were sometimes called (up to several hundred people) were for the sole purpose of servicing the small farmer and railway operations. The railway system was not only a transportation system but a communication system as well. An infrastructure was required to enable the transportation system to work efficiently. In each one of these small communities there may have been as many as 15 to 20 railway related jobs—a station agent or two was required to accommodate communication through the telegraph system as well as processing freight and

Steam locomotive under full steam pulling loaded grain cars passing through Hatfield siding. 1929

accommodating ticket sales to passengers. Communications was critical to the railway system, since trains had to arrive and depart on time to ensure the delivery of goods and passengers in a timely fashion. And where there were no twinned tracks to allow on-coming trains to pass safely, trains had to wait at a siding where there were twinned or multiple sets of tracks (for grain elevator purposes) to allow on-coming trains to pass each other safely. Station agents were the "official time depots" where railroad employees and townspeople would check and set their watches and clocks. The station agents would communicate via telegraph to Saskatoon or Winnipeg to verify times and schedules of trains for the railway employees. There were 5 to 10 railway maintenance employees per railway station, water tower/coal dock operators and extra gang workers along with railway passenger safety that had to be attended to.

Railway workers and their families enjoying a Sunday afternoon outing on the section foreman's "railway speeder" or "jigger" as it was called. Note the railway station loading platform in the background.

There would be telegraph line men to inspect and maintain miles of telegraph lines that accompanied the railway tracks. Everything moved by rail prior to the 1960's. Farmers sent their milk and cream, eggs and produce to the dairies and creameries by rail; commodities such as clothes, shoes, appliances and machinery were ordered through Eaton's mail order service and shipped by rail. Cattle and other livestock

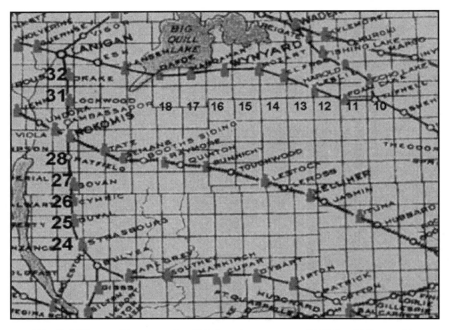

Hatfield located just south of Nokomis was one of Michael Tkaczyk's first permanent job locations. Source: Saskatchewan Wheat Pool Map/Calendar, Saskatchewan Wheat Pool Archives. 1924

were shipped to Saskatoon, Regina, Winnipeg or Edmonton via cattle cars. Train day was a special event in every prairie town. Mail came, and perhaps there was a word from a relative or acquaintance; perhaps a letter from the homeland; perhaps a cheque from the dairy for your produce; perhaps a new table cloth from Eaton's or those new shoes. The empty cream cans would be returned to the farmer to be filled and sent back to the dairy; a new canvas for the binder or threshing machine; most everything came by train. It was the life blood of every community. Communities were totally dependent on the railway and the telegraph system before telephones became prominent in communication and dirt roadways became highways and a highly efficient Trans Canada and provincial highway system. Since communities were so dependent on the railway system, railway and railway related jobs were treasured. The railway jobs provided a sense of security and long term employment which was an attractive feature. The negative side of railroad employment was the instability that was associated with it. Moving railroad workers was common for many reasons. Job enhancement was one reason and railway company needs being the other. Workers had to go where the company deemed they would do the company the most good. The railway was an Industry that helped build the prairies.

Michael wrote regularly to Mary. Even though she was an infant he wanted his mother-in-law and sister in law to talk to Mary about him and to explain to her that he was going to come for her in the near future. He would send photographs of himself and assisted in supporting the family financially. In return the family would send him photographs of Mary. He was determined to ensure that when he came for Mary in 1935, she would know who he is. He didn't want Mary to feel as he did when his father came back from Canada in 1907 and Michael didn't recognize him or relate to him. Michael was sure that Mary was being well looked after. With his late wife's family providing the major care and his family in close proximity he knew that Mary was getting care, love and attention from her three aunts and her Baba Kotyk. During the years between 1929 and 1933, with Michael working regularly on the railway, he received a few benefits from the C.P.R.

Mary, age two years, centre with her aunt Kateryna behind her, and Michael's sisters, Mary's aunt Maria Tkacz left and aunt ZoyaTkacz, right. 1930

He received railway passes to travel within the provinces of Manitoba, Saskatchewan and Alberta. He used these passes to travel to areas where he might want to settle down with Mary when he brought her over to Canada. In 1932 he travelled to Gonor, Manitoba to visit his sister-in-law Mafta and her husband whom Nick had sponsored out earlier. He later travelled to Edmonton, Alberta in 1934 and on to Edwand in the Smokey Lake area to visit a cousin from Uzhenetz who was related through his father. They had settled in the Edwand area taking out land grants or homesteads. Michael was looking for a Ukrainian community with a school, a church and social and cultural values that he grew up with in Bukovina. He was going to be bringing his seven year old daughter to Canada with no English background. He wanted a community where bridging the language gap would be as easy as possible, plus the added features of a church and cultural upbringing. This was not always possible in some of the Ukrainian communities due to the fact that in the late 1890's and early 1900's Ukrainian priests were not always available. The religious and cultural fabric was non-existent in some of the communities. Michael was not impressed with the Edwand situation. The lifestyle and opportunities available to him with a young daughter just didn't appeal to him. There were instances where families settled in the wilderness areas of the Prairie Provinces and were so isolated or affected by their surroundings that they lost their homeland values and traditions. Michael realized that the Ukrainian communities around Edwand were very leftist leaning, in fact the communist party of Canada had been making inroads in some Alberta Slavic communities, and he wanted none of that. He had just escaped that threat and was not to become involved in left wing politics in Canada. Michael was not impressed by what he saw and experienced during his brief visit. His political, religious, social and educational ideals for his daughter and himself were high and he wanted to keep it that way. He maintained contact with the Tkach's from Edwand and visited them in Edmonton during the 1950's. Later in the 1970's when Michael had moved to Edmonton he met up with Walter Tkach, a nephew from Edwand and visited with him frequently in the years thereafter. Conditions had changed. The social and political milieu had changed for the better.

GEORGE TKACHYK

In 1933, Nick Kotyk received a section foreman's position in Gronlid, Saskatchewan. Gronlid with a population of approximately 200 was located 30 kilometers north of Melfort, Saskatchewan and was the "end of the line" for that branch of the C.P.R. The Saskatchewan River flows from the West to Northeast about 20 kilometers north of Gronlid and forms a geographical barrier to towns north of the river. The railway bridge was built at Nipawin about 60 kilometers northeast of Gronlid, much too far for horse drawn wagons to transport grain, thus Gronlid as end of the line, became a busy trading center. The end of the line for the railway meant a beehive of activity for the community, since there was a" Y'" to facilitate for the train's turn around procedure. The railway tracks were configured into a "Y" shape and were fitted with a series of railway track switches that would allow the train, after dropping its caboose on another siding to stop near track's end. The locomotive and coal tender would be unhooked from the rest of the train and move in reverse backing into one branch of the "Y'" and then advance out the other end of the "Y". The locomotive and coal tender would then hook up at what was previously the tail end of the train. The caboose would then be attached to the rear of the train to complete the operation. That meant the train stayed overnight for locomotive servicing. All the wheels on all the cars would be greased, the brakes on each car checked, the hitches checked and all lights serviced. There was a coal dock to re-load the coal tender and a water tower to re-fill the locomotive's steam boiler. As well there was a stockyard to assist in loading cattle into the cattle cars bound for Saskatoon or Prince Albert, and four grain elevators to manage the grain handling. The trading area was large since there were no communities between Gronlid and the Saskatchewan River. The farmers had only one way to get their goods to market and supplies and farm equipment in from the large cities, and that was through Gronlid by way of the C.P.R. Gronlid was a bustling, thriving community in the 1920's, 1930's, 1940's and into the 1950's.

DREAM TO REALITY

Nick Kotyk advised Michael that since he was the section foreman in Gronlid, he would need some relieving assistance for his section men at Gronlid, and that with Gronlid being the "end of the line", there would always be the possibility of getting additional work there. In 1933, Michael moved to Gronlid. He enjoyed the community and work was plentiful. The railway workers were primarily Ukrainian. The farming community was a mixture of Europeans—Scandinavian, Ukrainian, Polish, British, German and Canadians of French and Anglo-Saxon origin. Neighboring communities such as Brooksby were predominately Ukrainian with Ukrainian Orthodox and Ukrainian Catholic Churches dotting the countryside with their hallmark onion-shaped domes. Michael enjoyed the Ukrainian cultural aspects of this community such as church, concerts, the arts and socials in general. In the rural Ukrainian settled communities, the social life was very active. While there were no modern amenities such as television, movies were available in town community halls usually once a week, but they cost money and money was in short supply during the depression of the 1930's.

Ukrainian Orthodox Church of St. Mary located several miles Northeast of Gronlid. Michael attended this church during the 1930's and early 1940's. Photo: Courtesy of Gordon Dobrowolsky

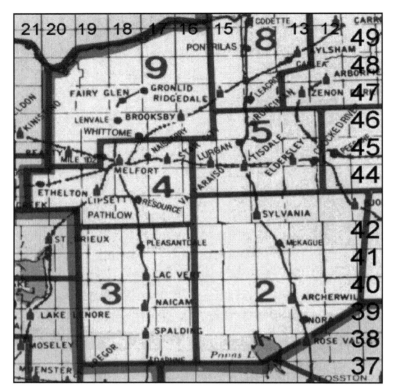

Gronlid, Lenvale and Brooksby, located in area 9 above, were to become Michael's home base for several years. Source: Saskatchewan Wheat Pool Map/Calendar, Saskatchewan Wheat Pool Archives, 1924

Farm families and towns people would get together for games nights of playing cards (whist drives), visiting, dancing, choir and drama nights. Community Halls or national halls (Narodny Deem in Ukrainian) were common in rural areas adjacent to churches, in villages and towns where immigrants from Europe would gather to recall, celebrate and promote their culture through language, song, dance, theatre and food. Today in Edmonton and other urban centers across Canada you still see vestiges of these community halls in the form of huge complexes such as the Ukrainian Center, the Italian Center, the Scandinavian Center, the German Canadian Cultural Center and others. Some of these cultural centers have gained national and international prominence through their dance schools and language schools, while others have morphed into full time private schools.

5

BRINGING MARY HOME TO CANADA

During the 1930's, The Great Drought and Depression were occurring in North America. The West was a dust bowl. Jobs were scarce as was money, yet Michael managed to work and save enough money to bring his daughter back to Canada. The only entertainment in the small rural communities were the activities that the people generated around their schools and churches—concerts, plays, choirs, traditional and folk dancing. Vacations were unheard of in these small farming and railroad communities. A radio was an absolute luxury, if you could afford to buy the radio. Then the battery, which was a series of dry cells (not re-chargeable) approximately the size of a car battery had to be purchased. The battery may last a year with very prudent use.

Michael split his work with the C.P.R between Hatfield and Gronlid. He was working hard to make sure he would provide the best for Mary. Medical services were few and far between in the 1920's to 1950's, especially the availability of Ukrainian speaking physicians. To ensure that he could provide health services for himself and Mary, Michael felt that he had to be informed himself. He bought himself a hard covered book called *"The Home Physician" (Domashnay Likar)* which was written by a team of leading physicians of the time and translated into various languages including Ukrainian. With the booming immigrant populations in the United States, Canada and South America and the lack of medical practitioners, this was a most useful book. This volume, 882 pages long, contained information from nutrition and meal planning to pediatrics; it dealt with serious ailments and chronic conditions from heart disease to communicable diseases. Michael felt this volume of information was necessary to help him bridge any communication gap between English speaking doctors and nurses and himself and Mary.

Michael had been working his way up on the railroad laborer seniority ladder. He started as a spare man, then worked his way up to a relieving section man and by 1934 he had moved up to a section man "B" status, which entitled him to permanent status with a higher rate of pay ($0.81 to $0.86 per hour) depending on the job description. However he was subject to moving anywhere in the Saskatoon division. Nick Kotyk was the section foreman at Hatfield prior to moving to Gronlid, thus Michael had worked quite extensively in the Hatfield area. While working in Gronlid and Hatfield, Michael was sent to relieve railway workers at Govan, Nokomis and Lanigan. While working at Hatfield and staying with Bill Kotyk, Michael applied for his Canadian Citizenship and on December 6, 1934, Mihaillo Tkaczyk received his *Certificate of Naturalization*, or as one would say today, "Mihaillo Tkaczyk became a Canadian Citizen". His Canadian Passport arrived at the same time, thus he was ready to go back to Bukovina unimpeded, to bring his daughter Mary to Canada without Soviet interference.

Michael Tkaczyk's Canadian Citizenship Certificate

September through December, 1934 was a whirlwind of activity for Michael. While he was preparing to go back to Bukovina to get Mary, he was buying her clothes to ensure that she would fit in with the Canadian school children with whom she would be associating. He was also contacting friends from Bukovina with whom he was working and that had supported him through his difficult times, since they would be passing letters and money packets to family and friends in Ukraine.

Steve Hryhirchuk was one such very close friend that Michael kept in close contact throughout his first seven years in Canada. Michael and Steve were childhood friends in Uzhenetz and maintained that friendship in Canada. They both worked for the C.P.R. and lived together in bunkhouses when they worked on the same work crews. Steve was a fun loving person, who lived for practical jokes. He frequented the Tkaczyk family

DREAM TO REALITY

whenever he was working in the proximity of the Tkaczyk home. He even lived with Michael's family in Sonningdale in the late 1940's. To the family he was known as "Uncle Steve". Steve was a support system for Michael in 1929 after Michael's wife Paraska had taken ill and passed on.

Michael got all his documentation together but in his communication with Immigration Canada, he received additional information that he could only bring Mary back when he returned. The immigration policy had changed in that one could only bring his spouse and children back as landed immigrants. His only option was to bring back Mary. His original plan was to bring as many of his brothers and sisters and his mother-in-law and sister-in-law Kateryna back with him. Mary's major care givers, her Baba Kotyk and aunt Kateryna would have to wait for George Kotyk to go back to Bukovina and bring them back to Canada since they were immediate family to him. December came quickly and Michael took leave of his relieving railway work, bade his friend Steve Hryhirchuk, and brothers-in-law George, Nick and Bill Kotyk farewell and left Hatfield by train on his trek to Montreal en route to Bukovina.

Michael Tkaczyk on the right with his friend Steve Hryhirchuk on left. Photo circa 1932

GEORGE TKACHYK

Michael arrived in Montreal on December 11, 1934. One of his requirements was to go to the Romanian Consulate to get his Romanian Visa #497 for which he paid the princely sum of $3.85. This document gave him access to Bukovina (a Romanian territory at the time) for several months so that he would have the time to procure Mary's travelling documents. Michael then travelled by train to Halifax where he would set sail from Pier 21 for Europe on December 15, 1934. He arrived in LeHavre, France on December 20, went through French Immigration and Customs as a Canadian en route to Chernivtsi, Bukovina and on to Uzhenetz and Stavchany. He then boarded a train for Paris. On December 21, 1934 Michael had to visit the Romanian Consulate in Paris to have his Canadian Passport verified, stamped and signed by Romanian authorities. He was to report to Romanian authorities when he arrived in Chernivtsi and then in Bucharest, Romania to verify his length of stay and his departure date. The political unrest was evident in all the checks and balances exercised on people travelling throughout Europe. Michael boarded the train in Paris and settled in for the last leg of his overland journey through Germany, Poland and into Ukraine to Lviv and Chernivtsi.

Michael's family knew he was making plans to come for Mary, but they weren't sure when he was arriving. Communications were by letter, and travel was not always time certain. Schedules were approximate at best.

Michael hadn't seen his daughter in seven years. He had corresponded by letter regularly and had received photographs of her so he knew she had grown and changed since he saw her as an infant. Would she recognize him? How would she relate to him? Would she want to leave her home, the only home she knew? Would she want to leave her Baba? Would she want to leave her caregiver Aunts; her cousins; her friends? Would she want to leave all that was familiar to her? Would she want to leave all her familiar surroundings and leave with this man she only knew through letters and photographs? Would she want to leave for a land so far away that she may not see again or see all those who she grew up with? These questions ran through Michael's mind as the train steamed on towards Chernivtsi. It provided for anxious days of travel. He was looking forward to their meeting, but anxiety was ever present.

The countryside approaching Lviv and Chernivtsi was so familiar. Not much had changed since Michael left in May of 1928. The countryside looked very much the same except it was winter with the country side covered in a deep blanket of snow. Memories came rushing back to Michael. Memories of his departed wife. Memories of him leaving his homeland seven years ago. Memories of him leaving an infant child and now coming back to her, a grown seven year old child. The stark reality of a changed Ukraine had hit him as well. It was 1934 and the Soviet Union was a fact, with the threat of the Soviets taking Bukovina over from the Romanians at any time.

Had the "Holodomor", The Great Famine of 1932-33 affected Bukovina as it had the rest of Ukraine? The Soviets had devastated Ukraine with their collectivization policy which had spearheaded the politically motivated and orchestrated famine. Had it reached Bukovina at all? Food was scarce. Males were being conscripted into the Soviet military. The people were under constant surveillance of the KGB. Romania seemed like a puppet government. It couldn't stand up to the Soviets, manpower wise. Yet the Soviets were allowing the Romanians to look after the civic administration of Bukovina. It was a very confusing and unstable time for the Ukrainians in Bukovina.

War clouds were on the horizon with Nazi Germany making threats on Poland, Czechoslovakia and Hungary. The Soviets were flexing their muscle on the Slavic countries as well. Michael had yet to arrange proof of parentage of Mary then apply for passport and citizenship documentation for Mary. The Romanians were still in control of Bukovina but Michael had to work fast to avoid Soviet intervention.

The train was slowing down and finally came to a stop. Chernivtsi at last. Michael disembarked from the train but his family was not waiting for him on the station platform. He had written a letter indicating that he was coming, but setting a specific date was impossible since communications and travel were not that exact and reliable.

It was December 25, another two weeks to Christmas. The Ukrainian Orthodox Church and Ukraine as an entity recognized the Julian calendar, thus Christmas Eve or Sviat Vechir is celebrated on January 6 and Christmas Day (Reez Dvo) is celebrated on January 7. Michael picked up his luggage and set about buying Christmas presents, a Christmas tree and Christmas tree decorations to bring to Stavchany. Christmas trees were not the norm in the rural areas of Bukovina. Christmas trees were mainly a city or urban tradition, so a real Christmas tree with decorations would be a great treat for Mary, her cousins and the rest of the family. Michael had, over his seven years in Canada, become accustomed to the North American tradition of the Christmas tree, so to him it was a natural thing to do. Michael caught a ride to Stavchany approximately 30 kilometers north of Chernivtsi.

Winter was in the air when he arrived in Stavchany with snow covering the fields and all the roads. Michael arrived with all his luggage, Christmas tree and presents for everyone. It must have been a sight to behold. The excitement of seeing Michael after a seven year absence was electric. The excitement of the Christmas tree, the tree decorations, the presents, the long awaited son, brother, brother-in-law, son-in-law, and most importantly the long awaited father finally arrived. Michael couldn't believe his eyes when he first saw Mary. His daughter was a young lady approaching her seventh birthday. She was everything he expected and more. Mary was six years old and would be turning seven on March 10, 1935. There were hugs, kisses and tears, then more hugs and tears from all members of the family. Almost seven years had passed since Michael had seen any of his family. There was much to talk about, experiences to share and catching up on the news from Canada.

Mary wearing her new Canadian clothes, a woolen pleated skirt, with a woolen sweater, western shoes and stockings. She is standing in front of the family stable. 1935

Mary and her cousins were ecstatic with the arrival of Michael, but they were also excited about their first Christmas tree and decorations to place on it. Then there were

Mary on left with her cousins in February, 1935 in Uzhenetz. Mary is proudly wearing her western style ensemble that Michael purchased for her in Canada. The girls are wearing "korali", red coral bead necklaces. Baba Kotyk is in the doorway with one of Mary's aunts behind her.

the presents to open. Christmas in January, 1935 was going to be something very special and memorable indeed.

Michael was pleased that Mary's care givers had done such an excellent job in preparing her for this meeting. Mary herself, was just proud to see her father and be just like the other children in Uzhenetz and Stavchany and have a real parent. Mary loved her Baba and her aunts, but a real parent was something very special to Mary.

In the days following Michael's arrival he made all his visits to family and friends, passed on letters and money packets and visited his wife Paraska's grave site. The Christmas season was a whirlwind of activity with all the relatives wanting to host a dinner or an evening with Mary and Michael. Mary, her cousins and friends were charged with decorating the Christmas tree, and what a time they had, A real tree with paper, tinsel and home-made decorations and garland. This was a first for the family. And then there were presents to go under the tree along with candy treats. For Mary this was a Christmas too good to be true; all this excitement and best of all, her father at home with her to celebrate Christmas.

January came and went for Michael primarily with socializing, visiting and renewing old acquaintances. February was busy with a Christening party arranged for Mary. She had been Christened before Michael left, but the social activity was put on hold since time was of the essence in 1928 for him to leave for Canada. Now Mary had a parent present and Michael was trying to regain some of the experiences he missed while he was away. Family and friends gathered in the community to commemorate this event.

DREAM TO REALITY

As February wore on, Michael started proceedings in Chernivtsi regarding the application for Mary's passport. He had to provide proof of marriage and proof of Paraska's death certificate to establish legal parenthood to the authorities in Bucharest, Romania in order to get the passport approved. Baba Kotyk was not pleased that Michael was making arrangements to take Mary to Canada and told Michael so. While Mary was excited about the prospects of going back to Canada with her father, her aunt Kateryna and Baba Kotyk were taking the upcoming separation hard. This was their little girl that they had taken care of, that they nurtured from the time that she was an infant to the present, seven years of care and now they were going to lose her. Michael talked the situation over with Baba Kotyk, explaining the legal rights he had, the advantages that Mary would have in Canada, and that this was the plan from the outset and he had explained that to her and she was aware of that. Baba Kotyk finally relented and agreed that what Michael was doing was best for Mary. She said, "Well, take her already, but I cared for her for all these years and now I won't have her with me." The parting was bittersweet for all concerned.

Mary's Romanian passport (Passport # 7639) was issued on March 15, 1935 in Bucharest, Romania. Michael travelled to Bucharest to pick up the passport on March 15, 1935 at what we would call the Romanian Consulate. He and Mary were now ready to leave Bukovina for their new home in Canada. Fortunately for Michael and Mary, the Soviets and the Romanians had not yet settled their boundary negotiations following the Great War of 1914-1918. Bukovina was still under the control of the Romanian government. The border dispute was later finalized in 1940, thus it was at that time that Bukovina became under the sole control of the Soviet Union. This also explains why the "Holodomor" did not affect Bukovina as seriously as it had affected other parts of Ukraine.

Little did Michael know at the time, that it would be 39 years before he would be able to travel back into Ukraine and Bukovina in particular to visit his family. The Second World War would start in 1939 and last to 1944. The Soviet Union would then impose the "Iron Curtain" on all Eastern Bloc countries making travel in and out of the Communist countries very difficult for non-communist citizens or citizens from the western bloc countries. It wasn't until the 1970's that travel became common for "Westerners" on "Tours" orchestrated by the Soviets to travel to Soviet Bloc countries, on their national airline, Aeroflot, then only through Moscow, then on to the large cities in Ukraine. There was no scheduled travel into villages as that was forbidden territory to Westerners. Travelers saw in the Soviet Union only what the Soviets wanted travelers to see. Money and political favoritism was the key in paying off corrupt officials to get out of the Soviet Bloc and to travel to Western countries. Most people in the Soviet Union did not have the money (the Soviets controlled that), and if you weren't a communist in good standing with a high rank, you simply would not be accorded travel privileges.

Michael and Mary, packed with all their belongings, made their last minute visits to grandparents and aunts and uncles who had cared for Mary for the past seven years and on March 19, 1935 they bade everyone farewell and boarded the train in Chernivtsi for their journey through Europe, on to Antwerp Belgium and on to Liverpool England. This train trip was an exciting event in Mary's life. It was her first train trip. She had never been farther away from Stavchany and Uzhenetz than Chernivtsi itself. Mary remembers the marvel of being able to walk around on the train, eating the lunch and suppers that

DREAM TO REALITY

her Aunt Kateryna had prepared and packed for them. The recollection of the roast chicken and the perizhky (baked or deep fried buns stuffed with cottage cheese or fruit filling) during the first few days of the trip still lingers with her to this day. Then it was the different sights that Mary would see on the trip as the train rumbled on. Travelling through the varying countryside and on into the large industrialized cities she marveled at the large brick buildings, apartment buildings, row houses and smokestacks of the factories spewing out their steam and smoke. All of these marvels gave Mary and Michael hours of conversation and different topics to talk about. What was Canada like? What do people do in those large cities? What kind of house would they live in? The questions were never ending. Travelling through the large cities was mystifying to Mary. There were no farms for miles and miles, just houses, factories, smokestacks, and motor vehicles. This was new to Mary, all this brick and mortar, and paved or cobblestone streets. Mary grew up in a rural agricultural area with small villages and the distances between the villages was short. These travelling distances by train were immense to a small child. Sleep and rest on the train eventually became commonplace to Mary.

Three days later they were disembarking the train at Antwerp and boarding a trans-channel ship to get them across the English Channel to Dover, England. Boarding a train they were off through the English countryside to London. For the first time since she left Bukovina, Mary saw emerald green countryside on the way to London. On they travelled through the industrialized area of London and again into the green countryside until they reached the port city of Liverpool on the Irish Sea.

Arriving in Liverpool, they went shopping where Michael bought Mary additional clothes. She especially remembers the burgundy woolen pleated skirt with matching shoulder straps. This was the perfect skirt for a little girl to twirl around in, with the pleats flaring out uniformly. Mary was quite excited about her new clothes. She was all set for her arrival in Canada.

Passing through Customs and Immigration was not an issue as they travelled through Europe and England. Their passports and citizenship papers were in order thanks to the advance planning that Michael had done. Arriving at the docks at Liverpool the immigration officials noticed that Michael was travelling with his daughter and had Romanian documentation. Since Michael spoke Romanian and they were travelling from Romania to Canada, the immigration officials asked Michael of a favor. They explained to Michael that they had an 8 or 9 year old Romanian girl travelling by herself to Canada to meet up with her parents in Toronto. The immigration officials requested that the little girl join them on the ship and stay with them during the trip across to Halifax. The ship would provide a third class cabin with an additional bunk so as to accommodate the little girl. Essentially they were asking Michael to look after the little girl for the Atlantic crossing. Michael could not refuse the request of the immigration official and steamship line, since he felt sorry for the little girl travelling alone, besides this little girl would provide companionship for Mary on the voyage across the Atlantic. Thus "Florika" joined Mary and Michael for the passage to Canada.

DREAM TO REALITY

Michaillo and daughter Maria Tkaczyk arrived at Pier 21 in Halifax, Nova Scotia aboard the MONTCLARE, Canadian Pacific Steamship Lines, on March 30, 1935 Source: Pier 21 Historical Society, Halifax.

Michael and Mary walked up the gangplank of the MONTCLARE, another of Canadian Pacific's fleet of passenger steamships. The MONTCLARE was laid down as the METAPEDIA, built in 1921 and completed in 1922. Upon completion and sale to Canadian Pacific, her name was changed to MONTCLARE, a sister ship to Canadian Pacific's MONTCALM and MONTROSE (the ship on which Mijaillo Nyczyk/Dido Nychyk came to Canada on February 11, 1928). The MONTCLARE was the last of and the largest of the trio to be built. Her Maiden voyage was made from Liverpool bound for Halifax on August 18, 1922. The MONTCLARE was 550 feet long and 70 feet wide with 542 first class cabins and 1268 third class cabins. During the Second World War the MONTCLARE was used as a submarine depot and supply ship, and following the war the MONTCLARE went back into Canadian Steamship

Lines passenger service. She was sold and scrapped in 1958 in Inverkeithing, Norway.

When Michael and Mary reached the top of the gangplank they were introduced to Florika. Michael had his work cut out for himself, except that he didn't know it at the time. Florika was a free spirit and was bound to explore the complete "innards" of the ship including the "First Class" sections, which were off limits to Third Class passengers. As Mary recalls, the "dynamic duo" explored everything, but especially enjoyed running up and down the long corridors of the ship and exploring the "boutiques" and fruit and candy shops. Mary mentioned that her dad saw much more of the MONTCLARE than he really wanted to, due to the "cruising" of the girls. The five day voyage went quickly for the girls. It didn't for Michael, since he was constantly trying to keep tabs on Florika and Mary. Halifax eventually did appear on the horizon with Michael breathing a sigh of relief. On March 30, 1935, the MONTCLARE docked at Pier 21 in Halifax harbor and Mary set foot on Canadian soil, her new home. Pier 21 was the point of entry to which all immigrants to Canada had to report to, when arriving in Halifax. Today Pier 21 is a Historic site as well an Historic Society in Halifax. It is also a part of Archives Canada that shares a data base in Ottawa for research and information. Much of the information and data on immigration as well as photographs of the steamships in this biography were researched and obtained from the Pier 21 Society.

After clearing Immigration and Customs at Pier 21, Mary received her landed immigrant status. She would receive her Canadian Citizenship automatically when Michael and Mary took up permanent residency and the routine paperwork was completed. Clearing immigration was a routine process since Michael was a Canadian citizen. Immigration officials in the meantime looked after Florika. They had transportation arrangements to get her to Toronto by train. Michael and Mary never saw Florika again after their trans-Atlantic journey. Michael and Mary were now set to start their cross Canada train journey from Halifax to Hatfield, Saskatchewan where they would stay with Bill Kotyk in the interim. Michael's railroad pass that Canadian Pacific Railways issued to him was coming in very useful at this stage.

The train trip across Canada was uneventful. They were into their second week of travel and to seven year old Mary this seemed like an eternity. Travelling through this vast empty country of Northern Ontario and on into the Prairies was interesting but very long. When would they get to their new home? Passing through Manitoba, Michael and Mary stopped at Gonor, Manitoba, north east of Winnipeg. They stopped to meet Aunt Mafta and her husband. Mafta had not yet met her niece, so this was a treat for everyone involved. Since Aunt Mafta didn't have any children of her own, she offered to look after Mary while Michael went off to Saskatchewan to work. Michael rejected the idea outright. He didn't go to all the bother of bringing Mary to Canada and have someone else look after her in another province. Michael didn't want Mary to grow up on someone else's farm working as a "servant". Mafta was a very nice and caring person, but from the old school of "girls didn't need an education". Michael was of another mind. He wanted Mary to have an opportunity to go to school and have all the opportunities he missed as a child and as a youth; and to grow up in a community he approved of and respected. Finally he wanted a hand in bringing up his daughter he had missed for seven years. To Michael, schooling and the opportunities that were available in Canada were too good to be true. He was going to make sure that Mary had all the opportunities for an education that he was deprived of in

Bukovina. A few days later they boarded the train for the trip to Yorkton, Saskatchewan and on to Hatfield.

Arriving in Hatfield was a relief. With all that travelling past her, Mary was going to meet her uncle Nick and uncle Bill and their families and renew acquaintances with her uncle George. There were new Canadian cousins to meet and play with. Michael and Mary moved in with the Bill and Ann Kotyk in Hatfield for the time being while Michael worked in Hatfield and Nokomis, a town just down the C.P.R. rail line from Hatfield. His work on the section crew at Hatfield and Nokomis lasted a few months. With Mary and Michael arriving in Hatfield during the first week of April, Michael decided that Mary would stay home for the few months and acquaint herself with the Kotyk families she had never met, and start school in September.

Mary, shortly after her arrival at Hatfield pictured with cousins Johnnie, left and Billy on her Uncle Bill's lap. May, 1935.

In the meantime, Nick Kotyk was busy as could be at Gronlid. He soon was in need of more men for his crew. He requested that Michael come up to Gronlid to assist him. This worked out very well for Michael since he had already worked in Gronlid and liked the area. He wanted to move from the Hatfield community because there were so few Ukrainian speaking people there.

Michael and Mary moved to Gronlid in July, 1935 and stayed with the Nick Kotyks until Michael found some housing to buy. The C.P.R provided the section foreman with a company house in every community large enough to accommodate a section crew. Nick had a two storey section house that was large enough to accommodate Michael and Mary for the interim. Michael wanted a place of his own and soon found a small dwelling to purchase. Mary recalls that it was a real treat to have a home of their own after living with aunts and uncles for so long. In reality this house was a small shack or lean-to with enough room for a table, a few chairs, a wood burning stove and a room for two cots. There was an outdoor toilet and no running water. Water for drinking and washing was brought in from the town well by pail. Water had to be heated on the stove for washing and bathing. It was primitive at best, but to Mary this was like heaven. It was better than Bukovina since she had her dad and it was their home. She wasn't living in someone else's house. By December, 1935 they were settled in their own home and had a routine. Michael worked six days a week and Mary learned to lock the door and be off to school with her "lunch pail". After school she would go to Nick Kotyk's or to a neighbor's until Michael got home from work at 5 o'clock. Mary became quite self sufficient in the days and months to come. She was helping with the household chores, making lunch, learning the English language and adjusting to school, a new country and life in small town Saskatchewan.

6

THE GRONLID YEARS

Mary used to help making her lunch every day and packed her lunch pail to school. The "lunch pail" was a common and necessary object for most school children, especially rural school children from the early 1900's to the 1950's. The lunch pail was a small metal bucket with a handle and lid. Originally lard, peanut butter, jam, honey, or syrup was packed and sold in these pails. These pails varied in size anywhere from one liter to four liters. These sizes of pails were very useful items to recycle. They were used in picking and collecting berries and to pack school lunches for school children. The pail would hold sandwiches, a jar of milk, a few cookies or cake, some vegetables and fruit. Most children of that era remember the lunch pail as a container for food, but on occasion it became a weapon of self defense against teasing or bullying peers. More than one person ended up with a welt or a "goose egg" on the head from this primitive weapon of self defense. Lunch boxes for children, as we know them today, the "Barbie, Flintstones, Superman or Spiderman cartoon themed lunch kits" did not exist prior to the fifties. There were adult sized lunch boxes or a "dinerka" (di-nerka) as they called it in Ukrainian, that men took to work in the fields or on railway or construction jobs. These lunch boxes were usually about twelve inches long, six to eight inches wide and eight inches high. The dinerka was large enough to hold several sandwiches, a large thermos of coffee or tea, deserts and fruits and vegetables.

Michael enrolled Mary at the Gronlid Public School a block away from their home, and Mary was off to a new beginning. School to Mary was an adventure. There were lots of children to play with and language was not a huge barrier. At the beginning she couldn't speak English but there were enough Ukrainian speaking children in school to help bridge any communication gap that arose. It didn't take long for Mary to pick up the English language and fit into the educational and social setting in the community.

Michael was no stranger to Gronlid and area, since he had been relieving for many section crews and the section foremen in the north-east division of Canadian Pacific Railways got to know him. Communities like White Fox, Smeaton, Nipawin, Tisdale, Arborfield and other nearby locations were places where Michael had relieved prior to bringing Mary to Canada. Gronlid was the community that Michael preferred because of its Ukrainian background and progressive outlook. Michael had befriended a couple who had just got married and opened a general store on Main Street in Gronlid.

John and Dorothy Panchuk were that couple. They were married on July 14, 1935 and with John working on his dad's farm and other farms, he managed to save a few dollars and set up a general store. Dorothy was the daughter of Michael and Anna Pohoreski of Trylid (northwest of Melfort) and later from Lenvale (north of Melfort), Saskatchewan. The building that John and Dorothy built was a two storey building on Main Street with the store on the main floor and the living quarters on the second floor. Building a store and investing in stock was a risky enterprise, since the economic depression of the 1930's was present. The crops, however, in the Gronlid, Melfort, Tisdale and Nipawin areas were bountiful since they escaped the severe drought and dust bowl that the rest of the Prairie Provinces suffered. The farmers in the Melfort area were reaping 40+ bushels to the acre crops of wheat during the drought compared to the rest of the Prairie Provinces harvesting 10 to 15 bushels to the acre on a good harvest. Many farmers in the drought stricken areas would have been fortunate if they could salvage their crops for cattle feed. The farmers in the Gronlid area could pay their bills and Dorothy and John prospered in their business venture. The general store carried groceries and food staples such as flour, sugar, spices, peanut butter (by the pail), seasonal fruits, dried fruits and vegetables, canned goods, cheese wheels, cured meats and bulk food products, nuts, fabrics, thread and basic clothing (coveralls, mitts, caps, underwear, shirts and footwear such as rubber boots, valyenky—knee high felt liners for rubber boots) and other assorted footwear. There were three other grocery/general stores in Gronlid plus a few hardware stores, a few implement dealers and garages that serviced cars, trucks and tractors for the few people that could afford them. A hotel, a café, a community hall, the Post Office, and a poolroom/billiard hall/barbershop completed the main business area. Adjacent to the railway tracks were four grain elevators, a flour mill owned by Louis Pohoreski, a brother to Dorothy Panchuk, the stockyard, railway station and its warehouse and platform, the coal dock and water tower to service the steam locomotives and several warehouses that stored coal and a variety of packaged feed and fertilizer. Gronlid was a bustling community with a population of several hundred people and a large farming community from which to draw. John and Dorothy Panchuk were aggressive and successful in their business venture. The community of Gronlid was growing and expanding in the 1930's and John and Dorothy were taking full advantage of the opportunities that were presented to them. John farmed as well, but soon realized that the store operation was a growing and lucrative business venture. They would soon expand the store operation to include warehouses to store more product such as flour, sugar and canned goods. In addition, John took over the British American Oil Company (B-A) bulk fuel dealership to deliver bulk fuel to farmers. They even hired a farm hand to look after the farm while they attended to their businesses.

Melfort, 32 kilometers to the south with a population of 5,000, was the closest large center to Gronlid. The residents of Gronlid accessed the larger centers such as Melfort by train. In the 1930's, motor vehicles were not that common and were the exclusive domain of the more affluent. Country roads were dirt roads with highways being gravel covered. Pavement was only used on main streets in cities. Travel by vehicle was either dusty or muddy in the spring, summer and autumn, and very cold in the winters, since cars were not equipped with heaters. Travel by train was cleaner and more reliable regardless of the season. Goods were transported by train throughout the year, thus communities like Gronlid would have regular mail service and food items were consistently supplied through the reliable railway system.

Michael and Mary set up their home in Gronlid during the spring and summer of 1935. Michael would get his groceries from Panchuk's General Store on a near daily basis since refrigerators were basically nonexistent in the 1930's. Grocery shopping for everyone in a small town of the day was a daily activity. Dorothy would assist Michael in selecting the groceries, and what would be appropriate for Mary's school lunches and what would be easy for Michael and Mary to prepare for themselves for their other meals. Dorothy looked out for Mary, since they didn't have any children of their own, and she admired Michael for taking on the challenge of raising a child on his own. Dorothy felt that Michael might need some assistance since he was a single father and in the 1930's that was rare. Michael would pick up his groceries after work, make supper for himself and Mary, then make their lunches for the next day. In the morning he would prepare breakfast, and after breakfast he would send Mary off to school with her lunch pail. He would set off to work himself and meet her at home after work or pick her up from the Kotyk's when she stayed there after school. Michael was concerned that Mary may need a snack after school, so to ensure that Mary would get a nourishing snack he set up an account at the store with Dorothy so that Mary could come in and get herself an apple, or an orange, some cookies, a chocolate bar, some peanuts or some other nutritional snack. Mary soon realized that this was pretty neat. She didn't have to pay for a treat and Dorothy was too happy to supply her with something to eat. One of Mary's friends came with her one day and got a treat too. This to a couple of seven year olds was too good to be true. Mary realized that it wasn't right but she just couldn't refuse her friend these treats of chocolates and fruits while she was getting them for herself. Mary hid the bills from her father. After a few too many trips to the store for treats, Dorothy realized that Mary was feeding her friends on Michael's tab. Dorothy advised Michael of what was going on and Mary's freedom of the "tab" was limited to her own purchases only. She was allowed snacks but that was where the line was drawn.

DREAM TO REALITY

Michael was a very good money manager, and even though the Great Depression and the drought of the 1930's was taking place, Michael managed to work extra hours and saved enough money to go to Europe and bring Mary back to Canada. In addition he saved enough money to buy a quarter section of land for $1100, about a mile north of Gronlid. Michael did not believe in borrowing money to make purchases. He did not want to be indebted to anyone, so his purchases were only made if he had the money in the bank. There were lots of trees on the land so Michael would have to clear some of the land if he were to cultivate it and settle on it. While he worked on the railway, he rented the cultivated portion to neighboring farmers. Michael envisioned the farm to be a place where he could grow a garden of vegetables, keep a cow and some cattle and chickens, but this would require some extra help such as a hired hand to look after the livestock.

Soon after Mary and Michael moved into the Gronlid community, they began to meet many new families which soon became friends. Church and cultural activities around community halls (Narody Domeh) accorded them many new acquaintances. John and Dorothy Panchuk became friends through the store and church activities.

John and Dorothy Panchuk had a car, so they offered to take Michael and Mary to church on Sundays and to church related activities such as choir practices and drama rehearsals at other times during the week. The Ukrainian Orthodox Churches traditionally were located in rural areas as opposed to villages and large towns, since farmers usually donated a small patch of land on their homestead, one or two acres, on which to build their church or locate their cemetery, or both. Another reason for rural churches was that most of the early Ukrainian settlers were farmers. Farms were small, mostly quarter section farms, so farmers lived quite close to one another. There were very few urban Ukrainians in Western Canada except for the large cities such as Winnipeg, Saskatoon and Edmonton. The two churches that the Panchuks attended were the Maryville St. Mary Ukrainian Orthodox Church (locally referred to as Franko Church, (named after the famous Ukrainian Poet Ivan Franko) since it was located across the road from the Ivan Franko Narodny Deem (Community Hall). This Church and Hall were located several kilometers north and east of Gronlid. The other church that the Panchuks attended was the St. Peter and St. Paul Ukrainian Orthodox Church, located just outside the village of Brooksby, the home church of Dorothy's parents, Michael and Anna Pohoreski. Mary enjoyed attending the Brooksby Church since Dorothy had younger siblings, two of which were approximately Mary's age; Tony, one year older, and Joanne, one year younger than Mary.

Michael and Mary attended Brooksby St. Peter and St. Paul Ukrainian Orthodox Church as often as John and Dorothy Panchuk attended. Michael and Mary were invited to the Michael Pohoreski home for dinners and family occasions thus they became better acquainted with the Pohoreski family. Michael liked the family oriented attitude of the Pohoreski family and their love for music, singing and maintaining Ukrainian culture in general. Michael Pohoreski was literate and very musical, playing the violin and dulcimer. He in fact, made his own violins and dulcimers. All of Michael and Anna Pohoreski's children played an instrument. They had their own family orchestra with Louis playing violin, Tena the organ, Dorothy the mandolin, Marie the guitar, Tony the banjo, Pauline the accordion and Joanne the piano.

DREAM TO REALITY

As Michael and Mary met with the Pohoreski's more frequently during the years of 1935 and 1936, Tena (Teklia) the eldest of the Pohoreski children caught Michael's eye and soon Michael and Tena were seen together more often. Both Michael and Mary liked Tena, and Mary enjoyed the large family atmosphere and the friendship of Tony and Joanne, Tena's youngest siblings.

Mary continued in her new school setting in Gronlid during the autumn of 1935 and into 1936. She was learning English quickly and assimilating into Canadian school routine. She completed her first grade without any difficulty and as June, 1936 rolled around she as most school children feel in June, was ready for summer holidays. During the summer of 1936 Mary journeyed to Gonor, Manitoba to spend the summer holidays with her aunt Mafta. The trip to and from Gonor was neat, since going down to Gonor she travelled by train (using her Dad's railway pass), and when she was ready to come back Michael went down to pick her up again by train via the railway employees' pass. Mary enjoyed her time at the farm just outside Gonor. This holiday worked out just fine for all parties. Aunt Mafta got to spend some time with her new niece. Mary had all this time to herself with her aunt and met some new friends in Gonor. Michael benefitted from Mary's summer holiday since he had time to attend to planning a wedding to take place in September of 1936.

Michael and Tena Tkaczyk, September 13, 1936

During the summer of 1936 Michael proposed to Tena and then went to ask the permission and the blessing of Michael and Anna Pohoreski for their daughter's hand in marriage. The wedding was set for September 13, 1936 at the Brooksby St. Peter and St. Paul Ukrainian Orthodox Church with the reception taking place at the Pohoreski farm. It was the norm with rural weddings that the wedding ceremony be held in the local church and that the reception take place at the farm. The meals were served indoors unless the weather was cooperative then they were held outdoors on long tables. A platform would be constructed for dancing and the local musicians provided the music. Most weddings were family and close friend affairs so the numbers of guests was not that great. With the Great

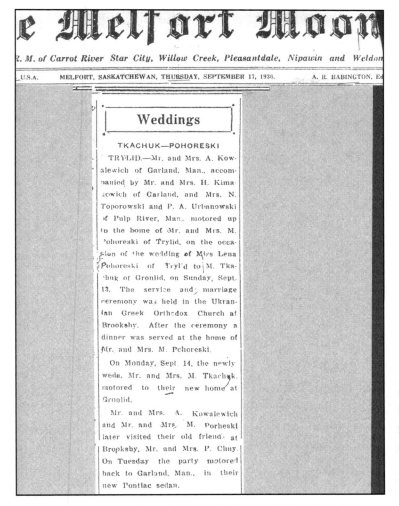

Front Page News Item in THE MELFORT MOON Weekly Newspaper September 17, 1936 Source: Tkachyk Collection

Depression taking place people did not have a lot of money to spare for frivolous things like large parties.

Mary was probably the most excited person in the wedding party. This was a hallmark day for her. She had a complete family. Not only did she have her dad, she now had a Mother. In addition to that she also gained an instant family—a Baba and Dido, lots of uncles and aunts and then there was Tony and Joanne, technically her uncle and aunt, but they were her age almost like brother and sister. They became close friends as well as family. During the year following the wedding, Michael and Teklia (Tena) decided to build a new house in Gronlid since the living quarters that Michael and Mary had been using were very cramped for three people. They moved into their new house in 1937 which was a much larger house (500-600 sq. ft.) than the previous dwelling. Mary, by this time was enjoying school and doing well, keeping up with the curriculum and mastering the English language. During the summer Mary and her new mother would go out to the farm and pick roots to clear the soil to enable the smooth seeding procedure for the wheat crops, tend the large vegetable garden and can preserves for the winter. Michael and Tena bought a pre-owned 1928 Chevrolet that served their local transportation purposes, since they had the use of railway passes for longer trips. Michael continued to work on the railroad and was established as a permanent section man (a permanent laborer maintaining the railway tracks) in Gronlid. In 1937 he became the "First Man" on the railway crew or assistant to the Section Foreman. Michael knew his job well and worked hard. His experience in the Romanian Army Engineers building roads and bridges was

Mary and Tena Playing Mandolin and Guitar on the Front Steps of Their new Home in Gronlid. 1937

becoming very useful in maintaining and building railway tracks and the track beds. Michael had also been learning to read and write in English which enabled him to keep books, maintain time sheets and file reports to the Roadmasters and the Superintendent of the Canadian Pacific Railways. Tena being Canadian born and having gone to school in Zalicia (near Garland), Manitoba achieved a grade eight education, before she had to drop out of school to help on the farm. She, along with Mary's mastery of the English language helped Michael sharpen his English skills. Before long Michael was elevated to a relieving foreman, taking over work crews for one to two weeks at a time to relieve existing foremen who were away on sick leave, holidays or who were transferred.

A Spring Sunday Afternoon in Gronlid. Michael Standing on Bed of Truck. Left to Right: unidentified, John Danyluk, Mary, Tena, Pauline Pohoreski, Louis Pohoreski. 1937

April of 1938 was an exciting time. A baby girl, Lessia was born to Michael and Tena, a baby sister for Mary. Mary was in grade four and progressing very well in school and enjoying her baby sister. The household was abuzz as was the rest of the family, since Dorothy and John Panchuk, that same year became the parents of a set of twins, Ann and Sylvia. Mary had her hands full in this new country and enjoyed every minute of it. She had her new found friends in Gronlid at school, her new mother's brothers and sisters, a new infant sister, Lessia and new infant twin cousins, Ann and Sylvia Panchuk as well as the Kotyk side of the family with all the aunts, uncles and cousins. Mary's summers were spent at the farm near Gronlid or visiting the Bill Kotyk's at Nokomis, Saskatchewan using her father's railway pass. She would spend part of her summers in Nokomis visiting with her cousins Peter, Johnny and Elizabeth Kotyk. By 1939, Michael, Tena, Mary and some hired workers cleared enough land that meaningful grain crops could be seeded. In the fall of 1940 they had a "bumper" crop that brought in a substantial harvest. After selling the grain and paying all the expenses, they had made enough money to purchase a shiny new maroon 1941 Chevrolet which they

Michael, Tena and Mary in a Family Photo 1937

Michael and Lessia, Feeding Chickens on the Family Farm. Gronlid, 1939.

kept through to 1954. They also bought two horses to pull the necessary farm machinery. A "disker" was purchased for $30 (two weeks salary working on the railroad) and a seed drill. They built a new barn for the horses, bought two cows, chickens and fixed up a two room house on the farm for a hired hand to live on the farm year round. And of course they had a huge garden that would provide them with vegetables and preserves throughout the year. The hired hand was John Mateyko, who had worked on the railroad with Michael, but loved farm work. Michael hired him to live on the farm and do the required daily farm chores of seeding, harvesting, milking cows, tending the chickens and clearing more trees to increase the cultivated acres. Michael was getting firmly established in this new country, something he never could have accomplished in his former home, Bukovina. As Michael was experiencing success in Canada, Europe was engulfed in the beginnings of a bitter conflict which was to become World War II. Ukraine and Bukovina would soon be caught in the middle of the Nazi–Soviet conflict.

Mary and Friend Feeding Cattle in Front of the New Barn under Construction, Gronlid, 1941.

In the meantime during this period of the late 1930's and on into the 1940's, John and Dorothy Panchuk's general store was a going concern. Business was growing despite the negative issues of the time. The outbreak of War with Nazi Germany, the Great Depression and drought of the 1930's did not have a negative effect on the businesses in Gronlid. John and Dorothy's hard work meant an expanding business and they had to bring in extra help. With the twin babies, Ann and Sylvia, and with the busy schedule of the store and their farm, they brought Dorothy's younger sister Pauline in to assist in the store. Pauline Pohoreski was a very capable assistant in the store. All the Pohoreski children were involved in farming or the Post Office and store operations that Michael and Anna Pohoreski had owned or operated in Zalicia, Manitoba or Trylid and Lenvale, Saskatchewan. As the saying goes," There were no free rides in the Pohoreski family"; everybody had to pull their weight or do their share of the work. Pauline was used to taking on responsibility and handled the work in the store very well. At age 16 she had mastered not only the store duties, but she also delivered groceries by car to the local priest, and older ladies in town, she also learned how to drive John Panchuk's grain truck in order to deliver grain to the grain elevators during the autumn harvesting season. She also delivered 45 gallon (180 liter) drums of gasoline to the farmers from John Panchuk's Bulk B-A (British American Oil Company) fuel station. But as a store clerk she had one weakness, she loved peanut butter. On one occasion Dorothy Panchuk asked Pauline to fill small jars of peanut butter from a large 12 kilogram pail. In those days peanut butter was not homogenized, thus it had to be thoroughly mixed before transferring into jars. Pauline mixed the peanut butter up and transferred the peanut butter into the small jars, but as usual there was some peanut butter that had not been mixed well and these dry leftovers were just too good to be true to a connoisseur of peanut butter. Pauline couldn't let that go to waste, so she scraped up the remnants of dry peanut butter, (about a tablespoon) and popped it into her mouth. As she tried to swallow the peanut butter, she realized she was in trouble. The dry peanut butter stuck to the roof of her mouth and lodged in her throat. At that moment, as chance would have it, the priest walked into the store. Here she was gagging on a mouthful of peanut butter as the priest started talking to her and she couldn't respond. She left the priest standing in the store, and flew down the stairs to the basement of the store where there was a rain barrel full of water. She madly started scooping the rainwater into her mouth with her hands to help dislodge the peanut butter. She loosened the sticky mass of peanut butter, swallowed hard and then tried to compose herself to go upstairs to serve the priest. The priest meanwhile, thought Pauline was trying to avoid him and started calling out her name. As Pauline came back upstairs still coughing from her ordeal with the dry peanut butter, the priest gave her a mild lecture about trying to avoid older people when they must be served. In spite of all the embarrassment she endured, the priest was served, the peanut butter got into the jars and Pauline got her peanut butter fix, albeit a very dry and trying experience.

The Pohoreski siblings were slowly leaving the farm at Trylid. Tena, Louis, Dorothy and Marie being the four oldest children did not get the opportunity to finish high school. They had to help on the farm, work in the blacksmith shop, help in the Post Office and store and help with the four younger siblings, Pauline, Adam, Tony, and Joanne. Marie, Tena's younger sister stayed on to help at home until 1943, when she married Harry Dobrowolsky from Gronlid. Pauline left to work at Panchuk's store in Gronlid. Adam was an excellent student completing his high school in Gronlid and was interested in pharmacy. He had no interest in the blacksmith trade of his father. In 1943 Michael and Tena encouraged Adam and assisted him financially to move to Prince Albert to work at Zubrack's Drug Store, earn some money for university and acquaint himself with the pharmacy profession before enrolling at the University of Saskatchewan. Adam, during that year had a change of heart about entering pharmacy studies and joined the Royal Canadian Air Force. Adam, after basic training and a year in Electrical Engineering at McGill University in Montreal was commissioned to the rank of Flight Lieutenant and served in England and Belgium during the final stages of the Second World War. Through Royal Canadian Air Force sponsorship, Adam gained his Master's degree in Electrical Engineering from McGill, and worked for Rockwell Industries in the United States assisting in developing the Redstone Rockets that initially powered Intercontinental Ballistic Missiles during the Cold War of the 1950's and 1960's and later the Redstone Rocket became the mainstay of the early space programs of the 1960's. Tony and Joanne continued their high school in Fairy Glen, six kilometers north of Lenvale. Tony went to Normal School (Teacher's College), taught for a few years then left for Hamilton, Ontario, where better paying jobs were more plentiful. He went on to became a successful business man in Hamilton and still resides there. Joanne completed her high school in Fairy Glen. She became a stenographer and was the stenographer for the head stewardess in Montreal for Trans Canada Airlines (Air Canada), and presently lives in Vancouver, British Columbia. Michael and Anna Pohoreski sold their two quarters of land at Trylid along with their store and Post Office and moved to Lenvale, closer to Gronlid and Brooksby. At Lenvale they would operate a store, the Post Office and blacksmith shop until 1961, when they retired to Prince Albert.

In the years 1937-1941, during the spring, summer and fall months, Mary and her new mother and later in 1938, with Lessia in tow, would drive out to the farm every day to tend to the chickens, tend to the large garden and pick up milk, cream and eggs that the hired man would have ready for them. In the late fall and winter there was less to do on the farm after the garden was brought in and the cucumbers and tomatoes canned and the potatoes, carrots, beets, cabbage and other produce put into storage. Winter was the quiet time with school work, visiting friends and family, attending church and community functions, sewing, embroidery, knitting and reading occupying everyone's time. Mary learned knitting, sewing and embroidery during those winter months.

Mary, Pictured in one of the Dresses that Tena Sewed for Her During the Winter Evenings in Gronlid. 1939

Michael loved to read and was very involved in supporting Ukrainian Institutions that fostered communication, education and the Church. He bought shares in, and subscribed to the "Ukrainian Voice" (Ukrainskey Holos), a Ukrainian weekly newspaper based in Winnipeg and whose editor was Myroslaw Stechishin, one of the three prominent Stechishin brothers. This publication gave him Canadian news, World news and news from the Ukrainian Canadian community. Radios were not common at this time and television was but a far off reality. Print media was the most common communication tool of the 1930's and 1940's, thus newspapers and the telegraph were the major media communications tools. Michael was also supportive of the Peter Mohyla Ukrainian Institute in Saskatoon that came into existence in 1916 and still exists today as the St. Petro Mohyla Ukrainian Institute. The purpose of the Institute was to provide a meeting place and dwelling for Ukrainian Canadians who wanted to further their education by attending high school or post secondary schools while maintaining their cultural roots. The Peter Mohyla Ukrainian Institute was also the birthplace and home to other Ukrainian Organizations but primarily the birthplace of the Ukrainian Orthodox Church of Canada in 1918. Michael had visions of Mary accessing the opportunity of attending the Peter Mohyla Ukrainian Institute and attain a post secondary education.

Michael was generally a healthy person, but in 1939 he came down with an infection. His legs would swell and ache. At times he couldn't walk because of the pain. He was physically weak. His medical home physician book "Domashnay Likar" was of no value to him with this illness. He went to doctors in Melfort but they could not pin down the source of the infection. He tried self healing by going to Watrous, Saskatchewan, where the healing waters of Lake Manitou were supposed to help, but the mineral laden salt water of the lake that helped others with their aches and pains did not help Michael. He had heard of the Sulphur Hot Springs from The Cave on Sulphur Mountain at Banff, Alberta that worked wonders with ailments. He set off to Banff via his railway pass. He soaked in the Sulphur Springs but they didn't help either. He felt a bit better but it still did not cure his weakness and pains. A chance conversation with a gentleman in the pool at Banff acquainted Michael with a physician who was staying at the Banff Springs Hotel. The Physician casually examined Michael and asked Michael if he had his tonsils removed. Michael explained to the physician that he had never had any kind of surgery. The Physician explained to Michael that there were no tonsils to be seen. Upon further examination the physician discovered that Michael's tonsils had deteriorated and had become infected and had fallen out of sight in his throat. The tonsils were so infected that they were causing a poisoning effect on the body, thus the cause of Michael's weakness, pain and swelling. Within a few days the physician had Michael admitted to the Banff Springs Hospital and Michael had his tonsils removed. A week later with tonsils removed, and penicillin doing its magic, Michael was a healthy person and he returned to Gronlid ready to continue his work on the farm and the railroad. This was Michael's

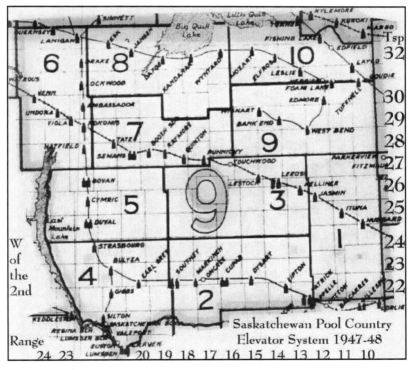

Michael's Promotion and Transfer to Sinnett, a Siding North of Lanigan, Top Left of Map Above Area 8, Was One of Several Promotions and Moves. Source: Saskatchewan Wheat Pool Archives, 1947-48.

only serious illness until his golden years in the 1980's.

Mary continued to do well in school. In 1940-1941, Mary completed her grade 6 and grade 7 by completing the curriculum requirements for both grades in the one school year. The school advanced her from grade 6 to grade 8 in the space of one year due to her academic achievements. Considering that Mary knew no English when she arrived in Canada in 1935, her progress in school was exceptional.

The Seniority List of "A" Section Men. Source: Brotherhood of Maintenance of Way Employees of the Canadian Pacific Railway Company. 1940

In 1941, Michael received a promotion to first man and then to relieving foreman and was transferred to Sinnett, a siding about 10 kilometers north of Lanigan. There was no town site at

Sinnett, nothing but a few elevators and a tiny railway station. The foreman and work crew were allowed to live in Lanigan where they could find housing and send their children to Lanigan Public School. The work crew would "commute" the ten kilometers to Sinnett. Michael and Tena moved to Lanigan with Mary and Lessia and all their belongings, including their cow. They moved into a small two storey house on the edge of town across the street from Tom Fraser, the C.P.R. foreman, and his family. According to the Lanigan town by-laws, since the house was near the edge of town, they could keep the cow. Michael built a small barn/shelter out of used railway ties for the cow to live in through the winter. The rent they paid for this house was a princely sum of $8.00 per month. In the mean time they rented out their home in Gronlid and John Mateyko continued to look after the farm and animals.

Michael's work crew would pick up their tools from the tool shed in Lanigan and with the C.P.R. motor car or "jigger" as they called it, would travel the 10 kilometers by rail to Sinnett to maintain the track and track bed.

As was the practice in small communities, Gronlid held a farewell party for the Tkaczyk's before they left Gronlid. After all, Michael had lived and worked in the Gronlid area for eight years, Mary lived in Gronlid and attended school in Gronlid for seven years and Tena had lived in Gronlid for five years. The Tkaczyk family had become an integral part of Gronlid life. At that farewell party, Michael presented the Gronlid School with a gift of a War Bond. War Bonds were marketed by the Dominion of Canada (the Federal Government of Canada) to raise money to pay the bills for the war effort. The Bond could be cashed with interest when it matured, then the Gronlid School could spend the money for books, equipment or supplies that they required. Michael was so grateful for the progress that Mary was making in school, he felt that this gift was the least he could do to show his appreciation for the freedoms that he and his daughter were experiencing and the fact that Mary was enjoying school and excelling in academics.

Michael, throughout his life would support and contribute to educational endeavors whenever the opportunity presented itself, whether it was a contribution to an institution or a contribution to assist an individual in need who wanted to further his or her education.

John Mateyko was left to run the farm in Gronlid. The farm operation was quite profitable even with the hired man running it. With the depression and drought taking place in the late 1930's in the Prairie Provinces, the Melfort-Nipawin area had rain and some very productive yields of grain. So even with the depressed world prices for grain, farmers in the Melfort-Nipawin area were making a very reasonable living because of the volume of grain that was harvested. John Mateyko, Michael's C.P.R. colleague and hired farm hand, got married, and he and his wife Helen eventually

> **Farewell Party Held in Honor of Tkachuk Family**
>
> GRONLID—In honor of Mr. and Mrs. Mike Tkachuk who are moving to Lanigan, a jolly farewell party was held in the primary school at Gronlid on April 14 with many friends and neighbors attending.
>
> The early part of the evening was spent in playing "Novelty Whist" in which prizes for high score went to Mrs. L. E. Lokken and Mr. Bill Tuffin while low score prizes went to Mrs. Collins and Mr. A. Sawchuk.
>
> After lunch had been served, H. M. Swisston expressed regret at the departure of Mr. and Mrs. Tkachuk and family and asked them to accept a handsome bedspread and tablecloth as a farewell remembrance from their Gronlid friends.
>
> Speeches were made by Mr. and Mrs. Tkachuk and Mary Tkachuk, H. E. Tanner, D. Pavelick, L. E. Lokken and Mr. Tkachuk presented a War Certificate to the school as a parting gift. The proceeds of the certificate, when matured to be used for some school purpose.
>
> Games and singing added to the pleasure of the evening. Mr. Tkachuk left for Lanigan Tuesday morning to take over the position of "First man" on the C. P. R. section crew.

began to rent Michael's land which was more profitable for both parties. The land was so productive that Michael bought another quarter section of land south east of Gronlid and rented it out until 1956 when he sold the land.

In the years between 1935 and 1941, Michael had done very well in his newly adopted country. As many of his countrymen had done, Michael took advantages of the opportunities that presented themselves and became financially independent. These opportunities required long hard hours of work farming, growing and producing your own food, holding down more than one job and watching how money was spent. Credit and loans were hard to come by, but Michael did not depend on loans since he paid for everything in cash. He could not have achieved this success in his former homeland. This new country was expanding and growing with jobs available to those who wanted them, and land was just waiting to be purchased and cultivated. To those willing to work the future was bright. Michael was financially stable and personally successful in the midst of severe economic times, through hard work and diligence. He established himself financially, brought Mary to Canada, bought two quarters of farmland, got married, learned English, bought farm machinery and livestock, bought an older car and later bought a new car.

Michael on the Front of a Railway Snow Plow at Lanigan. 1942

His daughter was succeeding in school and he was laying a ground work for the future. He was also raising a new family as well, with the arrival of a second daughter, Lessia. The land of opportunity that he dreamed of prior to 1928 was indeed a fact and the possibilities were numerous. Michael's future in Canada looked bright and promising.

The Lanigan years were busy years. Mary attended Lanigan School for grade 8, 9 and part of grade 10. Michael was busy with his railroad work and Tena was busy with Lessia and sewing and knitting and when time permitted on weekends they were off to Gronlid to tend to the farm and visit family.

The little two storey house in which the Tkaczyk's lived in Lanigan had electric lights, which was a first for them, but the house had no electrical appliances. Wood stoves and space heaters were used for heating and cooking. There was no central heating in most homes of the day. The electric lights were a novelty and most appreciated since they provided a steady and brighter light at night for fine needlework and reading; not like those dim kerosene lamps that they had been using in their other houses. To Michael these electric lights were astounding, since in Bukovina, electricity was unheard of even in 1935. The large cities like Chernivtsi and Lviv had electricity but many of the homes did not avail themselves of the new convenience due to the extreme costs involved.

During that first winter, on January 5, 1942, Mary and Lessia were taken over to Komar's, friends of Michael and Tena's for what would today be called a "sleep over". When Mary and three and half year old Lessia returned home the next morning of January 6, 1942, they had a new baby brother, George. Not only was this baby brother born on Christmas Eve of the Julian Calendar, this baby was the New Year's Baby in Lanigan. This was big news in Lanigan, mind you, in a town as small as Lanigan, a baby could be born in July or August and still be classed as a New Year's Baby. The award for being the new Year's baby in Lanigan was the awarding of a case, 24 cans, of Carnation evaporated milk from the Carnation Milk Company. Needless to say, everyone enjoyed the canned milk.

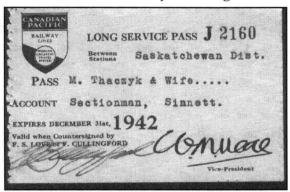

A C.P.R. Railway Pass that was Issued to Employees and Their Families for Complimentary Rail Travel in Canada

Baba Pohoreski, travelled out from Lenvale to Lanigan by train to assist with the cooking and cleaning and caring for the family while Tena and George got into a routine. Baba Pohoreski stayed in Lanigan for about ten days until some normalcy returned to the home then she returned to Lenvale.

During their tenure in Lanigan, the Tkaczyk's moved to another more comfortable house and for the last year they moved into the section foreman's house which was the traditional two storey deep red C.P.R. house with its matching outdoor pit toilet.

The young Tkaczyk family now numbered five. For Mary this was great. Not only did she have the Kotyk families in Gronlid, Nokomis and Gonor, she gained a mother and a sister and brother and all the Pohoreski's in seven short years since she came to Canada. From Lanigan Michael and Tena with Mary, Lessia and George would motor or travel by train to Gronlid to look after their farm affairs and visit family. They would spend weekends during the spring, summer and fall on the farm, expanding its productivity and making full use of the produce that they harvested. The Pohoreski clan was all living in close proximity of Gronlid so family visits with the Panchuk's, Pohoreski's, Dobrowolsky's and all their extended families made for fun-filled, loud and memorable visits. There were cousins galore on both sides of every family thus family gatherings of thirty or more people at a time was not uncommon.

George Tkaczyk, right and Cousin, Ted Panchuk, left, Sitting in the Grass on the Tkaczyk Farm. Summer, 1942

Michael and Tena were planning to settle down and farm in the Gronlid area, since they already owned two quarters of land, but the reliable and moderately well paying job on the railway was an opportunity that Michael did not want to give up. In addition Michael was advancing on the seniority lists, and the railway travel passes for himself and his family, were bonuses he didn't want to give up just yet. The railway travel passes were extremely useful within the Saskatchewan district since he and the family could travel at will any time they wanted to. For interprovincial travel, travel across Canada and the United States, Michael had to get a special extended travel railway pass. This extended travel pass depended on your seniority with the C.P.R. These incentives kept beckoning Michael to continue with the C.P.R. The uncertainty of the previous years of drought and economic depression made Michael cautious about leaving a steady paying job only to rely on farming two quarters of land for a living. While he was in good health and he was physically capable of handling the laborious work he decided to continue with the railway.

After spending three years in Lanigan as relieving foreman, Michael received another transfer in October of 1943 and

Michael, in 1941 was Transferred to The Siding of Buccleugh, west of Unity. Source: Saskatchewan Wheat Pool Archives, 1947-48

a promotion to permanent section foreman. This transfer and promotion was to take Michael and his family out of the familiar Ukrainian communities in which he had been working for so many years. This move was to Buccleugh, Saskatchewan, a siding west of Unity, Saskatchewan and south west of the Battlefords, near the Alberta-Saskatchewan border. Buccleugh was in the middle of nowhere. All there was at this siding was a small railway station with a platform (no station agent), a tool shed, a few small dwellings similar to lean-to's and a section foreman's house with its matching dark red outdoor pit toilet. There wasn't even a grain elevator there. All this was nestled in the hills about 20 kilometers from civilization, the community of Unity, where Michael and Tena would have to go to buy food and supplies. Rutland, a community with a population of 100 people was about 18 kilometers to the west. There was no highway to Buccleugh, just a series of dirt country roads. Michael did not want to turn down this move since he was receiving a raise in pay, a permanent position with the company, and he knew that he would move on to a more desirable location in a short period of time. He was moving up on the seniority lists and was getting into preferential positions. This Buccleugh appointment was an irritant in Michael's scheme of things, but it was a stepping stone and Michael wanted to take advantage of that. With all the hills surrounding Buccleugh, at night the coyotes would start their howling; an eerie and melancholy chorus that echoed and re-echoed in the quiet prairie summer air. It sounded like many children crying all at once. It really felt like this location was out of the civilized world.

Michael travelled by train to Buccleugh with all the household belongings and Jessie the jersey cow, safely secured in a cattle car. The C.P.R. paid for the moving expenses for their employees when they transferred them. Tena, Mary, Lessia and George travelled in the 1941 Chevy to Buccleugh, which was an adventure in itself. This was new territory to Tena. The highway system was in its infancy in the 1940's consisting of gravel roads which were dusty and rough with ruts and "washboard", a series of bumps in the road that were spaced closely together due to a combination of high traffic use and a sub-par road base. These series of bumps resembled a washboard that was a common household clothes washing device.

There was no school in Buccleugh so Michael and Tena made arrangements for Mary to travel by train from Lanigan to Gronlid and to stay with John and Dorothy Panchuk while she was completing her grade 10 during the 1943-44 school year. This was fine with Mary, since she knew most of the young people in Gronlid, she knew the school and its teachers, and Tony and Joanne Pohoreski were attending their high school in Fairy Glen just 10 kilometers away. There was family all around the Gronlid district so this was like home to Mary. Mary completed her grade 10 at Gronlid and started her grade 11 there as well, but there was an unexpected change in teachers at the Gronlid High School just prior to Christmas. It was decided that Mary would complete her grade 11 school year at the Nokomis High School in Nokomis while staying with the Bill Kotyk's. Mary enjoyed her year with the Kotyk's and did extremely well academically.

Michael, Tena, Lessia and George would spend the year in Buccleugh. The year was uneventful with Michael waiting for his opportunity to apply or "bid" for a more favorable location.

Lessia was turning six and ready to enter grade 1, but there was no school in Buccleugh. Michael and Tena were perplexed by this situation since there was no opportunity for Michael to "bid" out of Buccleugh. They were encouraged by Tena's sister Pauline who in 1944 married Jim Patrick, to let Lessia start Grade 1 in Goodeve, Saskatchewan. Jim Patrick was teaching at Goodeve, not far from Lanigan and Nokomis. It seemed like a good idea to leave Lessia with Jim and Pauline at Goodeve to attend Grade 1, while Michael's foreman assignment was stabilized. It had all the makings of a good plan except for one thing. No one consulted six year old Lessia about the idea, and she had a mind of her own. School started in September, 1945 but Lessia was homesick and she would have none of this new arrangement. She cried and fussed and fumed for two months. Life in Pauline's and Jim's home was not fun for anyone with this very upset child. Jim and Pauline were most accommodating and comforting but Lessia knew only one thing—she wanted her Mom and Dad. With Mom and Dad about 200 kilometers away even coming to see her on weekends was a near impossibility given the road conditions and train connections.

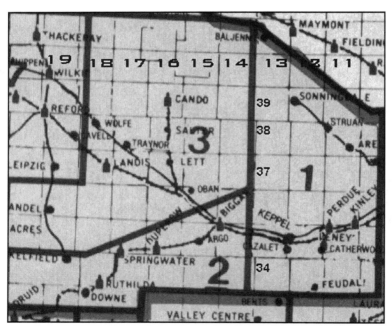

Sonningdale, Area 1, South of The North Saskatchewan River and the Village of Maymont on Today's Yellowhead Highway.
Source: Saskatchewan Wheat Pool Archives, 1924

DREAM TO REALITY

At this same time in late September of 1945 Michael received a transfer to Sonningdale, Saskatchewan as section foreman. Sonningdale had a school and that was all that Michael and Tena had to hear in order to solve a problem with Lessia's schooling; a problem that was most pressing. Sonningdale was about 90 kilometers from Buccleugh as the crow flies. There was no direct train connection or highway that connected the two communities. Travel by train would take one from Buccleugh east to Saskatoon then back west to Sonningdale on a different rail line.

There was the usual move by train and car to Sonningdale. The furniture, Jessie, the jersey cow and all the personal belongings were sent by train to Sonningdale. Michael accompanied the goods by rail while Tena and George drove to Sonningdale by car. Tena and George then drove to Goodeve to pick Lessia up and bring her back to Sonningdale where she started Grade 1 at Sonningdale School in November of 1945.

The move to Sonningdale for Michael and Tena was a more permanent move since Sonningdale was a village with a school. Lessia and George would have a neighborhood school to attend. Michael's previous two postings had been to sidings; temporary postings since there were no amenities at hand. Most postings to railway sidings were temporary by nature. The sidings would eventually close as work bases for railroad maintenance employees.

7

THE SONNINGDALE YEARS

Michael and Tena's move to Sonningdale was completed in October, 1945. The C.P.R. moved all the furniture and belongings including Jessie the jersey cow. The cow was like a family pet. In addition to the very rich milk and cream that the jersey cow rendered, she was very docile and had a mild temperament such that the children actually played with her. The family moved into the C.P.R. bunkhouse, while Michael built the usual small barn out of used railway ties for Jessie. The bunkhouse consisted of two rooms above ground and a root cellar to store garden produce. The two rooms of the bunkhouse were a kitchen and a bedroom; a humble but secure home but the most important issue was that the family was back together again. Bunkhouses were intended to house C.P.R. workmen, two or three to a bunkhouse, much like today's mobile work camps in the oil patch or in the forestry and lumber industry.

Lessia, after her brief attempt of schooling away from home, would successfully start grade one in November of 1945 in Sonningdale at Spartan School. George was three years old and was enjoying a group of young friends in the bustling community of approximately 150 people. This was a community that had a school encompassing grades 1-12, two general stores, two churches, two service stations/garages, a hotel, a community hall, a café or restaurant, a railway station and three grain elevators.

In 1946, Michael and Tena decided to send Mary to the St. Petro Mohyla Ukrainian Institute in Saskatoon, where she would attend Nutana Collegiate for her grade twelve year. Nutana was only two blocks from the Institute which made it very convenient for the students attending from the Institute. Saskatoon was only 90 kilometers away from Sonningdale so a quick trip into Saskatoon to see Mary was always possible. Michael's vision of Mary attending the Peter Mohyla Ukrainian Institute, completing her high school education and pursuing a post secondary education was nearing fruition. Mary would complete her grade twelve and enroll in the Faculty of Home Economics at the University of Saskatchewan the following year.

Tena, Baba Pohoreski and George, Who Wasn't Supposed to be in the Picture, on the Steps of the Bunkhouse in Sonningdale. 1945

The Sonningdale years for the most part were good years. The Tkaczyk's lived in the bunkhouse for a little more than a year while the C.P.R. was in the process of building a new section foreman's house. The Section house as it was called was a three bedroom bungalow painted in C.P.R. red and brown (actually maroon and brown) with the usual matching outdoor pit toilet sided and painted to match the house. All C.P.R. buildings that were built with wooden siding were painted in maroon and brown which included railway stations, ware houses, houses, garages, water towers, tool sheds and pit toilets. The huge yard was fenced and included a large garden. The positive thing about living in these small communities and working for the C.P.R. was that the C.P.R. owned a substantial amount of land along the railway right of way. This provided for large yards, large gardens, a subsequent abundance of produce and a large grazing area for the family cow. To Michael and Tena, the European and pioneering concept of being self-sufficient meant owning a cow that would provide milk and cream, some of which could be converted into cottage cheese and butter for the family. Michael twice built a small barn (shelter), from used railway ties. The first barn was built adjacent to the bunkhouse then later another barn was built across the road from the new section house, in farmer Ed White's field. The need for a family cow to provide fresh milk and dairy products for a family was a common reality in small communities. Transportation in the 1930's and 1940's did not have refrigeration units, thus perishable products were rarely ordered for and transported to small community stores. The majority of rural communities did not have an electrical supply for homes and businesses. A store or business that had its own power generator did not have such a powerful unit to power huge refrigeration units so substantial as to provide refrigeration for dairy products such as milk, cream, butter and cheese. Most stores may have had a soda pop cooler that was cooled by ice from a local ice house and perhaps an ice cream freezer that would hold six large 10 liter tubs of ice cream. That ice cream came packed in dry ice during regular train deliveries or on regular transport trucks. That luxury of large refrigeration units for produce, meat and dairy products was available in large cities. Electrification of rural communities did not occur until the mid to late 1950's. Commercial establishments in small towns that had electricity relied on their own electrical power generators. Lighting in homes was provided by kerosene or gas lamps.

The major stumbling block to completing Michael's dream for his family was that from 1941 to 1950, his C.P.R. job transfers took him and his family into communities where there were few Ukrainian families and more importantly there was no Ukrainian Church to attend. At Sonningdale, George and Lessia would attend the Pentecostal Sunday School program on Sunday mornings and would sing in the United Church Children's Choir on Sunday evenings for the evening Vespers. The United Church in Sonningdale didn't have Sunday morning church services on a regular basis since the United Church minister was shared by several neighboring communities such as Struan, Arelee and Baljennie. On occasion the Tkaczyk family would travel to Saskatoon to visit Mary and attend Sunday Divine Liturgy at the Ukrainian Orthodox Church in Saskatoon. That was a 90 kilometer trip over gravel roads which took several hours. Fortunately for Mary, as she was attending high school in communities away from her home and away from her immediate family, she was living in Ukrainian communities such as Gronlid, Nokomis, Foam Lake and Saskatoon where she had family and friends that were available to participate in these activities with her. The lack of a Ukrainian community was a stumbling block that Michael and his family would overcome, but it would take time.

Community life in Sonningdale was very active. The community hall was a beehive of activity. Once a week, one evening was set aside for the "showman" who came to Sonningdale from Asquith to show current movies on his 16mm projector. He brought his own electrical power generator to power the projector and a few light bulbs strung up in the hall. Normally light in the hall was provided for by four or five gas lamps. The movies that were shown covered the complete spectrum of Charlie Chaplin/Abbot and Costello slapstick comedies, to the Tom Mix/Hop-a-Long Cassidy westerns, to Dracula horrors and Humphrey Bogart dramas. The community hall movie presentations were common to all small communities, and the forerunner of movie theatres to which larger centers like North Battleford and Saskatoon were accustomed. On other nights the community hall was used for "carpet bowling", craft nights, card playing which included whist drives and bridge nights, Christmas Concerts and the traditional Saturday night dances. The Royal Canadian Legion and The Ladies Auxiliary of The Royal Canadian Legion met regularly in the United Church or the community hall raising funds through socials, dances and sales of various kinds to raise funds for the people in devastated parts of Europe following the Second World War. The community skating rink was busy during the winter and the school yard ball diamonds were busy with ball tournaments and sports days during the summer. The local hills were used for tobogganing and sledding in the winter and wagon races in the summer. There was never a lack of things to do for children from pre-school age to late teens and adults. The Churches

The Sonningdale Section House with its Matching Pit Toilet, "A One Seater". The Barn is Upper Left, The Garage is Middle behind the House. The Picture was Taken after a Severe Rainstorm that Flooded The Garden. 1948

played an instrumental role in community life as everyone attended one church or the other with all the children attending Sunday School and choir practices. Michael, Tena, Lessia and George participated in all of the events and activities on a regular basis.

In 1946 Michael and Tena moved into their new section house. They had all kinds of space, about 800 to 900 square feet of floor area, which was huge at the time. The house included a family type kitchen with room for a large dining table and six chairs, a living room, three bedrooms and a guest entry door with an entry closet. The back door opened directly into the kitchen. This was a fully modern house of the 1940's complete with full concrete basement. The house had no electricity since Saskatchewan had not yet started its province wide electrification program into rural communities and farms.

Lessia, Benny the Bull and George in Front of The Section House. Mary Washing Clothes on Washboard in Background. Note the Drain Pipe Sticking out of the House (1940's Plumbing) and the Barrel to Collect the Grey Water. 1948

Plumbing was absent from section houses except for a cistern in the basement to collect rain water from the roof that was directed into eaves troughs and through drainpipes down into the cistern. This "soft water" or rainwater was used for washing and bathing. Well water or "hard water" had minerals in it that made it best for cooking and drinking. This water had to be carried to the house from the local community water well. The kitchen sink was the only sink in the house. It was used for washing vegetables and dishes and was also used for washing hands, faces, ears, hair and brushing teeth. This single sink served all purposes and had a drain pipe that led directly through the wall and outside to empty into a 190 liter metal barrel. This barrel of grey water would be dumped out every evening so that the water would soak into the ground through the night. There was no bathroom in the house so a metal bathtub was located in the basement which was used by everyone for their baths. Plumbing in small rural communities was primitive if there was any at all. Later in the 1960's some communities through provincial initiatives would get water and sewer distribution systems based on wells pumping water into water towers to provide water to all homes in a village or town.

The Panchuks in Gronlid had installed in their store and house, a 32 volt electrical system that consisted of a 32 volt generator that charged a bank of glass, acid filled storage batteries that provided electricity for lighting purposes. But in Sonningdale the Tkaczyk's used kerosene lamps and gas lamps that provided a bright light for reading. Ironing was done with cast iron irons that would have to be heated up on the wood fired kitchen stove. A more modern innovation was the gas fired iron that had its own little gasoline tank which used air pressure to spray gasoline out of a nozzle to provide a flame with which to heat the iron. Primitive and dangerous? Yes! But it worked like a charm so long as everyone was careful with these gasoline lamps and irons. There were some clothes that ended up with a brown burn mark the shape of an iron, since controlling the heat of the iron was tricky at best, but those burn marks could be interpreted as a sign of modern technology in the home. The laundry was done outside in the summer in washtubs using wash tubs and a wash board. Clothes were hand wrung and hung out to dry on outdoor clotheslines. In the winter the washing of clothes was done in the basement or in the kitchen with water heated on the wood fired kitchen stove. The clothes would be hung outside or in the basement to dry. In the winter the wet clothes would freeze on the outdoor clothesline and be brought into the house to thaw and dry over chairs and racks or on clothes lines in the basement. Those frozen clothes smelled very fresh

THE POHORESKI CLAN IN SONNINGDALE

Front Row: Jim Patrick, Michael Tkaczyk, Louis Pohoreski, John Panchuk, Harry Dobrowolsky. Back Row: Orest Panchuk, Ann Panchuk, Ted Panchuk, George Tkaczyk, Lessia Tkaczyk, Sylvia Panchuk, Tena Tkaczyk, Mary Tkaczyk, Joanne Pohoreski, Dorothy Panchuk, Marie Dobrowolsky holding Vesper, Kay Pohoreski holding Diana. Railway station with train signal arms in background. 1946

when they were brought in from the freezing cold.

With all this extra space available in the new section house, Michael and Tena could actually buy furniture and have a place to put it. When Michael and Tena moved into the new section house, they purchased a piano and had Lessia begin music lessons at age seven. There was no music teacher in

Sonningdale so Tena drove Lessia to the neighboring village of Struan, 10 kilometers away to take music lessons from Mrs. Nestransky. Again the musical background of the Pohoreski's, and Michael's love of learning were the motivating factors to get Lessia involved in piano.

During the summer of 1946, Tena's side of the family came to Sonningdale from Gronlid to pay a visit. This was a journey of close to 320 kilometers, but John and Dorothy Panchuk, Harry and Marie Dobrowolsky, Pauline and Jim Patrick, and Louis and Kay Pohoreski all had relatively new cars so the journey was not as arduous as it could have been.

THE COUSINS Ted Panchuk, George Tkaczyk, Ann Panchuk, Lessia Tkaczyk, Sylvia Panchuk, Orest Panchuk, Vesper Dobrowolsky standing behind Diana Pohoreski in Basket. Sonningdale, 1946.

Michael and Tena enjoyed this visit as did all the cousins. This would be the first of many family trips back and forth across the province in the next five years as the families would get together for holiday or business reasons. The Panchuk's, Pohoreski's, and Dobrowolsky's from the Gronlid area, Louis and Kay Pohoreski from Middle Lake and later Saskatoon and the Patrick's from Goodeve, Bankend and later Saskatoon all kept in touch with each other and visited frequently. Most of the visits were to Gronlid and Lenvale, but on several occasions they all gathered in Sonningdale. The Pohoreski's were a close knit family as were most large families of the time. They were there to help one another in times of need, but most of all they loved to get their family orchestra together and play their instruments and sing along. Social life was a most important component of their existence and Michael and Mary loved every minute of it.

During the spring and summer of 1947, Tena was suffering from severe back pain problems. These back pains also affected Tena's legs as the pain shot down her sciatic nerve and into her legs. This was not a new problem for Tena as she had injured her back as a young teen in 1925 when a team of horses she was driving, got spooked and took off as a run-away team pulling Tena and her wagon box on a wild ride. As the wagon box weaved behind the galloping horses the front wheels of the wagon slipped off the shoulder of the road causing the wagon to tip and throwing Tena from the wagon box seat. Tena was thrown clear of the tumbling horses and wagon and into a bog landing feet first, jarring her spine. While suffering no ill effects immediately following the accident, other than a sore back, mud up to her waist and hard feelings due to the fact that she let the horses get away on her. Tena continued the farm work. As she got older into her thirties she began experiencing severe back and leg pain. She contacted doctors in Saskatoon and Regina, but the doctors did not have any answers for her. They knew of the injured back but in the 1940's they did not have the sophisticated diagnostic MRI's and radiology to determine the specific cause of her pain. Medicare as we know it today was in its formative stage in the late 1940's. The doctors recommended to Tena that she go to the Mayo Clinic in Rochester, Minnesota for a detailed diagnosis and possible corrective surgery to correct the problem. Upon hearing this, Michael insisted that Tena travel to the Mayo Clinic and seek a diagnosis and remediation for her back pain. Tena would have the use of a railway pass to cover transportation costs to and from Rochester, Minnesota. This process however, posed another problem. Michael could not leave work to assist in caring for Lessia and George while Tena was away. Lessia was in grade 3 but George who was 5 years old was still at home since school age children had to be six before they entered grade one. Mary was enrolled in Home Economics at the University of Saskatchewan and Michael was not about to interrupt her post secondary schooling to have her come home and baby sit. There was no family nearby for support as there had been at Gronlid. Michael and Tena approached the school board and requested special exemption for George to begin his grade one year in September 1947 at age five, one year earlier than usual. The school board granted the exception on the basis that George would have to maintain his grades in school to remain in school. This was not to be a babysitting project for the school.

Michael Tkaczyk, back row left, with his Sonningdale Section Crew. Andrew Chomyn, back row right, was Michael's First Man and Close Friend. Photo Taken in Front of Section House. 1947

George started grade one at Spartan School in Sonningdale in September, 1947. With both children in school and George holding his own in grade 1, the school board agreed to let George continue through to the end of the school year.

DREAM TO REALITY

Tena was getting herself organized to travel to Rochester, Minnesota. She prepared a large supply of baking to carry the family over during the time that she would be away. In October, Tena boarded the train in Sonningdale for her trip to Rochester, Minnesota and the famed Mayo Clinic in search of a remedy for her back problem. Mrs. Chomyn, a neighbor and the wife of Michael's First Man (assistant foreman), Andrew Chomyn was one of two other Ukrainian families in Sonningdale. Mrs. Chomyn offered to assist in Tena's absence and had lunches ready for Lessia and George when they came home from school at lunch time and provided after school care for them until Michael got home from work. Michael looked after preparing the suppers and breakfasts before getting the children off to school. Michael already had a routine established from when Mary came to Canada and they were living in Gronlid. This task of looking after two additional children instead of one was a little different since both children were headstrong. When it came to the treat of eating the baking, the pumpkin pie wars created the most angst for Michael. Both Lessia and George wanted to make sure that they each got their equal share of the pumpkin pies. When it came down to last pie and the last piece, Michael had to bring out the ruler to measure out the two equal portions to ensure absolute equality. To this day George still maintains that the older sister got more than her fair share of the pie. Fortunately for Mary, she was in Saskatoon attending school and didn't have to get involved in the great pie survey and debate. She only had to hear about it when she came home for long weekends and sympathize with her younger siblings, individually of course, so as not appear to be taking one side or the other. Outside of the pumpkin pie drama, the autumn of 1947 went well in Sonningdale.

In the meantime, at the Mayo Clinic, the team of physicians and surgeons discovered a crushed vertebrae and a slipped disc in Tena's spine. This problem with the crushed vertebrae and the slipped disc had caused a mis-alignment of the spinal column and the vertebrae and disk were pinching a bundle of nerves. This was causing the back pain and the pain down into her lower legs. Major surgery was required to correct the problem. Spinal surgery in the 1940's was not common. In fact, it was in its infancy. The surgeons took bone tissue from Tena's shin and grafted it into the space where they had removed the crushed vertebrae and the slipped disc completely. In its day, this was unheard of surgery in Canada. The diagnostics were unavailable in Canada let alone the surgical technique. Tena was hospitalized at the Mayo Clinic in Rochester, Minnesota for three weeks following the surgery for recuperation and rehabilitation before her three day train ride back to Sonningdale. The physicians wanted to monitor the spine for several weeks so that they could fit her with appropriate back braces and removable body casts (corset-like appliances) to ensure the proper healing for Tena's back. Return visits to the Mayo Clinic for Medical follow-up was not usual considering the distances and modes of travel. The Medical and Rehabilitation staff made special arrangements with the railway companies for Tena to be accommodated in a prone position in a sleeping car (Pullman Car) for the majority of the train ride back to Sonningdale, and that was possible for the entire journey except the last leg of the trip from Saskatoon to Sonningdale, where she lay prone on blankets on the floor of the baggage and mail car. The porters on the train and at the train stations would arrange for stretchers, then carry Tena from train to train when they were connecting with different trains in St. Paul, Minnesota, in Winnipeg and in Saskatoon. At Sonningdale there was no stretcher, so the station agent and the railway workers carried Tena from the railway station to the section house on a grain door. A grain door was a series of boards 1"X 6", six to eight feet long, nailed together to resemble a door. This set of boards was fastened across the opening of a boxcar sliding door to prevent grain from pouring out when the sliding doors were opened. Grain doors were a common item to be found in and around rural grain elevators. In this case the grain door became a stretcher. This was rural Saskatchewan ingenuity at its best. Tena was carried into the house and was placed on the bed which had been prepared with a sheet of plywood under the mattress so as to provide a firm support for Tena's spine. Tena was given an extensive exercise/rehabilitation regimen to assist in building strength up in her back. Tena walked around the house very gingerly for the first week back in her familiar surroundings.

The most important fact was that Tena was home with her family for Christmas. The community rallied around the Tkaczyk household. This was unheard of surgery at the time and the entire community wanted to know how Tena was doing and share in helping the family out. Complete meals were prepared and brought over to the house; chicken, ham, roasts, stews, vegetables and desserts. Oh those desserts! Pies, fruit preserves, cakes and cookies were continuously flowing into the Tkaczyk household. The church ladies and Ladies Auxiliary of the Royal Canadian Legion in Sonnigdale made sure there was food a-plenty through the Gregorian and Julian calendar Christmas seasons. There were more boxes of Christmas fruit cake, cookies and candies sent by mail from Tena's family in Gronlid to Sonningdale than the Tkaczyk's could eat. There was enough fruit cake and cookies to last to Easter. Of course the good neighbor, Mrs. Chomyn was there every day to assist and to make sure the food was looked after. It was a memorable Christmas on all fronts, with Mary home from University, Tena home after successful surgery, Lessia and George handling school well in Tena's absence and Michael able to get back to his work routine. Michael had reason to breathe a sigh of relief that all was unfolding as it should.

Tena recuperated quickly and the results of the surgery were positive. The exercise regimen, Mrs. Chomyn's assistance and Tena's tenacity all helped to get Tena back on her feet and handling household chores. Soon after the new year and into 1948, Tena was back to her industrious self—sewing, embroidering, knitting, gardening and travelling by car anywhere it was necessary for family related purposes.

Mary, in the meantime was doing well at University. Her roommate at the St. Petro Mohyla Ukrainian Institute was Sylvia Fedoruk, from the Canora, Saskatchewan area. Sylvia was studying nuclear physics, as well as playing fastball in the summer and curling in the winter. You couldn't find two fast friends as close as Sylvia and Mary, yet they were as diverse in their interests as could be. Mary wasn't athletic, but Sylvia was. Sylvia went on to win several Canadian Women's Curling Championships as the third for Joyce McKee's curling team, won several provincial women's fastball championships with her Saskatoon team, got her PhD in nuclear physics, worked with the Cancer Research Center at the University of Saskatchewan, assisting in developing Cobalt Therapy in the battle to defeat cancer. She later became the first female Lieutenant Governor for the Province of Saskatchewan. Sylvia and Mary became fast friends throughout their four year stay at the Peter Mohyla Ukrainian Institute helping each other with their course assignments and graduating with their Bachelor's degrees. In fact Sylvia was as close as family until they went their separate ways after graduation.

Michael, Tena, Lessia and George travelled to Saskatoon by car quite often to see Mary and her Institute friends. Michael and Tena visited with fellow Ukrainians at the Peter Mohyla Ukrainian Institute which was a meeting place not only for Ukrainian students but for their parents as well. Weekends would see parents from all over Saskatchewan coming into the institute to see their high school and post secondary school students and to bring garden vegetables and fruit and vegetable preserves for the kitchen to assist with keeping the food expenses lower. The days in Saskatoon were busy. On Sundays the Tkaczyk's would go to church while in Saskatoon, visit with Jim and Pauline Patrick and on Saturdays they would check in with Paul's Music and Book Store for the latest Ukrainian print publications for Michael, do some general shopping or go to the Saskatoon Exhibition when it was in progress.

In addition to her studies and socializing with her friends at the Institute, Mary met a young man by the name of Alex Hupka. Alex had just returned from England where he was stationed with the Canadian Army as radio operator. He had completed his military duty and was living at the St. Petro Mohyla Ukrainian Institute completing his university studies working towards his Bachelor of Arts and Bachelor of Education. Mary on occasion would bring Alex home to Sonningdale to meet the family. Alex in the meantime, was working during the summer months for the Institute, travelling around to the rural areas of the province of Saskatchewan fund raising, promoting the Peter Mohyla Ukrainian Institute to rural Saskatchewanites of Ukrainian origin and recruiting students that would be attending high school or post secondary educational institutions in Saskatoon. He had the prestige of using the "Institute car" promoting the necessity of the Peter Mohyla Ukrainian Institute as gathering place and a residence fostering Ukrainian values and culture. Of course during his journeys through the rural areas, if he was in the Sonningdale vicinity, he would stop in to Sonningdale to see Mary. George and Lessia enjoyed having Alex drop around to Sonningdale. The fact that Mary had all these neat friends such as Sylvia Fedoruk, Alex and others from the Institute that paid so much attention to them when they visited in Saskatoon, was right down Lessia's and George's alley.

Michael's work with the C.P.R. in Sonningdale was progressing well. He received safety awards relating to accident free days for himself and his crew. His crew was efficient and hard working thus it stayed constant, which was usually contrary to the migratory and transient nature of the railroad workers. His management style was low key and he led by example which also helped. Tena was constantly busy with her sewing and the Ladies Auxiliary of the Royal Canadian Legion and the Canadian Red Cross, assisting with benefit drives collecting, repairing and making clothes, knitting sweaters and making quilts for survivors, refugees and volunteers that were helping in the re-building of war torn Europe. George and Lessia were busy with their school work, their friends, United Church choir, Sunday School and of course their pets, Benny the baby calf and Rusty the cocker spaniel. Mary's university studies were progressing well as she was entering her final years before graduation.

During the summer of 1949, Michael and Tena with Lessia and George in tow embarked on a cross Canada trip by rail thanks to Michael's C.P.R. rail pass. His years of seniority provided Michael with the benefits of extended travel outside the prairie zone of the C.P.R. Visits to Toronto, Niagara Falls and Montreal were the main focus. Tena had cousins in Toronto, the Sobey's (Sobaschansky), which led to trips to Niagara Falls and picnicking in Central Island Park in Toronto.

They visited Tena's brother Adam who was completing his term with the Royal Canadian Airforce and attending McGill University where he was completing his Master's degree in Electrical Engineering. This trip would be the last big trip that Michael would make using the C.P.R. railway pass. The other trips that were taken in the previous years were to Banff, Vancouver, Winnipeg and to visit family in Regina and Saskatoon.

Change for Michael and his family was on the way. Labor unrest among the railway construction and maintenance employees across Canada was brewing for the past year and the national railway strike of 1950 was looming. Michael was not a union minded person. His dislike for unions and collectives stemmed from his bitter experience with the Bolsheviks and the Soviets. He would have nothing to do with the strike. Michael's love and belief of independence and freedom would not allow him to be shackled by union and collective thought and philosophy. This would lead to Michael and Tena to look at changing their focus from depending on railway employment for income. Leaving the railroad would not be that difficult since Michael already owned two quarters of prime farm land in the Gronlid area. His choices were to buy more farmland to enlarge his farming operation or to diversify by purchasing a business and continue to rent out the land. The rental income from his two quarters of land was soon going to come in handy when the railway strike would occur.

Meanwhile, other changes were on the way. The year 1950, was to become a hallmark year for Michael and his family.

In May, 1950 Mary graduated with a Bachelor of Science in Home Economics degree from the Faculty of Home Economics at the University of Saskatchewan. Michael's dream was coming true. He brought his seven year old daughter to Canada in 1935 and in 15 years she had mastered the English language, completed her high school and a four year degree program at the University of Saskatchewan. Soon she was about to set out on pursuing her new career as a Home Economist. Her first job opportunity came when she was offered a teaching position at the High School Collegiate in Smith's Falls, Ontario, near Ottawa. She left Saskatoon by train (using a C.P.R. railway pass) in August of 1950 to teach in Ontario during the 1950/51 school term. She completed her first year of teaching in Smith's Falls and returned home to Saskatchewan in the summer of 1951.

Mary's Convocation at the University of Saskatchewan, Bachelor of Science in Home Economics, 1950. Back row—Tena, Mary, Michael Front Row—George, Lessia

With the railway strike of 1950 looming, Michael decided he had better prepare himself for the worst. During the spring and summer weekends of 1950, Michael, Tena, Lessia and George travelled by car throughout the province of Saskatchewan looking at business opportunities, particularly hotels. Marie (Tena's sister) and Harry Dobrowolsky had purchased the Gronlid Hotel and were doing very well in the hotel and restaurant business. This gave Michael and Tena the impetus for looking at getting into the hospitality industry. They looked seriously at a hotel in Rouleau, Saskatchewan, 40 kilometers south east of Regina, the setting for the TV sitcom "Corner Gas". The business in the hotel was thriving, however there weren't many Ukrainian communities in Southern Saskatchewan, outside of Regina and Moose Jaw. The social and religious issue was a major consideration for Michael and Tena since they wanted to settle down in a community where they would feel comfortable and bring their children up in a Ukrainian community where customs traditions and religion were the focal point. The Saskatoon region which housed many communities with a Ukrainian influence was the area upon which they focused their hotel search.

Driving north from Sonningdale one weekend, led the Tkaczyk's across the North Saskatchewan River via the Maymont Ferry to the town of Maymont, onto Highway 5 (today the Yellowhead Highway) to North Battleford, then approximately eighty kilometers east on Highway 40 to a village called Krydor.

Michael and Tena had heard that there was a hotel for sale in Krydor that was actually going to shut down. The owner, Mr. Andrew Worobetz, a long time Krydor resident and business man was leaving the hotel business for health reasons. He was going to retire to Saskatoon where his family had already taken up residence. Michael and Tena had done their due diligence in examining the books and financial status of the hotel. They realized that the hotel had not turned a large profit in the last few years. This was in large part due to the failing health of Mr. Worobetz. Michael and Tena saw potential in this business that was run down. Mr. Worobetz was a successful farmer, general store owner and as of late the hotel owner, but age and ill health was taking its toll on him. The building was relatively new but it needed work. The beer parlor was dingy, the walls discolored from the smokers. This was the time period before mixed drinking and the beer parlor was the man's domain. Brass spittoons were located throughout the premises, the hardwood floor showed stains from beer and burn marks from cigarette stubs. There was no central heating, no electricity in the community or the hotel and no running water and sewage in the village. However the village of approximately 170 residents had a large drawing area of successful farmers. There were four grain elevators in the village which was an indicator of the successful farming that took place. And a few kilometers east and west from Krydor were located the sidings of Tallman and Redberry with two and one elevators respectively. The Krydor district was certainly a generous grain producing area. That was what every prospective entrepreneur wanted to see. There were four grocery/general stores, two hardware stores, a café, a confectionary store, a post office, a lumber yard, three service stations/garages, one implement dealer/blacksmith, a livery stable, a telephone office/exchange, two trains per day (one passenger and one freight) between Prince Albert and North Battleford, daily bus service between Prince Albert and North Battleford and Highway 40 connecting North Battleford and Prince Albert. The highway ran right past the hotel door providing heavy hotel traffic for meals, rooms and beer parlor activity. There was a community hall (Narodny Deem), a Ukrainian Catholic Church, a Ukrainian Orthodox Church, a Polish Roman Catholic Chapel, an outdoor skating rink and a school that accommodated grades 1 through 12. The community was 99% Ukrainian with the remaining 1 % of the population made up of people of German and Polish origin. The neighboring town of Hafford, twenty two kilometers to the west was comprised of a population of primarily Ukrainian Canadian residents with a mixture of Anglo-Saxon, French, and German people. Blaine Lake, seventeen kilometers to the

DREAM TO REALITY

east was primarily Ukrainian and Doukhobor with a minority of French, Anglo-Saxon and German settlers.

Driving back to Sonningdale, there was much talk about the possibilities and the potential of the Krydor Hotel.

On one of the Tkaczyk's trips to Gronlid prior to the railway worker's strike, John and Dorothy Panchuk upon hearing that Michael and Tena were looking for a business in which to invest, mentioned the possibility of Michael and Tena buying the Panchuk's general store business. The Panchuks would look after the bulk fuel distributorship to farmers, run the Massey Harris farm implement dealership and run their farm operation. Michael and Tena could run the store and look after their own farm as well. The business proposition sounded like it had possibilities, but Michael and Tena would have to think about it. Again the trip back to Sonningdale was filled with discussion about the pro's and the con's of the business ventures in Krydor and Gronlid.

The summer of 1950 was filled with talk of what could be. Michael was sure that he wanted to leave the railway. The work was physically demanding plus the fact that he truly disliked the trade union movement helped make up his mind. He didn't want any part of the trade unions.

On August 22, 1950, Canada's railway unions launched a nation-wide labor strike, shutting down the rail system from coast to coast. At that time Canada depended on the railways for the shipment of everything, from food to clothing, from raw materials to manufactured goods across the nation from coast to coast. The goods and raw materials were transported from the most remote locations to the population centers; from cities to small towns and villages and vice versa. The delivery of mail was dependent on the railway system. Due to the strike, the nation came to a grinding halt. The highway system and trucking industry was in its infancy. Highways were not built for load bearing trucks; they were primitive gravel surfaced two lane roadways. Without freight trains to haul the goods, there were fears that factories would not be able to ship their goods to market, receive raw materials for manufacturing, thus factories would have to shut down creating job losses and lay-offs. Farmers were particularly concerned that they would not be able to get their food products to market. The economy would be affected by this railway strike in a major way. As well the railway workers were branded as unpatriotic because their job action did not support the Korean war effort which depended on railway transportation of military goods, supplies and troops to the port of Vancouver for trans-shipment to Korea to supply the Canadian and American troops.

On August 29, 1950, Prime Minister Louis St. Laurent introduced Bill-1, The Maintenance of Railway Operation Act. It ordered an end to the strike and imposed a process for settling the dispute between the workers and the railway companies. The Bill was passed by the House of Commons and the Senate and within days the railway workers were back on the job. A by-product of the of the strike was that it gave a boost to the fledgling trucking industry and the impetus to complete an all weather Trans-Canada Highway and provincial highway networks with appropriate load bearing limits to allow highway transportation of goods and commodities.

Michael breathed a sigh of relief with the mandated end to the strike. He disliked the strike in general, but what he disliked most of all was the fact that all railway maintenance employees were being branded as unpatriotic for disrupting the rail service during a time of war. He loved Canada and the opportunities that it had provided for him and his family. He disliked strike action, period! He disliked the unions for forcing the strike. He loved independence and felt that he could contribute more to Canada as an independent worker, rather than a union worker. In order to accomplish that, he had to leave the railway since all railway workers were forced to join the union.

In September, 1950, Michael served notice to Canadian Pacific Railways that he would be leaving their employ at the end of the month. With that notice Michael and Tena would have to move out of the C.P.R. section house at the end of September. John and Dorothy Panchuk had suggested that Tena and Michael could move in with them above the store and give the store business a trial run while they were deciding upon which business venture they were going to choose. Michael and Tena were leaning toward the purchase of the hotel in Krydor because they felt it had more potential than the store, but took John and Dorothy up on their offer. For Lessia and George it was like a grand holiday. They would be living with their cousins, going to school with their cousins and visiting with their other aunts, uncles and grandparents.

With that offer of John and Dorothy Panchuk's, Michael and Tena hurriedly sold Jessie the jersey cow and Benny the little bull to a local farming family, the Muzyka's. They packed their furniture and belongings and sent them to Gronlid by train. In mid October of 1950, the Tkaczyk's were moved to Gronlid and were living with the Panchuks. George in grade four and Lessia in grade seven were enrolled in the Gronlid

GEORGE TKACHYK

Public School following in Mary's footsteps. George and Lessia fit in well in the Gronlid School and community since they knew some of the students from their previous visits with their cousins Anne, Sylvia, Orest and Ted Panchuk and Vesper and Gordon Dobrowolsky.

Two families living under one roof for two months led to some interesting moments, especially with six precocious children between the ages of 8 and 12 years occupying the same living space. There were many "time outs", primarily for the boys, even before the term "time out" was invented. Actually, the two months sped by uneventfully in spite of the time outs, except for a case of tonsillitis for George. He had to spend a week in hospital, then had his tonsils removed in the Melfort Hospital at the end of October, marring George's Hallowe'en. The cousins however made up for this disappointment by sharing their Hallowe'en loot with George.

On the business side of things, Michael and Tena decided that they didn't want to be in a partnership in the general store. Michael was an independent minded person and did not want to be tied to a partnership, especially when he could manage to purchase the hotel on his own. Thus, during their time in Gronlid, Michael and Tena were negotiating the purchase of the Krydor Hotel and looking into the licensing regulations with the Saskatchewan Liquor Control Board.

On November 1, 1950, Michael and Tena purchased the Krydor Hotel. In order to do so they sold one farm. They had an instant and willing buyer in John Mateyko, Michael's former railroad work mate from his Gronlid years with the C.P.R. and hired man who looked after Michael's farm. In addition, Michael used his savings and borrowed $1,000 from Steve Hryhirchuk, Michael's best friend, to make up the $17,000 purchase price of the hotel. Michael still owned another quarter section of land in the Gronlid area, but he wanted to retain it for future needs. He would gain in the short term by renting the land to a local farmer, but his thought was that the land could serve as a backup should the hotel business not pan out as planned. While Michael was independent minded and an entrepreneur, he was also cautious in that he wanted a safety net. He had just come through the Great Depression and knew that he should always provide for unexpected eventualities. Possession date for the hotel was set for December 1, 1950.

This decision of purchasing the hotel was going to make a tremendous change in Michael's life. From a life on the railway where moving from community to community was a commonplace occurrence; from living a life under a trade union cloak (which he detested); to a life of self determination in the business world; and to a life of selecting the location where he would raise his family, was part of Michael's dream that was becoming Michael's reality. Michael was seeing that all of his planning and labor was coming to fruition. Michael's dream for a new life in Canada was truly becoming reality.

John Panchuk and Michael loaded all of the Tkaczyk family's furniture and some of their other belongings on to John's red Chevrolet three quarter ton truck, and with Tena, Lessia and George following in their 1941 Chevrolet loaded with suitcases and boxes, the two vehicle caravan set out for Krydor, 300 kilometers south-west of Gronlid. The move was made on a cold December 1, 1950. There were many stops for this two vehicle group since car heaters were primitive thus leading to cold toes and hands and constant scraping of frost off the interior of the windshields since defrosters and heaters were not that functional in vehicles during the 1950's, especially on long trips such as this.

GEORGE TKACHYK

It was late afternoon on December 1, 1950 when John Panchuk and Michael Tkaczyk pulled up in front of the Krydor Hotel. The hotel was busy as one could tell by the hitching rails filled with teams of horses and their sleighs. The horses were waiting patiently for their owners who were in the beer parlor consuming a few cool ones before heading home to their respective farms with the day's grocery shopping done at the local general stores.

Mechanization on farms and in rural Saskatchewan was in its infancy. Any farmers that did have tractors, trucks or cars would have had them winterized by December. Winterized meant that the vehicles would have had the water drained from the motors and radiators and the vehicles would have been parked in shelters for the winter. Anti-freeze or engine coolant as we know it today for vehicle motors, was a rare and expensive commodity. With only water used as a coolant for engines, the water would have to be drained in cold weather or the water would freeze and crack the engine blocks and radiators necessitating replacement of the engine and radiator, which was an expensive, and to most farmers a prohibitive repair. In addition, motor oils were not as sophisticated as they are today. There were usually two weights of motor oil—summer weight which was about 40 SAE and winter weight which was about 5 SAE. There were no blended oils or synthetic oils. Thus with the primitive stage of motor vehicles and motor vehicle servicing, the vast majority of vehicles were "winterized" and stored for the winter and horses and sleighs put to use for local transportation. Only if one was going on a long trip to one of the major cities would one "un-winterize" a vehicle. Today, winterizing a vehicle takes on a totally opposite meaning where we actually prepare a vehicle for winter driving. John Panchuk and Michael Tkaczyk had put anti-freeze into their vehicles along with the winter weight oil for easy starting on cold mornings, since they would use their vehicles constantly throughout the winter, thus they were safe from having their motors freeze up on them. Since the late fifties, coolants have been devised for motors that would stay in the motors year-round to prevent them from overheating in the summer and freezing in the winter.

There was the "romantic" aspect of the horse and sleigh. The farmers would dress up their teams of horses with decorative harnesses and bells, and as the horses and sleighs moved through the towns, villages and countryside, the melodic and pleasant symphony of sleigh bells was a common sound to be heard. Hitching rails were found in front of every business establishment. The horses were housed in livery stables during the day of shopping in the village or while children were in school. The farmers and their families by late afternoon would drop by the businesses to pick up their groceries and supplies and in doing so would tie up their teams of horses to the hitching rails so that they wouldn't wander off. The sights and sounds of the horses and sleighs were common to all small towns in the years leading up to the 1950's.

Tena, Lessia and George arrived shortly after Michael and John, and pulled up alongside the hotel. The sun was just going down, casting long shadows on the new blanket of snow as George and Lessia walked past the horses in front of the hotel. The Tkaczyk entourage entered the hotel, made acquaintances with Mr. Andrew Worobetz the owner, and subsequently started moving their clothes, furniture and other belongings into the hotel. In very short order the patrons of the beer parlor joined in to help move the items into the hotel as a gesture of welcome to the new "Hotelnic" and "Hotelnychka" (hotel owner and the hotel owner's wife). The moving of items took very little time, and of course following the patrons' welcoming gesture, Michael Tkaczyk and John Panchuk entered the beer parlor, introduced themselves formally and Michael bought the patrons several "rounds" of beer. These patrons as it turns out were the regulars that patronized the beer parlor throughout the years. Tena was not allowed to enter the "licensed premises" as the beer parlor was called, since the Saskatchewan Liquor Control Board forbade the female gender, anyone under the age of 21 years and all First Nations People from entering licensed premises or anywhere beer, wine and spirits were sold or served. However, Tena did pop her head into the beer parlor to say hello and thanked everyone for their helping hand.

Tena, Lessia and George proceeded to unpack their belongings, pick out their bedrooms upstairs and in short order Tena was in the kitchen of the hotel getting something together for supper. Mrs. Worobetz had already moved to Saskatoon to set up their new home thus Mr. Worobetz was fending for himself and his cupboards were quite bare. Needless to say there were several trips over to Dragan's Red and White Store to procure enough food items for supper for the hungry new arrivals in Krydor.

The next morning John Panchuk left for Gronlid. Michael and Tena waved good-bye then settled in to take over the reins of a business that was new to them, but that would prove to be a very successful and rewarding move.

News in the Village of Krydor spread like wild-fire. "The new hotel owners were in town". Krydor Hotel was a busy place for the first few weeks with the curiosity seekers and well wishers popping in to meet the new village residents.

DREAM TO REALITY

The first order of business was a letter to Mary in Smith's Falls, Ontario where she was in her first year of teaching home economics in the Smith's Falls High School Collegiate. Mary knew nothing of Krydor except for the bits of information that would arrive in the letters that Michael and Tena wrote to her. Mary would be coming back to a new home in the summer of 1951, but this was nothing new to Mary. She was used to moves throughout her life since coming to Canada.

There were further changes in the family that would be coming in 1951. During the winter of 1950-51, Mary and Alex through their long distance correspondence had decided to get married. Alex was teaching high school in Drumheller, Alberta during that year. They had both applied for and received teaching positions at Spirit River, Alberta for the 1951-1952 school year. Mary's homecoming to Krydor in the summer of 1951 was going to be very busy and of course short lived. A wedding was being planned for July 22, 1951 and then Mary and Alex would be leaving for the Peace River Country in Alberta, shortly thereafter.

8

THE KRYDOR YEARS

The small village of Krydor was but a whistle stop in 1950. Michael and Tena had first and foremost wanted to get into the business world, but they were also looking for that elusive community that would satisfy their other needs and values such as a positive cultural, religious and educational environment.

The Krydor years were unique in many ways in the life of Michael Tkaczyk. Since Michael came to Canada in 1928, this was the first community that Michael would settle in and call home. After years of moving, the longest stay in any one place was 4 years. Now having purchased a business in Krydor, Michael had long term goals for his business and the Tkaczyk family had an opportunity to put down roots. This community seemed to have everything to which they aspired. It was a community where churches were the main pillar, and with the education, cultural and economic presence, the remaining foundation or building blocks for success were in place. In addition, there was the proximity to larger centers such as Saskatoon that housed the St. Petro Mohyla Ukrainian Institute and the University of Saskatchewan. It was Michael's

DREAM TO REALITY

expectation that Lessia and George would follow in Mary's footsteps and stay at the St. Petro Mohyla Ukrainian Institute and attend the University of Saskatchewan or some other post-secondary educational institution.

The day after John Panchuk's departure, Lessia and George were off to Krydor School to meet their new teachers and classmates. Michael and Tena were busy getting into the routine of hotel life and meeting their business and social neighbors. Mr. Worobetz was staying on for a few weeks to assist Michael with the transition of the hotel take-over. There was much to do, even in a small village like Krydor. There was the transfer of the mail box at the local post-office; transfer of telephone service; arranging the municipal change of title and tax responsibilities; and then there were several trips into Saskatoon and North Battleford to arrange for food wholesale access and Saskatchewan Liquor Board purchase agreements for the purchase and delivery and beer orders. It was a busy and an exciting time for everyone involved.

The Village of Krydor was incorporated in 1914, but the first Ukrainian settlers in the region of present day Blaine Lake, Krydor and Hafford, arrived at the turn of the century. The settlers were looking for larger tracts of land than the 40-60 acre land tracts offered to them in the Fish Creek area (near Wakaw, Alvena, Cudworth) east of Rosthern and across the South Saskatchewan River. Their opportunity came when the Doukhobors (a communal Russian religious sect who settled in colonies) could not fulfill their Canadian Government contracts for land purchases west of the North Saskatchewan River in the district of Petrofka (near the present day site of the Petrofka Bridge that crosses the North Saskatchewan River).

GEORGE TKACHYK

Thus in 1904, the Canadian Government offered homesteads of 160 acres to whomever wanted to buy them for $10.00 and a written promise to live on the land for three years, build a dwelling and cultivate crops on that land. Needless to say, Ukrainian settlers immediately began to purchase their homesteads and encouraged friends and relatives to come to the area as well. By 1910, all of the available land in the Krydor District had been purchased. This district was comprised of rich promising farmland just north of the North Saskatchewan River and around Redberry Lake, a stream and spring fed lake that was a great attraction to settlers. While Redberry Lake is a heavily salt saturated lake due to the natural springs percolating up through the potash sub strata, there was an ample supply of fresh water from a high water table, the North Saskatchewan River, streams, ponds and lakes left over from the glaciation periods of the ice age. With all the streams, lakes and ponds, there was wooded land which would supply wood for dwellings and firewood. There was ample water for settler use, water fowl, and animals. Today Redberry Lake is the centre piece for Redberry Provincial Park as well as a United Nations Environmental and Ecological Preserve with research and ecological studies on going at the lake and its adjacent drainage area.

The Krydor district got its name from two early settlers in the area. Peter Krysak purchased the first homestead in 1904 and was the first Postmaster for the district. Teodor Lucyk was one of the early settlers whose homestead was the closest to the actual village site. So as not to offend either of the first settlers, they took the KRY from Krysak and the DOR from Teodor to form the name KRYDOR.

Trips for supplies for the settlers from the Krydor District and points West, were made on foot to Rosthern, a large community north of Saskatoon. There were no roads or railways at the time, only trails. One of Western Canada's more historical trails runs through the Krydor District—The Carlton Trail. Fur traders, settlers, the Northwest Mounted Police, military personnel and gold miners, used the Carlton Trail on their trek west and for their regular trading trips to larger centers.

Archeological evidence has shown that the Carlton Trail Route had been in use by aboriginal hunters more that 6000 years ago following the river valleys and flatlands which were animal migration routes from the Rocky Mountains to the flatlands near ancient Lake Aggasiz (Lake Winnipeg). The trail was named after Carlton House (Fort Carlton) which was a Hudson's Bay Trading Post established in 1810, on the North Saskatchewan River, half way between Fort Ellice/Fort Gary (Winnipeg) and Fort Edmonton. (Carlton House was named after King George III's house in London). The Carlton Trail connected Fort Gary to Fort Battleford (the capital of the Northwest Territories) and extended on to Fort Pitt (north of Lloydminster), on through the Victoria Settlement (near Smokey Lake Alberta) and on to Fort Edmonton. The Carlton Trail was used by fur traders and colonists with their Red River carts when the North Saskatchewan River could not be used in the late autumn, winter and early spring to transport goods with the York Boats. The North West Mounted Police used the Carlton Trail to as a highway as a means to get to their forts, since they were the only law and order in the west. They had to deal with whiskey traders from the United States, uprisings among the aboriginal and metis insurgents which included the Riel Rebellion, Frog Lake massacre (north of Lloydminster) and settling treaties with Chief Poundmaker, after several uprisings in the Fort Battleford area. The trail was used in the settling of the North West by the Barr Colonists in the Lloydminster area, and later by the Doukhobors, Ukrainians, French, and

English settlers in the Blaine Lake, Krydor, Hafford and North Battleford districts.

To go East from Krydor, the North Saskatchewan River would

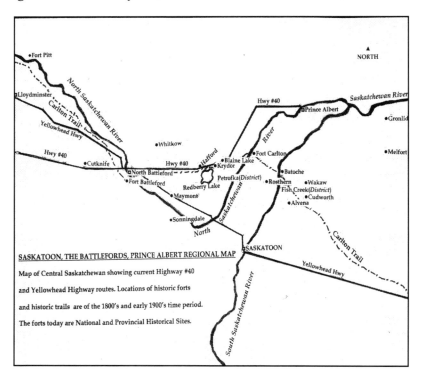

SASKATOON, THE BATTLEFORDS, PRINCE ALBERT REGIONAL MAP

Map of Central Saskatchewan showing current Highway #40 and Yellowhead Highway routes. Locations of historic forts and historic trails are of the 1800's and early 1900's time period. The forts today are National and Provincial Historical Sites.

have to be crossed by ferry at Petrofka in order to get to the large town of Rosthern, Saskatchewan. The settlers would walk the Carlton Trail to get supplies and get their grain milled into flour at the flour mill in Rosthern. Settlers from further west, such as the Kowalsky's, from as far away as the Battlefords would walk the Carlton Trail to Rosthern to mill their grain into flour and buy supplies. They would stop over in Krydor to stay with relatives or close acquaintances since the trek would take several days one way. Today the Yellowhead Trail and Highway 40 pass through much of what was the Carlton Trail.

In order to have contact with the outside world a post office was set up in the home of Peter Krysak, the first Ukrainian settler in the Krydor District. The Krydor Post Office became a hub of communications for the new settlers. Peter Krysak would make a weekly trip to Petrofka on foot or by oxen and wagon or sleigh, depending on the season. This trip to take outgoing mail to Petrofka and bring in the mail that would contain news from their homeland, was approximately 30 kilometers, but it would take the better part of a day to go to Petrofka and back. (Tena's father, Michael Pohoreski performed the same task when he was the postmaster while homesteading at Zalicia, Manitoba, picking up mail in Garland, Manitoba and transporting it by oxen and sleigh/wagon some 20-25 kilometers to Zalicia).

The railway came through Krydor in 1913 when the Shellbrook extension was built, connecting Prince Albert with North Battleford. This provided a reliable mode of transportation and communication for everyone. No more travelling to Rosthern on foot or by oxen, no more travelling to Petrofka on foot to get mail. Grain and farm products along with the Royal Mail moved with ease from Krydor to North Battleford, to Saskatoon and Prince Albert. The farm products could easily be shipped to the dairies and creameries. The livestock was shipped to the packing houses in Saskatoon and Prince Albert and the grain could reach the Lake Head port terminals at Fort William and Port Arthur (Thunder Bay), within very short timelines. Krydor and all the other villages and towns were now connected to the world to deliver their

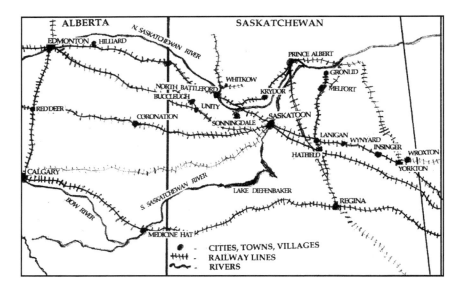

products to world markets, along with reliable communication in the form of daily mail and telegraph.

The Canadian Northern Railway (later the Canadian National Railway) wanted to name the village located at SE 15-44-8W 3rd meridian, "Bullock" after one of the C.N.R.'s officials, however the residents petitioned the railway to have the village maintain the name of the Krydor Post Office and the Krydor District. They were successful in doing so and the incorporation of the village of Krydor became a fact in 1914. The village of Krydor grew quickly as reported in the North Battleford News, January 22 and February 5, 1914 where Krydor was called *"a brand new settlement typical of Western Canada's great development—no paint on the buildings, but no weather stains either"*. The buildings listed were: two or three general stores, two lumber yards, a hotel, two livery barns/stables, a blacksmith shop, a railway station, a garage to repair vehicles, two dray (delivery) lines, two implement firms, a pool room (billiards), a harness shop, grain elevators, a real estate office, stock yards and homes. The early 1900's were booming in the Krydor District.

As was the custom in Ukrainian communities, as soon as homes were built, churches, schools and community halls were soon to follow. Church services for the early immigrants took place in their homes. As soon as the homesteads were established a church would be built, since religion played a very important part in the immigrant Ukrainian's life. Ukrainian immigrants were also eager to foster reading and learning. Shortly after the abolition of the feudal system in Europe in 1848, a renaissance of learning occurred in Ukraine. The common people suddenly had the freedom to enlighten themselves and would establish libraries or learning centers for adults. This pattern would follow in Canada. Soon after a church was built, Ukrainian communities would build a "Narodny Deem" (National Home-directly translated) or community hall. This hall would be the home of a library of Ukrainian reading materials and a meeting place for cultural activities — drama, dancing, public speaking and a venue for wedding celebrations and concerts.

A Ukrainian Catholic Church was built in the Krydor District about three miles from the present town site, in 1910. The school was built in 1915, a community hall in 1916, a Roman Catholic Chapel in 1914-15, and the Ukrainian Orthodox Church in 1934-35. The Ukrainian Orthodox congregation was formed in early in 1921 with church services being held in peoples' homes and in community halls. The first Ukrainian Orthodox baptism was held on July 12, 1921 at the home of Peter Chuhaniuk with John Nemish of Blaine Lake being baptized. Since the first baptism was held on St. Peter's and St. Paul's Feast Day the parish adopted St. Peter and St. Paul as their Patron Saints. The first marriage ceremony to be conducted in the Ukrainian Orthodox congregation was that of Stephen Mulka and Pauline Chonko in 1929. Stephen grew up in the Krydor District and was a school teacher at Krydor. They later moved to Alberta. Stephen and Pauline's son Orest, was born in Krydor, grew up

GEORGE TKACHYK

in Alberta and was married to Michael and Tena's daughter Lessia, from 2003 to 2010.

Mr. Andrew Worobetz had moved to Krydor from the Wakaw district in 1913. He opened a general store in Krydor on Main Street. This building burned down and he immediately built a new store on Railway Avenue. Buildings were prone to burning down in small frontier communities in the early 1900's, since firefighting equipment was not always available. The risk of fire in the buildings at the time was high since all buildings were of wood frame construction, insulation in the walls and ceiling was usually wood shavings with no fire-proofing, heat was provided by wood or coal burning stoves or space heaters, and light was provided by kerosene lamps, coleman-type lanterns or candles. The modes of heating and lighting and the absence building codes and fire regulations added to the potential fire hazard in these buildings.

In 1926, Andrew Worobetz built a hotel on the former, burned out store site on Main Street, Lot 1, Block 1. The hotel still exists, the only active business establishment in Krydor today. He operated the hotel from 1926 until he sold it to Michael and Tena Tkaczyk in 1950.

- Historical Note: With the coming of the railroad, every community had a Railway Avenue running parallel to the railway tracks with a Main Street intersecting Railway Avenue near the railway station. This was common to every prairie village and town plan.

Telephones came to Krydor in 1920. The telephone system was the famous "Party Line" system that had five to ten clients on each line. At this stage of telephone development there was no such thing as direct dialing. The telephone operator in Krydor had a switchboard and would have to connect the caller and listener by physically plugging the caller's line into the listener's line so that both parties could communicate. Each home that subscribed to the telephone service would have a distinct ring similar to a Morse Code, to distinguish to which home the call was intended. Although it really didn't matter who the call was intended for, since there were interested eavesdroppers picking up the local gossip or news. Obviously there was no "Privacy Act" in those days. This made for very interesting community gossip and interpersonal dynamics in the community. If farmer Jim's cow had a two headed calf, the party lines were buzzing near the melting point, distributing the news, thus the entire district knew of the event. In some ways it was like living in a glass house. Some creative neighbors who couldn't afford a phone line connection would make their own connection by patching in some barbed wire fencing to connect their phone with the regular phone lines. Long distance calls had to be routed through North Battleford, Prince Albert and Saskatoon to a long distance telephone operator who would then make the necessary connections to the community outside the local telephone exchange. It was a cumbersome system compared to today's digital and cell phone technology, but at the time the telephone system was a communications marvel compared to the telegraph. There was no isolation of pioneer communities. The modern era of communications and travel with the railroad, telegraph and telephone had arrived in Krydor as it had in all rural communities across the West by the 1920's.

Since the main economic activity was farming, as soon as the railway came through, four grain elevators sprang up in Krydor. The Saskatchewan Grain Elevator was built in 1913, McLean's Grain Elevator in 1914, The Ruthenian Grain Elevator in 1917 (a

Ukrainian grain buying co-operative based in Winnipeg) and the Saskatchewan Wheat Pool in 1925. By the mid 1920's Krydor was a thriving, bustling community with all the amenities that an agricultural grain producing community could want.

The greater majority of settlers in the Krydor District were from Western Ukraine. Names like Krysak, Lucyk, Cyba, Romaniuk, Saganski, Korolewich, Kozak, Checknita, Borycki, Charko, Bazarkewich, Korpan, Worobetz, Tkachuk, Wawryniuk and Hawryliak were some but not all the Ukrainian names among the many early settlers. There were a few Doukhobor families living closer to Blaine Lake and Petrofka and a few Polish families settling closer to Krydor. The farming community was one hundred percent Slavic which aided the settlers in their communications with one another.

The majority of the business establishments that arose in Krydor, Hafford and Blaine Lake were owned and operated by English, French, Jewish or German entrepreneurs. Where there were settlers, there was a need for basic supplies and services. The Ukrainian settlers had agricultural roots from their homeland and their interest first and foremost, was the item that they rarely could own in their homeland which was land-real estate. They hungered for the privilege of land ownership, plus they were a self sustaining, self reliant people. Then there was the initial language barrier which steered them to their own cultural communities. Life on agricultural land was near and dear to their hearts. Here in Canada they could claim an entire quarter section of land and build on that acquisition, whereas in their homeland land ownership was but a dream; they were limited in their agricultural aspirations and by social and political structures. Whether the acquisition of land was a deep seated desire that brought them to the new land or whether it was just a natural and functional activity to them, agriculture was the endeavor that the majority of Ukrainian immigrants chose. With the Ukrainian settlers interested in land and agriculture and with no seed money to start businesses, the business community in most settlements was largely non-Ukrainian. The early business owners in Krydor set up a village council. It was made up of H.F.Dodd, overseer (mayor), George Heuring, J.P. Lauriault, J.J. Loepky with J.D. Michasiw as secretary-treasurer. It wasn't until 1915 and later that the business community was to become largely Ukrainian.

Besides becoming landowners and being involved in the business community, the settlers set their sights on one other elusive target: Education. Education had been an elusive objective in their homeland for several reasons. Peasants in a feudal society rarely had the opportunity to achieve an education. They were locked into a social structure that would take years and eventually generations to overcome. Two of Ukraine's great poets and political and social activists, Ivan Franko and Taras Shevchenko constantly urged the people of Ukraine to shed the veil of ignorance by enlightening one's self through education. There was this constant and inherent desire to read, write and further one's self through education. However, with the constant threat of war in the late 1800's and early 1900's in the Western border areas of Ukraine, and with the coming of the First World War, few if any immigrants were educated due to the constant disruption and devastation of war in their homeland.

Krydor was the birthplace or home town of many successful and forward thinking individuals. The settlers realized very quickly that while the agricultural lifestyle was essential for survival and making a living, education was also essential if they wanted to further their own and their children's aspirations. The children of the pioneer families set the educational and career standard and consequently the late comers to Krydor were encouraged to follow in their footsteps and pursue their education and career dreams. Many children of the pioneers from the Krydor area went on to become authors, agronomists, academics, medical doctors, lawyers, pharmacists, accountants and teachers. As a result the children and the grandchildren and great grandchildren of the Wawryniuk's, the Worobetz's, the Michayluk's, the Melnychuk's, the Mulka's, the Marko's, the Shklanka's, the Pawlyk's, Wawryk's, the Tkaczyk's, the Hnatiuk's and others continued their education through high school and pursued higher education at universities and technical institutes throughout Canada, the United States of America and the United Kingdom. A few of the notable leaders that emerged from Krydor were:

- Savella Stechishin (nee: Wawryniuk) at the age of 10 emigrated to Canada from Western Ukraine and settled in the Krydor District with her family in 1913. After attending elementary school at Krydor, she completed her high school education in Saskatoon, then received her teaching certificate. In 1921 she married Julian Stechishin, a prominent Saskatoon lawyer of Ukrainian heritage and a leader in the Ukrainian community. By 1930 she was raising three children and was the first Ukrainian woman to graduate from the University of Saskatchewan with a Bachelor of Arts degree majoring in Home Economics. She was the co-founder of the Ukrainian Women's Association of Canada and assisted in founding the Ukrainian Museum of Canada in Saskatoon. Her further contributions included being a columnist and women's page editor of the Ukrainian language weekly newspaper "The Ukrainian Voice", writing about nutrition and health. In 1957 she authored an extensive and comprehensive cook book in English titled "Traditional Ukrainian Cookery". This book went into reprints and is a common fixture in Ukrainian homes across Canada. In addition, she authored and co-authored several books on Ukrainian culture. She received many awards during her lifetime including the Order of Canada, the Saskatchewan Order of Merit and she received an award by the President of Ukraine. She died in Saskatoon on April 22, 2002.

- Honorable Dr. Stephen Worobetz was born and raised in Krydor (no immediate relation to Andrew Worobetz). He went on to the University of Saskatchewan, completing his Bachelor of Science, then completing his Medical Degree at the University of Manitoba. In 1944 he joined the military and served with the Princess Patricia Canadian Light Infantry Medical Corps serving in Italy where he was awarded the Military Cross for courage under fire. Following his post-graduate studies at the University of Pennsylvania in Philadelphia, he returned to Saskatoon where he became a General Surgeon and President of the Medical Staff at St. Paul's Hospital. He was a clinical lecturer in Department of Surgery in the College of Medicine at the University of Saskatchewan. He was appointed Lt. Governor of the Province of Saskatchewan and served inn that office from 1970 to 1976.

There were many more settlers' children from the Krydor District that went on to vocations and positions of prominence. Dr. Marko (Toronto), Dr. Melnychuk (New York), Mr. Shklanka (author) and Dr. Julian Michayluk (University of Saskatchewan) were a few of the children of immigrant settlers that progressed into positions of prominence. This was true of many of the immigrant settled districts, villages and towns across the prairies. These newcomers to Canada had a thirst for knowledge and education and subsequent leadership that was unavailable or unattainable to them in their homeland. These immigrants ensured that their children had those opportunities and made them available through education. It seemed that the success of prairie communities was often marked by the departure of their sons and daughters for academic and business successes farther afield. The departure of these sons and daughters ironically often led to the decimation and stagnation of prairie villages and towns until they became virtual ghost towns. Other factors came into play such as technological advances in communications and travel, but the loss of the potential leaders hurt these small communities.

Michael and Tena, meanwhile, were very pleased to be able to settle down in a community where there was a positive attitude toward the fostering of high educational ideals.

While Lessia and George were becoming familiar with their school and their new school friends, Michael and Tena were busy starting up their business and getting involved in the community.

Taking over the Krydor Hotel was a full time job. The building was relatively new and was sturdy for its 24 year existence. The two story frame structure had an exterior that was clad in wooden siding with cedar shingles on the roof. The interior was plaster on wood lathe construction with hardwood floors throughout, except for the kitchen which had a linoleum covering on the floor. The exterior of the building had been

DREAM TO REALITY

recently painted, thus it was presentable from the exterior. The interior was a different story. It needed cleaning, needed paint and many utility renovations. The walls were dingy with years of smoke build-up from cigarette, pipe and cigar smoke, not to mention the smoke from the coal and wood stoves and space heaters and their leaky stovepipes. There was no electricity, no central heating and no running water and no sewage facilities. With no present day utilities, life in the hotel for the first two years was primitive by today's standards.

Since there was no electrical supply to the community, the lighting was supplied by gas lamps (similar to Coleman camping lanterns) and kerosene lamps. That meant live flames in six lamps on the main floor and a kerosene lamp in each of the 10 guest rooms on the second floor. To go to the basement one had to carry a kerosene lantern to provide light. The walls and ceiling were covered in soot from years of using this lighting system. With the coming of spring Tena, Lessia and George would be scrubbing walls and ceilings of the hotel in preparation for Mary's and Alex's wedding.

Food and beer was kept in the basement during the winter since there was no refrigeration in the hotel. Outside in the back yard was a building the size of a double garage. It had two wide doors at one end and a walk-in door at the other. This was the ice house. Inside the ice house was a hole the size of the double garage and about six or seven feet deep. This hole was lined with sawdust and large blocks of ice about one cubic meter in size were placed in the hole then layered again with sawdust, with another layer of ice blocks, then more sawdust and so on, until the hole was filled with ice. The sawdust acted as an insulator to prevent the ice from melting too quickly in the summer. The ice was replenished in the winter months with river ice from the North Saskatchewan River. This ice house was the equivalent of a walk-in refrigerator. Food and beverages could be kept on ice during the spring, summer and autumn months. The water well which was about 4 meters from the back door of the hotel was used as a cooler as well, with food, primarily dairy products lowered in a pail and kept just above the water line. The coolness of the well preserved perishable foods which could be brought up any time they were needed.

There was no central heating in the hotel. The wood/coal stove in the kitchen provided heat for the kitchen and part of the dining room. There were two additional wood/coal burning space heaters on the main floor to provide heat in the dining room and the front lobby. The beer parlor had two wood/coal space heaters to provide heat in the beer parlor. The 2nd floor with the guest rooms had two wood/coal burning space heaters in the hallway to heat the upper hall and the guest rooms. The doors to the guest rooms had transoms above the doors that would allow heat to transfer into the guest rooms even if the guest room doors were closed. The 180 lineal feet (59 meters) of shiny blue/black exhaust/smoke pipes were suspended one meter from walls and ceilings, leading to the central brick chimney. This was a marvel in itself and a fire hazard at the same time. The pipes, where they passed through the walls from one room to another, were lined on the outside surface with asbestos sheets (as a fire prevention measure). In the years leading up to the 1970's asbestos was not considered to be a dangerous life threatening substance. It was used quite liberally wherever heat and fire transfer might be evident. Feeding the wood and coal stove and space heaters and removing the ashes was a twice daily job in the winter. Michael and George looked after that task as well as chopping all the wood for the stoves and space heaters. Michael would order two or three two ton truck loads of wood for the winter and he would order a railway box car of coal from Drumheller or

DREAM TO REALITY

Coleman, Alberta to last the winter. The wood would have to be split by axe and the coal transferred from the box car to the hotel basement. One third of the basement would be full of coal. The coal management was heavy and dirty work with the coal dust filtering throughout the hotel. Each stove and space heater had its own coal scuttle (bucket) and wood box that had to be kept filled throughout the day during the winter months. As well, the ashes from the stove and space heaters had to be removed and disposed of outside in a hole in the ground to prevent the live coals and ashes from being blown around and setting other buildings on fire. The management of the coal, wood and the ashes were time consuming tasks that Michael and George had to tend to every morning and evening.

The hotel had no plumbing system, thus water for drinking and washing had to be brought in from the water well just outside the back door. There also was a large water cistern in the basement that was 4 meters by 4 meters by 4 meters, that collected rain water off the roof of the hotel. This cistern was made of concrete and was located under the floor of a store room adjacent to the kitchen. The water was hand pumped into pails for use in doing the hotel laundry. Water was heated on the stove top in a large copper boiler for washing and bathing. There was also a water reservoir attached to the side of the wood stove that kept approximately 5 to 8 gallons of water warm so long as the wood stove was fired up and hot. The bathroom was a two hole outdoor pit toilet near the back lane. There was an indoor toilet for the hotel guests on the upper floor, however the bucket from the toilet would have to be emptied into the pit toilet every day or more frequently at times, then sanitized with bleach several times a day to keep it fresh and free of germs. As well, the guest rooms had a wash basin stand with a porcelain wash basin and pitcher. Warm water would be brought up for the guests in the morning at their wake up call.

Inside the wash basin stand was a large porcelain chamber pot for guests who had to relieve themselves during the night.

The main and upper floors of the hotel were all oak hardwood and had to be waxed and polished regularly. Waxing meant applying a paste hardwood wax to the floor and then polishing the wood on your hands and knees with a polishing cloth. This was made easier on all when Lessia and George would put on some old heavy woolen socks of Michael's and slide over the floor in their stocking clad feet polishing the floor. That sure beat polishing on your hands and knees. The floor in the beer parlor was hardwood as well. However it had seen such abuse from spills, muddy boots, burn marks from cigarettes being butted out on the floor, and the grain and grit from farmers' coveralls scoring the wood, this floor had to be scrubbed daily. Its finish was . . . . rustic.

Laundry day was a day long enterprise. It started at 6:00 a.m. with water being drawn from the cistern and heated in the 5 gallon copper boiler on the wood stove. The bed linens and towels would be set to soak in a washtub of hot water and bleach solution on the stove. The washer was originally a washtub with a manual agitator that Tena, Lessia and George manually operated by rotating a handle that was attached to the agitator. The manual wringer was comprised of two rubber rollers that were operated with a crank. The pressure of the rollers caused the rollers to squeeze the water out of the sheets, towels and other clothes. This process was very labor intensive, but much better than washing the clothes on a washboard and wringing the water out of the clothes with your hands. After the water was squeezed out of the clothes with the wringer, the clothes were then hung outside on the clothes lines to dry. There were six clothes lines outside in the back yard, each about 10 meters long. Wash day usually ended by 8:00 or 9:00

p.m. In the winter, the sheets would freeze and would have to be brought into the hotel, like sheets of plywood and carried into the basement to be hung on clothes lines and finish the drying process. The basement of the hotel was long enough that the clothes lines were a match to the outdoor ones. The smell of the frozen sheets was a fresh smell, one that lingers in memories from those years in the 1950's. During all their years in the hotel from 1950-1965, Michael and Tena never did have an automatic washer and dryer. They laboriously washed the hotel bed linens and hung them out to dry.

Ironing all the sheets by hand for hotel use was a massive job. After a few months of hand ironing, Michael and Tena acquired a "mangler". Mangler was an appropriate vernacular term for this cold press, due to the potential injuries a person could inflict upon one's self. A hand operated mangler was a press made up of three wooden rollers that was cranked by hand with the rollers used to cold press sheets, pillowcases and other flat items. The pressure to press the sheets and linens was provided by turning an adjustment wheel at the top of the mangler to provide pressure on a large leaf spring. This spring would in turn press the rollers closer together. Too much pressure and the sheets would not pass through the rollers; too little pressure and the sheets would not get pressed. The odd finger could and did get caught in the rollers, thus the appropriate name of "mangler". One could even press slacks with a mangler if care was used on the creases. Dido Pohoreski, after seeing a mangler built for commercial purposes, built a mangler for the hotels in Gronlid and Krydor, from spare and discarded gears, pieces of angle iron, a car leaf spring and three hand turned wooden rollers about four inches in diameter.

Dido Pohoreski was in his glory when he was challenged to invent, fabricate or reconstruct a wood or steel object with his welders, hammers, forge, anvil, lathes and saws. He was always manufacturing garden tractors, motorized two wheeled scooters, motorized or electric lawnmowers, implements and electronic objects such as radios for himself, family or friends.

A sketch of a hand operated mangler

Ironing other clothes would depend on flat irons heated up on the wood stove. A handle would be attached to the flat iron and would be used to iron a garment. The next advancement in ironing clothes arrived in the late 1940's. This new iron had a gas tank and a burner fastened to a thin flat iron base. The open flame heated the flat iron to provide heat for the iron. It wasn't until 1952-1953 when 110 volt electricity became available to the rural areas that electric irons became the norm.

From the outset in December, 1950, the hotel business was thriving. Michael and Tena were the new business couple in Krydor and everyone had to come and check them out. The primary trade initially was the beer parlor with its beer parlor clientele with unusually large off premises sales of beer. There were no liquor (wine and spirits) stores in smaller communities, so the nearest liquor stores were in North Battleford, Prince Albert and Saskatoon. In fact Michael and Tena had a difficult time with people coming to the back door of the hotel late at night or on Sundays to try and buy beer during off hours. In addition to the brisk beer trade, the guest room trade and dining room/ restaurant trade began growing almost immediately when the travelling public caught wind that there was new ownership and a new eating establishment had opened up. Saskatchewan Highway #40 passed within a few meters of the hotel thus it was a usual and convenient stopping place for commercial travelers, inspectors, and supervisors who made their weekly, monthly and yearly visits to the various businesses in Krydor. During the 1950's all goods in stores were ordered through commercial travelers representing the various wholesales, meat packing plants and dairies in North Battleford, Prince Albert, Saskatoon, Edmonton and Winnipeg. In addition to the commercial travelers, there were grain elevator inspectors, grain elevator repair crews, fish hatchery workers who came out to stock Redberry Lake with whitefish fingerlings for the winter commercial white fishing season, highway repair crews, an optometrist (Dr. Proctor) who came out to Krydor from North Battleford to set up practice for a day every week and other travelling public. The hotel lodging and boarding business in small towns was very active, and Krydor was no different. The need for modernizing the hotel became very evident, shortly after Michal and Tena settled into their business. The turn-around time for laundering the hotel sheets and linens had to be shortened. The wood stove was not always reliable for preparing meals. A constant hot water supply was needed for hygienic purposes, particularly for washing dishes, silverware and beer glasses from the beer parlor. Lessia and George were the dishwashers and servers in the dining room with Tena doing all the meal planning and preparation. Homemade bread, pies, and other baking was a feature that the travelling public enjoyed thus Tena's kitchen was a going concern from early morning to late at night. Often Tena would hire high school girls for noon hours, after school periods and on Saturdays and school holidays or summer vacation to assist with the cleaning and meal preparation. The hotel was definitely a full family operation that was also dependent on some outside help.

During the spring of 1951, Tena got a gas powered washing machine which had to be vented to the outside of the hotel to get rid of the engine exhaust and carbon monoxide fumes. This innovation certainly speeded up the laundering process. During the spring and summer months the washing machine would be moved outside and the laundering was done outside. The gas motor was the size of a gas lawn mower engine which operated the agitator and the wringer. The next washer would have an electric motor in place of the gas motor, which was much quieter and safer, but that giant leap in technology wouldn't come until 1954.

As technology progressed quickly in the 1950's, work that was often time consuming and tedious, and referred to as drudgery, began taking on a more expedient form and providing for a more labor efficient operation of the hotel. By the mid 1950's Krydor Hotel was going to be transformed from a once primitive operation to a streamlined and a very profitable enterprise.

Michael and Tena were soon becoming involved in the cultural fabric of the community. Michael purchased shares in the Ukrainian National Home (Narodny Deem) or community hall. Whenever a Ukranian institution was getting started, shares were sold as a form of raising money for the venture. Michael bought shares in order to financially support many Ukrainian organizations such as the various Narody Domeh, The Ukrainian Voice (Ukrainksi Holos), a Ukrainian weekly newspaper edited and published by Myroslaw Stechishin and The St. Petro Mohyla Ukrainian Institute in Saskatoon just to name a few. Today the shares in those ventures are worthless, in fact they were not meant to create a monetary return for the investor, but a return in the form of cultural maintenance. The shares indicated a membership, a commitment, a voice in running the organization or paying the bills. Any community where a Ukrainian Church was built, a Narodny Deem would follow. The hall would be used for church dinners, concerts, staging of dramas or plays, for church and community meetings, community dances, socials and wedding receptions. It was the focal point of the community along with the churches.

Michael and Tena became members of the St. Peter and St. Paul Ukrainian Orthodox Parish in Krydor and before the year was up, Michael was the Palamar and chairman of the Church Board of Management. There was only a handful of parishioners (five or six families) who lived in the village of Krydor itself. The rest of the parishioners lived on farms nearby or in neighboring towns and districts such as Blaine Lake and Tallman. Most of the Church preparation and cleaning was left to the Krydor townspeople. Michael, being the Palamar and Tena the head of the altar guild, the Tkaczyk family soon became responsible for the Church cleaning, Church yard maintenance and snow clearing chores.

The parish priest, Father Aponiuk, was located in Hafford, 23 kilometers to the West of Krydor on Highway #40. He served four parishes—Hafford, Krydor, Dominion (near Richard) and Whitkow. Father Aponiuk would take the bus from Hafford to Krydor on a Saturday and spend the late afternoon and evening at the hotel visiting with the Tkaczyk family or visiting the parishioners in town. He would conduct the Divine Liturgy on Sunday morning, have lunch with the Tkaczyk's at the hotel and then Michael and Tena would drive him back to Hafford on Sunday afternoon. Church services were held in Krydor at least once a month.

Soon after arriving in Krydor, Michael and Tena found out that there was no piano teacher in Krydor. In order for Lessia to continue her piano lessons, they started a search and soon located a piano teacher with excellent credentials who came to Hafford on Saturdays and taught piano in the Hafford Elementary School. This teacher was Mrs. Wier from Speers, 16 kilometers west of Hafford, who had her A.R.C.T. (Associate of The Royal Conservatory, Toronto) in piano and piano theory. Tena would drive Lessia to Hafford every Saturday for her piano lessons, but that soon became a problem with the busy hotel and dining room schedule. The daily Saskatchewan Transportation Company (STC) bus schedule was a blessing. Lessia and George would board the westbound bus coming from Prince Albert at 10:30 a.m. and travel to Hafford. Lessia would have her piano lesson at the Hafford School by 1:00 p.m., then George and Lessia would spend the afternoon in Hafford doing some shopping for sewing items for Tena that were not available in Krydor, or spend time with friends, usually the Mitchell's, since their daughter Christina also took piano lessons. Lessia and George would catch the 5:00 p.m. eastbound bus from North Battleford back to Krydor and be home for supper. At 35 cents per return ticket, it saved Tena her valuable time in baking, serving meals or sewing clothes for family or for people in the community.

The weekly trip to Hafford for Lessia and George was an adventure in itself. It was the twentieth century version of Chaucer's Canterbury tales. The bus was usually full of people, some of them very unique characters, travelling to North Battleford or Prince Albert or any points beyond, or in between.

Every one of them, and the cast of characters changed, had a unique personality or a story to tell. On the 14 mile (23 kilometer) one way trip to Hafford, the bus would make frequent stops along Highway #40 to pick up passengers travelling to Hafford or North Battleford to do their weekly shopping. A regular passenger was Mrs. X who lived 8 kilometers west of Krydor. Every Saturday morning she would take her 10 dozen eggs to sell to Mr. Herman, the owner of Herman's Nu-Way Store. Mrs. X was the "atypical" Ukrainian Baba wearing several skirts of varying lengths, one on top of the other, a colorful, flowered baboushka (a colored or embroidered head scarf) and for safe keeping she carried her money wrapped up in a red and white polka dot handkerchief. She would stand well into the middle of the road so that the bus driver couldn't miss her imposing figure, to stop the bus. She would climb into the bus with her crate of eggs and stand at the bus driver's seat and admonish him, in Ukrainian of course, for not assisting her with her crate of eggs onto the bus. Then standing astride her crate of eggs, with her hands on her hips, she would start haggling, in Ukrainian of course, over a discount on her 25 cent return bus fare to Hafford. The English speaking bus driver could only guess at what she was demanding and communicated with gestures, hand language, body language and the bus fare chart until a deal was completed and bus could move on to its destination. Lessia and George would cringe and slide low into their seats since they did not want to become part of this bizarre scenario of bus fare bartering and verbal bashing of the bus driver; and then have to sit next to her for the remainder of the trip to Hafford. She would eventually spot Lessia and George because after paying her reduced bus fare she stood and gazed at all the passengers and studied them as though she was a detective looking for a possible fugitive. Then spotting someone she recognized, usually Lessia and George, she would proceed to sit near them literally moving people out of the way to achieve that end. Lessia and George knew that the trip back to Krydor would be eventful since Mrs. X would be waiting for them and specifically pick a seat across the aisle from them. On the trip back to her drop off point on Highway #40, Mrs. X would relate to everyone within earshot (which was the entire bus load of passengers) of stories of how the shop keepers in Hafford were dishonest and constantly under paying her for her eggs and stealing her blind when she tried to purchase items. Then she would inform the entire busload of passengers that the only honest business person in the area was the "hotelnik" (hotel owner) in Krydor (only because she was sitting next to the "hotelnik's" children).

Michael knew her well. She was one of Michael's usual customers, making a weekly visit to the hotel. She couldn't legally enter the beer parlor and sign for an off sale beer purchase, since only males were allowed into the beer parlor. Legislation would change that in years to come. She would come in through the back door of the hotel without knocking, walk through the kitchen, checking out what Tena was baking or cooking and taste it if she so desired, then moved on into the dining room and demanded (she never asked), that Tena get Michael out of the beer parlor because she wanted to buy her weekly six-pack of "stout" dark ale, or as she called it "to chorne pevo" (that black beer). She considered Michael a good man since the hotel owners in the area wouldn't give her the time of day; they couldn't be bothered with her and her antics, and refused her attempts to purchase her ale. Michael always sold her that six-pack, mainly to get rid of her, since she would cause a disturbance of one kind or another.

The bus trip home from Hafford on Saturday evenings couldn't end soon enough for Lessia and George, who would relate their bus adventures to Michael and Tena around the supper table.

DREAM TO REALITY

Each week was a new and exciting adventure with Mrs. X. The bus drivers in Prince Albert and North Battleford, for that Saturday run surely drew lots to avoid the assignment.

Krydor, as every small town on the prairies, had its share of characters. Michael dealt with all of them since they usually ended up in the beer parlor at one time or another. One person that was near and dear to Michael and Tena was "Matzko" Mike Tywoniuk. Matzko was a frequent hotel customer, in his fifties, a short slender man about five feet tall, but with the heart of a giant. He was a railway "extra gang" worker who worked during the summer, drew unemployment insurance during the winter and ran the livery stable that was left to Matzko after his father's passing. The livery stable was in use in Krydor until 1956 when horses weren't used for travel any more. During the winter, Matzko would spend most of his days working in the livery barn, playing pool at the local pool hall, playing cards (rummy, poker or Kaiser) or spending afternoons and evenings in the beer parlor spinning yarns with his cronies. He was a constant in the beer parlor. He had a story for everyone, about everyone, but no one ever got offended. He would spin yarns so that everyone "came out a winner". He was a rural bar room psychologist ahead of his time. Matzko was well liked by everyone and when the beer parlor became busy, he helped Michael wait on tables and served beer while entertaining the customers with his stories and yarns. He refused Michael's offer to pay him, only accepting Tena's home cooking as payment. Michael had Matzko look after the beer parlor when Michael and Tena had to travel to Saskatoon or Gronlid for a day or two to contend with business appointments or family gatherings.

Often, Matzko would come into the dining room for a meal. The piano was in one corner of the dining room and Lessia would be practicing her scales on the piano for her Saturday piano lessons. After listening to the scales for a while, Matzko would ask Lessia to play some polka's or kolomaykas. Of course Lessia would oblige him, since she wanted to get out of the practicing of scales anyway. The interior walls of the hotel were not insulated, and with the beer parlor being on the other side of the wall from the dining room, the sound of the music carried right through into the beer parlor. With all this music going on, soon there would be clapping from the bar patrons and requests for more music. As Lessia would keep playing, Matzko would "pass the hat" and the beer parlor patrons would send money to Lessia via Matzko for more requests. Matzko took great delight in that he was procuring entertainment for the beer parlor patrons and Lessia was making a few dollars for her effort and talent. Tena would have to step in and take control so that this situation would not get out of hand, and that Lessia could get some serious piano practicing done. When Michael and Tena would eventually leave Krydor in the 1960's, Matzko was very despondent since he claimed he was losing his only "family".

The first winter in the hotel was a totally new experience for the Tkaczyk family. The business component kept Michael and Tena very busy. The maintenance component alone, the chopping of firewood, bringing up coal from the basement, for all the space heaters and the stove, removing ashes from them, bringing in water from the water well, washing dishes, clearing snow and of course school work and piano kept Lessia and George very busy the rest of the time. Tobogganing, skating, broom ball, shinny (hockey) and moccasin dances (outdoor dances held at the skating rink to the tune of scratchy 78 rpm records on an old antiquated record player) were Lessia's and

George's recreation that first winter in Krydor. Contact with the outside world took the form of a large cabinet style radio that could receive about four or five radio stations with an appropriate antenna mounted to the roof of the hotel. The dry cell battery pack for the radio was twice the size of a 12 volt car battery. The battery usually lasted the winter if the family used it judiciously. Programs that were allowed were the news in the morning and evening, special programming such as the A.C.T. (Associated Commercial Travelers) Amateur Hour and Hockey Night In Canada with Foster Hewitt on Saturday Night from Maple Leaf Gardens. Sunday evening was a special time on radio with radio plays that everyone listened to. Fibber McGee and Molly, Henry Aldrich, Our Miss Brooks, The Lone Ranger, The Cisco Kid, The Green Hornet, The Shadow Knows and Matt Sevetic, Agent for the F.B.I were the more common radio plays that were followed from week to week. Occasionally George and Lessia would sneak in the "Top Ten Hit Parade" with the top DJ's from radio station CFQC in Saskatoon.

Michael wrote to his family in Ukraine on a regular basis. Writing and receiving letters from family members in Canada or Ukraine was a regular activity for the Tkaczyk's. Mail day was every day in Krydor as there was twice daily train service between Prince Albert and North Battleford until about 1956 when it changed to once daily train service. Picking up mail at the Post Office was an exciting event. There were letters from Mary in Smith's Falls, letters from Gronlid, from Ukraine, from Michael's brother's in law, the Kotyk's in Hatfield, Wynyard and other Saskatchewan locations. Mail order catalogues were a much awaited item. Eaton's, Simpson's, Army and Navy and McLeod's were but a few of the usual catalogues by which people in rural communities made clothing, household furnishings and equipment purchases. Christmas was an especially exciting time since there were always the Christmas cards and Christmas presents from aunts, uncles and cousins.

By the time Christmas of 1950 arrived, Michael and his family were comfortably settling into the routine of the hotel and community. Michael continued his correspondence with his family in Uzhenetz, Kitsman and Stavchany in Bukovina by writing letters on a regular basis. He, Mary and Tena did so through the 1930's, 1940's and continued to do so into the 1990's. There was constant concern for Michael's father, his brothers and sisters and his in-laws throughout the periods of famine, the entire Second World War and throughout the Stalinist purges following the war. Having lived through the First World War as a pre-teen and as a teen ager, Michael knew well the ravages and hardships that his countrymen faced under the brutal and heartless Stalinist regime. The Bolsheviks or now the Communists were a heartless and corrupt society. The Bukovina region of Ukraine was fortunate to escape the full brunt of the Communist induced famines of the 1920's and the 1930's, thus Michael and his family did not suffer as did the central and eastern regions of Ukraine. Stalin's collectivization of farms and harsh quotas on all produce left nothing for the people to eat. Stalin's quotas were not as harsh in Bukovina since Romania still maintained administrative control over the region. Yes, there were food shortages and hunger prevailed as times were tough, however not to the starvation extreme.

The added political conflict between the Soviets and the Romanians assisted Bukovina in that Romania held administrative control over the region. Even though Romania exercised control over Bukovina, the communists and the KGB kept a close eye on the people and their farming activities. Anyone with more food than was allowed or if someone displayed a surplus of food, currency or wealth, they would be severely punished, put to death or exiled into the Siberian work camps. Any display of excess or wealth was considered treasonous to the Communist state. There were food shortages in Bukovina but not the starvation and cannibalism that occurred elsewhere in Ukraine. The political map was re-drawn in 1940 when the Communists militarily took over Bukovina and pushed the Romanian Military back. In doing so the communists massacred many Romanians, their families, children and whoever got in their way. Josef Stalin was infamous for his orchestrated famines and the brutality of his KGB (secret service). He had complete control of Eastern Europe (Berlin and east from the Berlin Wall to the Pacific Ocean was under his control) either directly or through satellite powers such as Poland, Hungary, Czechoslovakia, Romania and East Germany. The Iron Curtain as it was called, let very little through from 1944 up to the 1990's. Letters were opened and screened, parcels were opened and inspected (and most times pilfered by officials); people could not enter or leave the countries as they wished, unless they were given special permits to do so. Once inside the Iron Curtain, one was at their mercy. Travel and visits were limited and overtly watched by agents. During the war from 1939 to 1944, very little could be mailed to Michael's family. The need for clothing was great. Michael's family would beg him to send winter clothing, shoes, leather, fabric, anything that they could use as garments and protective clothing and footwear to protect them from the cold winters. Michael communicated often and tried to send parcels of clothing to his family members, however the corrupt Soviet postal officials would intercept the letters and parcels and steal or pilfer all or select items from the parcels which would then be kept or sold on the Black Market. The Black Market was officially banned in the Soviet Union, however the corruption was so great that the Soviet officials thrived on it. The families were benefitting in a small way from Michael's generosity, but Michael continued to send clothing, even if some of it was being stolen by the Soviet authorities, some of it was put to use by his family. Michael knew what was getting through since his family would always confirm what was sent through thank you letters. Michael was extremely angry that his parcels were pilfered, however he felt that if he sent nothing, his family would suffer more. It was the least he could do.

January through to March of 1951 was extremely busy. With all the hotel work, community activities and school for Lessia and George and Lessia's piano lessons, there was a wedding to plan. Mary and Alex had informed their families that they were planning to get married in July of 1951 and take on new teaching positions in Spirit River, Alberta (Northwest of Grande Prairie). During the spring of 1951, the regular hotel cleaning was ramped up and the hotel was washed from top to bottom, ceilings, walls and windows. The smoke from years of kerosene lamps and wood and coal stoves and heaters had turned the ivory colored paint to a brown. Michael and Tena hired a group of high school girls to help with the cleaning. The high school girls were eager to get a paying job, and Michael and Tena were pleased to have this capable work force assisting with the mammoth cleaning task.

It was an exciting June when Mary arrived from Smith's Falls, Ontario and the final preparations for the wedding were taking place. The invitations had been sent out earlier, since the wedding date was set for July 22, 1951. There were all the other preparations that Michael and Tena had to look after—the food, the refreshments and the accommodations for the guests. The hotel had enough rooms and any overflow would be accommodated by some of Michael's and Tena's friends in Krydor. The guests would be arriving from Gronlid, Saskatoon, Insinger, Foam Lake and Regina. The wedding was a relatively small affair as far as Ukrainian weddings go, due to the fact that the family was spread all over Saskatchewan and distances were an obstacle unless the family had a vehicle. The small wedding included guests from the Kotyk families, Hupka families and the Pohoreski families. Very few Krydor townspeople were invited since no one knew Mary and Alex and the Tkaczyk's were relatively new to the Krydor Community. The wedding took place at the Krydor Ukrainian Orthodox Church of St. Peter and St. Paul with Father Kowalishin from Saskatoon officiating. Father Kowalishin was the Rector and Chaplain of the St. Petro Mohyla Ukrainian Institute when Mary and Alex stayed there throughout their University of Saskatchewan years. He was also a Chaplain in the Canadian Army when Alex served overseas, so it was fitting that he officiated at the wedding ceremony. The reception took place in the dining room of the Krydor Hotel. Mary's and Alex's wedding was the only wedding reception that was ever held in the hotel during the years that Michael and Tena owned it. Weddings in succeeding years became larger and larger, such that the wedding receptions were held in the Narodny Deem or community hall. Michael and Tena catered to the large banquets for local groups and weddings in the community hall many times during their Krydor years.

Wedding Party-Ukrainian Orthodox Church of St. Peter and St. Paul Front Row: Vesper Dobrowolsky, Diana Pohoreski, Jimmy Kotyk Second Row: Lessia Tkaczyk, Sylvia Fedoruk, Mary Hupka, Alex Hupka, Nick Hupka, Johnnie Kotyk Back Row: Michael Tkaczyk, Tena Tkaczyk, Aunt Ann Kotyk, Aunt Mafta Foreground Right: Elizabeth Kotyk, Kay Pohoreski, Louis Pohoreski,

Mary and Alex had a very busy summer collecting all their belongings and packing them into their new blue 1951 Pontiac, and venturing off to visit all their immediate relatives in Insinger, Alex's home town, then visiting family that couldn't make it to the wedding, before venturing off to Spirit River in Northwestern Alberta. They had to find accommodations in that small community north west of Grande Prairie and get set up for the upcoming school year. Mary would be teaching home economics and Alex would be teaching math and physics in the Spirit River High School. Mary and Alex wrote often and would come back to Krydor and Insinger for the two weeks of Christmas Holidays, but that would be their only year in Spirit

River since it was so far from their families and there was no Ukrainian community to which they had become accustomed. They made the best of their year in Spirit River. You know that Mary and Alex had time on their hands when they surprised George at Christmas with a pair of genuine "Indian knee high moccasins" complete with fringes around the top and made by the famous Indian "Chief Thunderbird" himself. Now only an eight year old, eagerly waiting for these moccasins would believe a story like that. It was a few years later that Mary and Alex admitted that they had crafted those moccasins themselves from some heavily smoked and tanned moose hide they had purchased from a local native band around Spirit River. Those moccasins were so heavily smoked that George couldn't even wear them to school. The smell was so strong that it bothered everyone in the building. It took years to get rid of the smoke smell out of the leather. The hotel smelled of smoke if the moccasins were kept indoors. The moccasins spent a good part of their existence in the ice house and garage. Everyone had a good laugh about those moccasins, even to this day the topic of Chief Thunderbird brings a smile to certain family member's faces.

Michael and Tena worked long, hard hours under primitive conditions to turn the hotel business around from one of neglect and barely existing financially to a profitable enterprise. They pinched pennies when it came to personal expenditures and in doing so poured all their resources into the infrastructure in order to maximize their business and profit margin, by every way imaginable. Because of their hard work, personal sacrifices and entrepreneurship, business was booming. The beer parlor was a going concern with on premises customers providing much of the business and the off sales of beer providing a surprisingly large volume of business. In the 1950's the nearest liquor stores to Krydor were located in North Battleford, Prince

Albert and Saskatoon. Smaller centers did not have liquor outlets, thus off sales beer was a very large sales item in small town hotels. Wine and spirits had to be ordered from the large city liquor stores and would be shipped via train or bus service to individual customers in the rural communities. Individuals making pleasure or business trips to the larger centers usually got bogged down with orders from their friends and neighbors, especially around the holiday season. In the 1960's Hafford and Blaine Lake would get their liquor outlets as the liquor licensing regulations were being upgraded.

The other side of the booming business was the dining room/restaurant and room rental trade. A day didn't go by when Michael, Tena, Lessia and George weren't serving meals to locals, to the travelling public or to work and maintenance crews. Michael and Tena had a large garden beside the hotel for ready to eat vegetables such as onion, chives, carrots, lettuce, dill and some other herbs. They also had a large garden at Ference's farm which was located about 5 kilometers out of town. This large garden included potatoes, peas, corn, cucumber, beans, broad beans, tomatoes, dill, garlic, onions, beets and turnip. This garden would provide produce to last a year or more in terms of canned, fresh or frozen vegetables. George, Lessia, Michael and Tena had their summer mornings cut out for them with watering, weeding, hoeing, hilling potatoes, and then autumn harvesting and vegetable gathering and canning and later freezing of these vegetables. Canning time during the summer and fall was a full time job for three or four people in order to put away enough food for the fall and winter for the hotel operation. Fruits and vegetables had to be washed, jars had to be sterilized, vegetables peeled or shelled, blanched, cooked and vacuum sealed in jars and stored in the basement. A large portion of the canning included the canning of dill pickles, sweet pickles, relishes and borsch. Jams and fruit preserves (pears, strawberries, Saskatoon berries, pin cherries, high bush cranberries or kalyna, plums, peaches, apricots etc.) were also a huge part of the canning process. By the time canning season was over there were 500 to 600 jars of preserves in the basement. Commercial jams and fruit preserves were only purchased in an emergency. The money saved by producing and canning their own produce rather than purchasing them from wholesalers was most profitable during those early years in Krydor. When Michael and Tena were busy with hotel work and serving meals during the day, George and Lessia would cycle out to the farm to do the garden chores. As soon as Lessia (age 14) and George (age 10) were taught to drive the 1941 Chevrolet, they drove themselves out to the farm to do much of the gardening, harvesting and berry picking.

Under age children driving vehicles in rural areas of the prairie provinces was a common sight in the 1950's. Children growing up in rural areas were taught to drive vehicles as soon as they could reach the foot pedals and see over the steering wheel. They were invaluable to their parents with completing farm and rural chores. It was not uncommon to see 10 to 15 year olds driving tractors, trucks and cars to and from towns for supplies, water or repair parts for farm equipment and implements. The Royal Canadian Mounted Police at the time had large areas to patrol and they were understanding of the difficulties rural people had in finding farm help. So long as young people were reasonable and responsible in their driving on the rural roads and kept off the major highways, the Mounted Police were lenient in administering the traffic laws away from major highways. Warnings to the parents and under age drivers as opposed to traffic tickets were the order of the day.

Then there was the Krydor Hotel chicken raising process. Between 100 and 200 baby chicks were ordered from the chicken hatchery in North Battleford during the months of April and May. The Krydor Hotel housed these baby chicks by the wood stove in the cardboard chicken "condominiums", in which the baby chicks were shipped. The box was large and divided into quarters with 25 chicks in each compartment. The box was placed near the wood stove so that the chicks would be warm. The were fed "chick starter" and water for days until the chicks would lose their soft down and start to develop feathers. Then Michael and Tena would take the chicks out to Ference's farm to be "range raised" on the farm during the summer. Michael, Tena, Lessia and George would spend the better part of several days in late August or early September at the farm, butchering, plucking, eviscerating and cleaning chickens. Michael would have to go back to tend the hotel and sometimes Tena would have to hire some high school girls to serve meals in the dining room while the chicken harvest was in full swing. The chickens would be harvested in the fall and when they were cleaned and eviscerated, approximately one third of them were canned in jars and the other two thirds would be taken to the "quick freeze locker plant" in Hafford to be frozen for future use in the kitchen of the hotel, where gourmet delights such as home-made chicken noodle soup, creamed chicken, roast chicken and fried chicken were dining room favorites.

DREAM TO REALITY

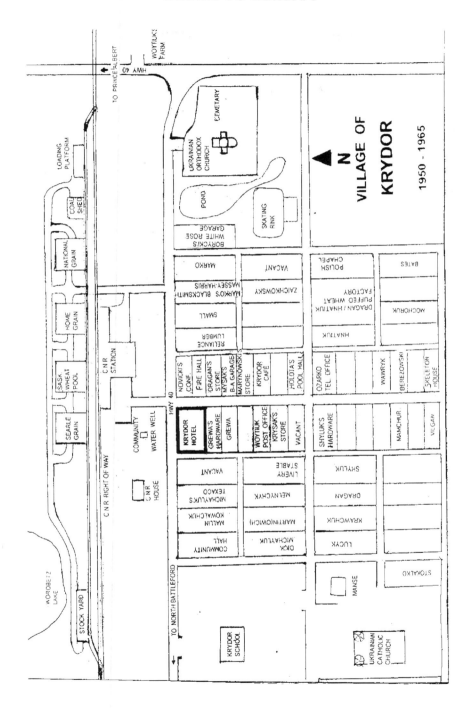

Michael bought a hand meat saw and would purchase a whole beef and several porks for the winter and would cut them up into roasts, steaks, chops, ribs and stewing beef for freezing. Of course the pork hocks and pigs feet were saved for "studenetz", the jellied pork hocks and jellied pig's feet which were Ukrainian traditional and festive favorites. Michael and Tena would take the meat to Hafford to the "quick freeze locker plant" and store the meat in the commercial freezer during the warm months and get sufficient quantities when they would need it and keep it in the ice house until the meat would eventually thaw. In the winter months they could keep larger quantities of meat on hand in "Mother Nature's" freezer in the trunk of the car or in the ice house. Hams and bacon sides were ordered from the meat packers, since Michael and Tena did not have a smoke house to cure and smoke the meats. Some hams and side pork were cured with a product called "Habacure". This was a type of chemical crystal that included salt and smoke flavoring that was used to tenderize ham and bacon and to give it a smokehouse flavor. The ham or bacon would be rubbed with Habacure then set in a brine solution containing the Habacure. This cured or pickled ham and bacon would last for several months without refrigeration, and would actually have the taste of smokehouse ham or bacon. Today the product (Habacure) is not allowed to be produced or marketed due to its extreme salt content and other chemical constituents that are harmful to human health. The maintenance of a meat supply for the hotel's dining room was a time consuming endeavor, but one that Michael and Tena managed to master.

As one can see, life was anything but dull at the hotel. There was never a dull moment or a lull in the calendar throughout the year. Summer holidays were non-existent for farm families prior to and into the 1950's, and living in a small rural community and running a small business did not allow for the luxury of a summer holiday or a vacation at any time of year. Family run enterprises were year round operations. The odd Sunday trip to Gronlid or Saskatoon, a picnic at Redberry Lake, or going out berry picking were the usual breaks from the busy hotel schedule. In fact Michael and Tena never did take a holiday in all the years that they lived in Krydor during the years from 1950-1965. With the regular hotel maintenance, gardens, canning and freezing, tending the chickens, meat cutting and looking after guests and customers, idle time was not to be found around the hotel. The only times when there were fewer tasks to complete was during the Christmas and New Year season. The rest of the year was a constant blur of activity.

The concept of growing, processing and preserving your own food and cutting out the "middleman" costs in the dining room component of the hotel operation was very labor intensive but very profitable to Michael and Tena. However, handling all this food and the associated chores in the "primitive" conditions in the hotel required serious changes to the building itself.

After Mary and Alex's wedding, Michael decided that changes had to be made to the building. Michael and Tena paid off the $1000 loan to Steve Hryhirchuk in the first year. Michael and Tena tackled the heating and electrical systems. For the interim time period they purchased a 32 volt generator and electrical system from John Panchuk, who was upgrading to the more common 110 volt electrical generator and electrical system. The Province of Saskatchewan was installing an electrical supply grid in the entire province in the 1950's. All towns and farms would be able to tap into the grid for a reliable electrical supply. But in the meantime, Michael's 32 volt system would provide the hotel with an inexpensive source of lighting. The 32 volt generator was housed on a platform in the ice house, with the power source wire attached to the hotel then leading into the basement where there were eighty acid filled batteries that were waiting to be charged. These batteries were car type, glass batteries that sat two deep across the entire width of the basement of the hotel. The generator would run most of the day operating the lights and equipment and at the same time charging the batteries for night use of lights and small appliances. Tena did have a 32 volt toaster and iron but those were the only appliances to run off the low voltage system. The time saving alone from not having to fill the myriad of kerosene and gas lamps daily, cleaning the glass chimneys, trimming the wicks and replacing the mantles to the coleman type gas lamps was very noticeable, plus the fire hazard of all those open flames was eliminated. The electrical wiring was temporary surface wiring, since Mr. Lucyk the electrician, advised Michael that the 110 volt wiring would soon become necessary and that 110 volt wiring would be installed inside the walls.

The heating system was next on the list of upgrades for the 1951-1952 winter season. There was a huge coal-fired furnace in the basement, but it had never been connected with air ducts, nor was it mounted on a cement pad. Mr. Worobetz had purchased the furnace but had done nothing with it. The basement floor was only half finished with the furnace and glass batteries sitting on wooden platforms on the gravel base of a floor. Michael had a cement pad poured for the furnace and had some air ducting installed. The heating contractor designed a system of hot air ducts and cold air returns, to heat the main floor and second floor through gravity heating—hot air rises, cold air sinks—the advent of high tech heating. Until the hotel had a 110 volt electrical system, there wasn't a 32 volt fan to be found to force air throughout the hotel. The hot air ducts could not be mounted on the inside of the walls due to the wood lathe and plaster wall construction, so the air ducts were mounted to the inside corners of the walls and ceilings, so as not to be too obtrusive. The coal fired furnace was a vast improvement over the series of space heaters and stove pipes running throughout the hotel. Again, the central heating system was a vast improvement in heating efficiency plus the fire hazard was substantially reduced. There was also a great reduction in time spent in cleaning ashes, from space heaters and supplying coal and wood to the space heaters. There were only two coal and ash locations—the furnace and the kitchen stove.

In 1952 Michael received some very disturbing news from his family in Ukraine. The Stalinist Purges were in high gear. Soviet Russia took over Bukovina in 1940, and during their ouster of the Romanians and the infamous Fontana Alba massacre of thousands Romanians, Bukovina became a part of Ukraine. Stalin forced collectivization of farms upon the Ukrainians and if anyone was suspected of having wealth of any sort, they were stripped of the wealth and persecuted. The KGB was apprehending all goods, money and land that seemed to be out of line with the communist collectivization policy. The communists wanted total control of the people and their holdings. George Kotyk (Michael's brother-in-law) and his wife were suspected of withholding money and land. The communists knew that George had been to Canada, had family in Canada and therefore he must be hiding money or goods. The only land that George and his wife owned was the land for which Michael and Bill Kotyk had had loaned George money, back in 1929-1930. Since the KGB couldn't find any money, they confiscated the land and arrested George Kotyk and sent him to a labor camp in Siberia. Several weeks later the KGB returned and demanded all of George Kotyk's wife's household furnishings, even little wooden trinket or jewellery boxes (that were empty). Then they arrested her, since they still believed she was withholding information and goods, and sent her to a labor camp in Siberia. Both George Kotyk and his wife had been charged with being "kulaks". Kulaks were "hoarders of wealth from the state" and were severely punished by the communists when convicted, and suspects were usually convicted. Convicted kulaks were sent to labor camps, tortured and even executed. George Kotyk and his wife were sent to Siberian labor camps not knowing each other's fate. Their children aged 8 and 10 years, were left on their own. Villagers under cover of darkness would leave food, clothing and firewood for the children so they could survive. The KGB in the meantime would watch the house and punish anyone who was caught assisting the children.

It was late November when Michael received that letter from his sister Zoya. Winter was setting in. It was a dull grey day and this disturbing news just added to the mood of the day. Zoya wrote, "George's children are alone . . . ." The dots finished the sentence, but Michael was reading between the lines. No one knew what had happened to George and his wife. Zoya couldn't spell out the details for fear of the letter being screened by the KGB. Zoya knew that if she disclosed too much information, she could meet the same fate as the Kotyks. Michael spent several years fearing the worst, not knowing what had become of his brother-in-law and his sister-in-law. Were they dead? Had they been tortured? Are they alive? Are they in a dread labor camp in Siberia? Would they ever be released? Was it something he said in one of his letters to George that provoked the KGB and the authorities to take such action? He wrote back to Zoya asking careful, non provoking questions wanting to get more information without getting her into trouble with the authorities. The Kotyk's were released after two years of incarceration in separate labor camps. They made their way back home independent of one another. They had no knowledge of each other's location until they got home to rejoin their children. The children's childhood was obviously stolen from them. The children had to live in a small closed community with the knowledge that their parents were enemies of the state, and the authorities would have the community know that there were enemies of the state living amongst them. Michael's dislike of the Russians and the Soviets grew more intense than it had ever been before. Michael would not get the entire story from his family until 1974, when he visited his family in Ukraine and spoke to them personally, with no eavesdroppers.

During the early and mid 1950's Saskatchewan was becoming serviced with electricity and a more sophisticated telephone system. This meant conveniences for the population, but for Michael and Tena it meant a boom in business that could only be dreamed of. Construction companies were installing electrical power lines and telephone lines. These were not only the main trunk lines but the subsidiary lines to all towns, villages and farms. This boom of construction crews, land surveyors and roadway workers requiring rooms, three meals per day, lunches and refreshments in the beer parlor would last for three or more years. It meant that during those years, 35 to 40 men were waiting for breakfast, dinner (lunches were an additional snack during the work day) and supper. Room rentals and meals were required seven days a week throughout the spring, summer and fall months. Winter months were a bit slower and more manageable. Then there was the beer parlor with its on premises and off premises beer sales to the construction crews and locals. Michael and Tena were hiring high school girls to assist in the food and lodging area since the laundry, cooking, waiting on tables and cleaning was too much for the family to handle. Michael had to hire on some extra help as well and "Matzko Mike" was his right hand man. Since Matzko could only speak limited English, he served the locals in the beer parlor, while Michael who had a better command of the English language handled the travelling public and work crews. These construction and maintenance crews were a boom to the entire village economy. All businesses thrived, from service stations to grocery stores, from dry goods (clothing and boots) to hardware stores and the pool hall. Everybody was busy and required extra help. Krydor Hotel was hiring full and part time help throughout the boom years of 1952-1955.

While this boom was occurring, Michael and Tena did not lose focus on the education of Lessia and George. Lessia continued her piano lessons. George was enrolled in voice lessons in North Battleford with Mrs. Girling, a noted voice teacher. George would travel to North Battleford by bus every Saturday throughout the winter for his voice lessons. At age 10, his was a soprano voice. Lessia took several voice lessons per year as well. Other students from Krydor became involved in music and voice on these Saturday excursions to North Battleford. With these voice and piano lessons, Lessia and George would participate in the Kiwanis Music Festival every spring in North Battleford. George continued with his voice lessons until his voice started to change at age 13. Even though business was booming for Michael and Tena, Michael never lost the vision of education for his children.

In the meantime grass was not growing under Mary and Alex's feet. Mary and Alex would spend only one year in Spirit River, since it was too far north for their liking. They applied

DREAM TO REALITY

to Mundare, Alberta for the 1952-1953 school year and were successful in getting teaching positions there. They would spend the next three years in Mundare. It was a much better setting for them since it was on Highway 16, later to become the Yellowhead Highway, and a direct route to Krydor, Saskatoon and Insinger, Alex's home town near Yorkton. There were many more and frequent trips to Krydor and Insinger for Mary and Alex during those three years.

The mid-fifties were very busy for the enterprising Michael and Tena. Besides the very busy and lucrative hotel business, they were upgrading the building continually. They found that the 32 volt electrical system was inadequate and could not handle the workload in the hotel, and in 1953 had to upgrade to a 110 volt electrical generator system. A year later in 1954 the provincial electrical grid extended to Krydor and the hotel was re-wired with permanent wiring inside the walls. Then came an electric range and electric wringer clothes washer, a refrigerator and a freezer. The kitchen was becoming more labor efficient and profitable. In the beer parlor, Michael installed a walk in beer fridge that could store large quantities of beer and food. He even had a spring loaded beer bottle dispenser installed in the fridge so that when he opened the small fridge door the bottles of beer were automatically pushed forward when one bottle was removed. Constant ice cold beer was a treat that the locals never had before, since the beer was kept cool in the basement, but never ice cold.

Two of the social hubs of any prairie village or town were the skating rink and curling rink. Krydor only had a skating rink and that is where the community gathered to for social skating, hockey, broomball, and moccasin dances. Moccassin dances were outdoor dances held on the ice surface, usually after skating or hockey so that the ice surface wasn't too slippery. The rink shack was large with wooden benches around the perimeter. There was the reliable pot bellied cast iron stove in the center of the rink shack where one could place his or her frozen feet on the warming rail that circled the stove to warm up after a few hours of skating, playing hockey or broom ball. That pot bellied stove warmed the rink shack when it was used as a dressing room for hockey, skate changing area for social skating, or when it was used as a seating area for the moccasin dances. During the time period when the village had no electricity, an electrical line was strung from Borycki's Garage down the street to get electrical power from his 110 volt power plant to the rink. This power source provided lighting for the ice surface, the skate changing area and electricity for the water pump to flood the ice surface and to power a 78 rpm record player that would play scratchy old records for the moccasin dances. Inside the rink shack in a separate room there was a well that provided the water for flooding the ice. In 1951 the village bought a 110 volt power plant for the rink so that Mr. Borycki wouldn't have to run his power generator for rink purposes. In 1950 through to 1952, the village of Krydor hired a rink caretaker, who was a local

Michael supported community activities such as the skating rink. Krydor High School Hockey team. George standing to the left of the goal tender. Walter Borycki, teacher and coach.

DREAM TO REALITY

railroad worker, to look after the rink. In 1953, the railroad worker was transferred and with no one to maintain the rink, the school boys in town took on the job voluntarily. It became a community effort with all students pitching in to make the ice, clean and sweep the ice, flood the ice, paint the hockey lines and circles and generally maintain the rink. Michael and a few other businessmen made sure that the village council provided funds for the maintenance and running of the rink which was the main recreational activity in town.

While Michael was busy with the hotel, rink ventures and village council work, Tena was organizing a 4-H Girls Sewing Club affiliated with the Extension Department of the University of Saskatchewan. The high school girls would meet during the evenings at the hotel and proceed with learning how to sew and complete sewing projects. These sewing projects would also count as projects toward their grade 10, 11 and 12 home economics classes that they were taking by correspondence.

Tena's Krydor High School 4-H Sewing Club. Tena, Center, second row. Lessia, Left front row.

Krydor School was comprised of grades 1 to 12 in three classrooms. The high school teacher taught all high school subjects, but he couldn't teach home economics, thus the girls who wished to take the course took it by correspondence and Tena looked after the sewing projects in the hotel. In a way she also looked after the cooking classes since the high school girls also worked part time in the hotel during the busy line construction season. Tena had only completed her grade eight in formal education, but she had all the skills of a seamstress and chef through practical and self help courses through the Department of Extension at the University of Saskatchewan. The hotel became a hub of activity. There was the sewing club and school hockey team with their social gatherings and lunches at the hotel that Michael and Tena hosted. After moccasin dances at the rink on Saturday nights, the students would all gather at the hotel for hot chocolate and snacks. Michael and Tena were more than pleased to host and encourage the youth activities in the community.

With all this activity occurring in the community and directly affecting Michael and Tena and consequently the hotel, Michael decided that he would tackle the problem of the water and sewage system for the hotel. There was a water well just outside of the hotel a few meters from the back door, so water supply was not an issue. During the summer of 1953, Michael had a huge septic tank—4 meters by 4 meters by 5 meters deep, excavated and poured in concrete with a concrete top, adjacent to the rear right of the hotel. The hotel had been built on one lot with the adjacent lot purchased by former owner, Andrew Worobetz for future expansion. Mr. Worobetz had a sheet metal warehouse sitting on the front portion of the vacant adjacent lot that contained store fixtures and dry goods from his previous ownership of a general store. The septic tank was built just behind the warehouse and was hooked up to the hotel plumbing system that Michael had simultaneously installed. Now the hotel had a water supply system from its own well which provided for water to the kitchen sinks which drained into the septic tank. No more five gallon pails of waste wash water to carry outside to the grey water pit. The upper floor had one central bathroom with a flush toilet, sink and bathtub. This was marked improvement over the previous toileting. This new plumbing and water supply system contributed significantly to the convenience of every one concerned. The beer parlor had a regular bathroom with flush toilets, and Michael had running water to wash his glassware in the bar.

The septic tank, even though it was huge (close to 2000 gallons), needed to be emptied three or four times a year depending on the usage of water. Usually it was emptied in the early spring, during the summer and in late fall. Michael bought a used 300 gallon fuel tank from a farmer. The tank would be lifted by a few men onto a cradle which was on the truck bed. Michael bought a motor and pump which was used to pump out the septic tank. George was trained to use this high tech machinery and was placed in a position at age 11 to haul out the contents of the septic tank. Michael would rent a ½ ton truck from Stan Woytiuk for the day and George had the privilege of emptying the septic tank and driving the waste to the garbage dump which was about 2 kilometers south east of Krydor. It would take five to eight trips to the garbage dump for this "honey wagon" as it was fondly referred to, to empty the septic tank. George then had to wash the truck to get rid of the odious smell. But this job was worth it to an 11 year old. As far as George was concerned this was a plumb job. He got to operate the machinery (pump and motor and truck). He drove this loaded ½ ton International truck out to the garbage dump several kilometers out of town, emptied the tank, drove back, filled the tank and repeated the task over and over until the septic tank was empty. The emptying of the septic tank would take most of a day, usually a Saturday, unless it was during a school holiday break. For an 11 or 12 year old, this was quite the task. The first few trips with Stan Woytiuk to learn the "tricks of the trade" were true learning experiences. The shifting liquid load of 300 gallons/1200 liters of sewage when taking corners, made one very aware of the dangers of tipping the loaded truck. This task was one where speed was not of the essence.

In the eyes of George's 11 and 12 year old peers in the village, this was an enviable and prestigious job. Thus George, being the "big man" driving this truck around town, was the envy of his friends. He always had able and willing helpers to accompany him with his "professional" responsibility. Not only was this a neat job driving the truck, but it was unsupervised by an adult. While George and the boys were driving the truck to and from the garbage dump and unloading the sewage at the dump, the opportunity was ripe for the experimentation with cigarettes and smoking. Now for 11, 12 and 13 year olds in 1954, having a smoke on the job was just emulating what adult males did. George had access to cigarettes since they were sold in the hotel. He had a job that would take him out of town for a half hour to forty five minutes, and the status that would attract peers. In an exaggerated way it was the Tom Sawyer and Tom's fence painting scenario, only transferred into the 1950's. George had plenty of help and able assistance for the honey wagon task. As one would expect, in later life George omitted this work experience from employment application resumes.

That same year, Michael decided it was also time to change over from the coal fired furnace. Coal energy was very labor intensive. It involved ordering a box car load of coal, delivering it to the hotel, unloading it into the basement, cleaving the coal into manageable pieces, then having to deliver the coal to all the space heaters and the kitchen stove. After the coal was burned the ashes then had to be removed to the out of doors. Michael had the coal fired furnace converted to an oil burning furnace. Now this was a huge move in the right direction, since the furnace oil was delivered to the hotel by tanker truck and transferred into a 200 gallon oil tank outside the hotel. The furnace oil was transferred into the hotel by a pipe that fed the fuel oil to the furnace. There was no manual labor required for the oil furnace operation. There was no delivery of coal, no cleavage of coal, no coal dust, no ashes to remove, just clean reliable heat. With the provincial electrical grid providing a constant 110 volts to the hotel, Michael had a furnace fan attached to the furnace to provide forced air throughout the hotel. Out from the primitive conditions of the 1920's, 1930's, 1940's and into a modern age of heat, plumbing and electricity of the 1950's. 1954 was a banner year for Michael, Tena and the Krydor Hotel. Krydor Hotel was truly on the cutting edge of building technology at this point in time.

The mid to late 1950's were very good to Michael and Tena. The 1950's were good to them because they worked extraordinarily hard; long hours, no breaks or holidays, just dedication to a dream of business ownership and business success. The hotel business thrived. In fact business had been so good that not only did they complete all the changes in the hotel, they bought a new car in 1954. They traded their maroon 1941 Chevy in for a new white and blue 1954 Ford "Custom Line" sedan at Kindrachuk Motors in Wakaw, Saskatchewan. This was the first V-8 powered car in the extended Pohoreski family. The trips to Gronlid became somewhat shorter due to increased power of the flathead V-8 and the greater speeds that were generated. It was on their first visit to Gronlid with the new Ford that the higher speeds were checked and confirmed by George and his cousins Orest and Ted Panchuk. When the three cousins got together, there usually were anxious moments for them and their parents. Dorothy Panchuk asked the boys to drive out to a local farm and to pick up some cream for dinner. George age 12, Ted age 12, and Orest age 14 were just too happy to get out of the house and asked if they could take the Ford. Michael handed over the keys and asked Orest to drive since he was the eldest and probably more responsible than the two younger cousins. The boys promptly drove out to the farm, picked up the cream and then proceeded out to Highway #6 South of Gronlid where the highway had a six mile stretch of straight, smooth gravel road. Orest promptly had the Ford revved up and had the speedometer buried at 110 miles per hour for the six mile stretch. At that speed the cream certainly didn't have time to turn sour. The parents were quite surprised that the boys had returned so quickly with the cream. They assumed that the boys would have taken some other friends out for a ride to show off the new car. The boys were satisfied that they did a favor in bringing home the cream and at the same time had tested the speed limits of the new V-8 powered vehicle.

1954 was also the year that Michael and Tena sent Lessia to St. Andrew's College Ukrainian Summer School in Winnipeg, and George to Green Grove Summer Camp (Zeleniey Hai) at Wakaw Lake. Micheal and Tena were interested in their children taking the advantages of the cultural and religious milieu and continued to enroll them in educational opportunities that became available. To assist the camp that was in its formative years at Wakaw Lake, Michael decided to buy a row boat for the camp. He ordered the boat from the Eaton's Spring and Summer mail order catalogue and in a week or so the boat arrived at Krydor from the Eaton's Winnipeg based mail order house via the daily train service. The boat was beautiful. It was a green slender row boat with a grey painted interior with three rows of seats, space for five people and a set of oars and oar locks. Mary Hnatiuk, who helped Tena out in the hotel during the busy times, offered to paint the name of the boat on its bow. She painted in white block letters CYMK on one side and BUKOVYNA on the other side of the bow. Michael was very proud of the boat. He hired a ½ ton truck to deliver it to the Zeleney Hai camp at Wakaw Lake which was 80 kilometers away. Michael and the family followed in the car that Sunday in late June of 1954. Arriving at the lake prior to noon they unloaded the boat and Michael, Tena, Lessia and George along with the camp director and several other bystanders watched as the boat was eased into the water. The CYMK promptly took on water through the floor boards and sank! Everyone was most disappointed since everyone wanted to take the rowboat out onto the quiet waters of Wakaw Lake; but on that day it was not to be. Michael and the other men quickly realized that they should have tarred the bottom to seal the bottom of the boat. The boat was pulled out of the water, emptied and turned over to have the hull dry in the sun. Michael in the mean time drove into Wakaw, and even though it was Sunday, he tracked down the hardware store owner and purchased a five gallon pail of tar and some tar brushes. By early evening the boat bottom was tarred twice and by the following Sunday when camp officially opened and George and his cousins arrived at camp, the CYMK was ready for ferrying children and adults around the lake. Later that week, George caught a 6.25 pound pickerel (walleye), a camp record that lasted several years.

Television and transistor radios were the big technological advances in the mid 1950's. Television was being introduced into the prairie provinces in 1952 and 1953. Television was truly a marvel. Moving pictures being brought into your home via magnetic waves travelling through the air and projected through a tube into your living room was a new and an astounding concept in communication during the 1950's. The Tkaczyk's first glimpse of television was in early 1953, when they drove up to Mundare to visit Mary and Alex. Mary and Alex drove everyone into Edmonton on the Saturday and the

GEORGE TKACHYK

Tkaczyk's saw television for the first time through a store display window.

Saskatoon got its first television station in 1953—CFQC TV. There was only one television network in Canada thus every large city had only CBC programming. But by the 1960's that would change, with CTV entering the television broadcasting arena. Michael and Tena bought their first television set in 1954. It was an Electrohome 21 inch black and white cabinet model that cost approximately $500.00, and in 1954 that was a huge sum of money considering that Michael's and Tena's new Ford car cost $1800. There were only a few people who had television sets since they were quite expensive. Krydor Hotel was on record for the shortest external television antenna in town. The hotel required only a 10 foot antenna mounted on the roof of the hotel to pull in the television signal, since the hotel was the tallest building in town, except for the grain elevators of course. Most houses had to have 20 to 40 foot antennas on their roof tops anchored by guide wires to the corners of the roof or sometimes anchored to the ground. The tall TV antennas were required to pull in the television signal through the air from Saskatoon which was 100 kilometers away. At times the black and white signal would turn snowy or became non-existent due to electrical disturbances in the air, stormy weather or even due to aircraft flying overhead or between the transmission tower in Saskatoon and the receiving antenna in Krydor. In general, television reception in rural areas by today's standards was very poor, but at the time it was considered marvelous. Rabbit ear antennas were only good for short distances within the city of the television transmission tower. Television viewers thrilled at the aspect of viewing the Ed Sullivan Show and his cast of star performers on Sunday evenings and Hockey Night In Canada and All Star Wrestling from Maple Leaf Gardens on Saturday nights. Technology in the 1950's was on the upswing and growing fast. Michael saw and experienced many changes economically, socially and technologically from the time he came to Canada in 1928 to the prosperous post-war 1950's. He took these changes in stride adapting to the changes as well as adapting the changes to his mode of operations as well.

During those boom years of 1953, 1954 and 1955, when not helping with the hotel work, Lessia was pursuing her piano and voice studies and at the same time played piano and piano accordion in a local dance band while completing her high school. George was playing hockey in the winter and trying to get out of hotel chores the rest of the time. Actually, for George, much of the spring, summer and fall was spent in helping Michael and Tena in the hotel and to help cater to banquets in the community hall. His major job was to haul water from the community water well to the community hall in five gallon cream cans for cooking and washing of dishes and utensils, since the community hall did not have any plumbing or water source nearby. Between the hauling of water to the community hall, helping with the gardening and being master of the "honey wagon", George did get the privilege of taking the car during the summer months, for an afternoon of swimming and tanning on the white sandy beaches of Redberry Lake which was about five kilometers south of Krydor. Summers and winters were anything but dull for George and Lessia in the mid-1950's.

Mary and Alex moved from Mundare, Alberta to Canora, Saskatchewan during the summer of 1955 where both of them received teaching positions in the Canora High School. This was more convenient for them since Alex's parents farmed near the village of Insinger, which was about 40 kilometers from Canora. In addition, Alex knew many people in Canora from his years growing up in the Insinger area and from the days when he travelled the province working for the St. Petro Mohyla Ukrainian Institute. During that same summer of 1955, Michael and Tena sent George to St. Andrew's Summer School in Winnipeg for five weeks. Lessia spent the summer in Saskatoon at the St. Petro Mohyla Ukrainian Institute while furthering her piano studies in piano and music theory at the Lyle Gustin Studio of Music. Lessia by this time was focusing on attaining her ARCT in Piano, Music Theory and Voice training. Again, Michael's dream of providing the best possible educational opportunities for his children was becoming a reality. He couldn't achieve educational goals for himself in his home country due to the social, political and economic turmoil. The least he could do is try to live that reality through his children.

During the summer of 1956 Mary and Alex were involved in the educational program at the Ukrainian Orthodox Church Camp at Good Spirit Lake near Canora. George attended that camp while Lessia pursued her piano studies in Saskatoon preparing herself for the winter term at the Lyle Gustin Music Studios. Michael and Tena continued their feverish pace at the hotel providing meals and rooms for the various work crews. By this time the hotel had been repainted on the interior and exterior. The electrical wiring, plumbing and heating systems had all been installed allowing for the finished product to be painted. The hotel had undergone a very major facelift and was a vast improvement over the building they had purchased six years earlier. In addition Michael and Tena were totally involved in the community. The hotel was the hub for church meetings, 4-H Sewing Club activities which Tena organized and operated, high school hockey team lunches and banquets and general youth socials.

Michael and Tena saw their second daughter off to the St. Petro Mohyla Ukrainian Institute in Saskatoon for her post-secondary studies in music. Lessia studied piano and piano theory under the tutelage of Lyle Gustin and voice training under the direction of Mrs. F.B. Morrison during the winter of 1956.

Back at Krydor during the winter of 1956, a small town drama was unfolding. The Blaine Lake School Unit had announced that they would be closing some small town high schools due to declining enrolments. Small town Saskatchewan was changing. The demographics were such that farming was increasing in scale. With the increase in mechanization, farmers could cultivate more land and produce more grain per farm operator than was possible with teams of horses or other draft animals. The ¼ section homesteads were being enlarged as the older homesteaders were leaving the land and younger farmers were buying up the available land. Farms were becoming larger—½ section, ¾ section and even one section land tracts were starting to become common in the mid 1950's. This meant fewer families on the farm in the mid 1950's and fewer children to populate the schools. Also, with the predominance and economic availability of road worthy vehicles, farm families would travel to larger towns and cities to purchase commodities. The small villages were feeling the squeeze of progress. The school districts were attempting to consolidate schools thus larger towns were gaining in school population and the subsequent spin off was that the larger towns were gaining in economic growth as well.

With the prospect of Krydor High School closing down, and George beginning grade 11 in September of 1957, Michael and Tena were caught on the horns of a dilemma. They were not fond of the idea of George travelling to Blaine Lake by school bus for his grade 11 and 12. Added to the equation was the fact that by contributing to the closing of Krydor High School by sending their son to Blaine Lake High School, they were actually assisting the larger communities to destroy their own village and the trade that went with it. Most of the high school students who attended Krydor High School were rural students who stayed in Krydor during the winter months or for the entire school year. Some rural people built homes in Krydor, rented homes or paid for room and board for their students while they attended high school. This brought the families to Krydor to purchase supplies, see their children, support the school and its programs and sports activities, and in so doing the community thrived economically and socially. The business owners, because of the Blaine Lake School Unit's decision to close the high school, were in an uproar. If the rural people who normally would have had their children attend high school in Krydor, had them attend Blaine Lake High School, they would then take their business to Blaine Lake as well. The Krydor general stores, service stations, café and hotel would lose clientele and eventually would have to close. The businesses in small villages were largely dependent on the local rural consumer for their existence.

Krydor High School

Michael and Tena made a dramatic decision when the Blaine Lake School Unit would not change their stance on closing Krydor High School. They decided not to have George attend Blaine

DREAM TO REALITY

Lake High School but to send George to The St. Petro Mohyla Ukrainian Institute and have him complete his grade 11 and 12 in Saskatoon just as Mary had done earlier. In this small way Michael and Tena were protesting the closure of Krydor High School. This in effect had bumped their plans up by two years, since George would have gone to Saskatoon for post secondary schooling after he completed his grade 12 at Krydor.

This decision of Michael and Tena's had another effect. The townspeople and some rural people whose children would have been in grade 11 and 12 as well were also incensed by the school unit's decision to close Krydor High School, they also decided to follow Michael and Tena's lead and decided to send their children to Saskatoon and The St. Petro Mohyla Ukrainian Institute to complete their high school education. The facilities and staff in Saskatoon high schools were certainly much better than those in rural Saskatchewan high schools. In all there were six students who left Krydor for Saskatoon, an additional four students went to Hafford High School and only two students ended up attending Blaine Lake High School. This was small village political drama at its best. This small village was boycotting Goliath, the large town and its controlling municipal councilors. The neighboring town that was to gain substantially ended up receiving the least number of students and consequently very little in additional provincial grant money for the students, and little in economic spin-off since those parents were not shopping in Blaine Lake. The students were the ones that gained the most since they attended the St. Petro Mohyla Ukrainian Institute and gained from the all the advantages that the Saskatoon high schools had to offer in their superior facilities, programming, arts and athletic activities and specialized teachers. However, for the village of Krydor, the writing was on the proverbial wall. Krydor School enrollment was declining and eventually the school would close. With a school closure the eventual demise of a village was imminent. The question for Michael and Tena was . . . . When?

Michael and Tena continued to be active in church and church related organizations. Michael served as chairman of the board of St. Peter and St. Paul Ukrainian Orthodox Parish in Krydor in 1953 and 1954. In 1954 the parish celebrated its 20th Anniversary by hosting the Ukrainian Orthodox Metropolitan Ilarion, the Metropolitan of Winnipeg and all of Canada. On this occasion the church was blessed and the cemetery consecrated by the visiting Metropolitan. Michael, along with Zenoviy Dragan, Mr. William Martinovich and Mr. Anton Marko were instrumental in organizing this auspicious

Michael, back row third from left, and Tena, third row sixth from left, at a Ukrainian Self Reliance League convention in Saskatoon at the St. Peter Mohyla Ukrainian Institute. Circa. 1956-57

occasion. There were invited church dignitaries, the church choir from Prince Albert and visitors from miles around that attended. Michael was a keen supporter of the Ukrainian Self Reliance League, an organization that supported the Ukrainian Orthodox Church of Canada, the St. Petro Mohyla Ukrainian Institute and Ukrainian culture in general. They travelled to Saskatoon and other centres in Saskatchewan to attend the Ukrainian Self Reliance League conventions.

Lessia and George in the meantime, continued on with their studies in Saskatoon during the years of 1957 through to 1960. Lessia completed her A.R.C.T. in piano, music theory and voice. She then went on to the Saskatchewan Teachers' College in Saskatoon and received her teaching certificate. In 1960 she moved to Edmonton where she obtained a teaching position with Edmonton Public Schools. George completed his high school spending his grade 11 school year at the Saskatoon Technical Collegiate and completing his grade 12 at Nutana Collegiate, the same high school that Mary attended. George then completed one year in the Faculty of Arts and Sciences at the University of Saskatchewan and then completed one year at the Saskatchewan Teachers' College. In 1961, George received a teaching position at Coronation, Alberta, taught there for one year and moved to Edmonton so that he could complete his teaching degree at the University of Alberta. George received a teaching position with Edmonton Public Schools where he taught and later became a consultant and an administrator with Edmonton Public Schools.

Krydor Hotel with the addition built on at the left of the photo.

Michael and Tena as members of the Saskatchewan Hotels Association attended hotel and hospitality conventions around the province with a view to enhancing their business. In 1960 the Saskatchewan Liquor Control Board yielded to pressure from the Hotels Association and announced that the hotels of Saskatchewan could opt to change from men only beer parlors to mixed drinking beverage rooms. The change would take place in 1962. This would mean a major face lift to the hotels across Saskatchewan, if they wished to participate. With the loosening up of liquor laws, the smaller towns were beginning to receive their liquor store outlets. The hotels had to keep pace by altering their mode of operation. Not only were ladies permitted into drinking establishments, but food and wine were introduced onto the menu of the beverage room.

Michael and Tena jumped at the chance to enhance the environment of the alcohol serving component of the hotel. They began making plans immediately. They wanted to be on the forefront of this change, but this would mean major renovations and an introduction of a food and beverage menu. The old style saloon or beer parlor with spittoons and rough language would become but a memory of the past and a more sedate and refined atmosphere would prevail. Some males of the community grumbled that their "turf" or domain was being invaded by women. The beer parlor was the last bastion of the male dominated world in their view, and they wanted none of it. Women's lib was coming to Krydor in the 1960's.

Michael and Tena drew up their plans for the extension to the beer parlor and got busy hiring tradesmen to expand the hotel with the building extension, installing extra washrooms, added seating, redecorating the interior with pastel shades of paint, adding new flooring, color coordinated chairs and tables, menus, flower centre pieces for the tables (which really irked the male chauvinists) and decorative window coverings. Krydor Hotel was going upscale and cleaning up the rough and tumble image that all rural hotels had prior to the mixed beverage room concept. This was going to increase business in a huge way. People from several communities along highway # 40 and from the rural areas would drop out to the renovated Krydor Hotel for an evening of socializing, just to experience the new mixed drinking phenomenon. Other towns along highway #40 would soon get on the same bandwagon of the beverage room concept.

Michael behind the bar in the renovated beverage room with recessed ceiling lighting, new flooring, new tables and chairs and new paint.

Michael with Baba and Dido Pohoreski enjoying a cool one in the newly decorated beverage room.

Michael serving patrons prior to the official opening of the Krydor Hotel beverage room.

Beer & Wines				Light Lunches	
DRAUGHT BEER ON TAP				**SANDWICHES**	
GLASS 8-oz.			15c	Ham	30c
BOTTLED BEER, ALE, STOUT			36c	Beef	30c
				Cheese	25c
WINE BY THE GLASS				Egg	25c
	3-oz.	Tax	Price	Tomato	25c
Port	38c	2c	40c		
Sherry	38c	2c	40c		
Chateau Goi Sauterne	43c	2c	45c	Potato Chips	10c
Crackling Rose	48c	2c	50c	Cheezies	10c
South African Muscatel	48c	2c	50c	Beer Sausage	10c
				Pickling Eggs	10c
JUICES			15c	PLEASE ASK WAITER	
SOFT DRINKS			10c	FOR CIGARS AND CIGARETTES	

Michael and Tena's menu for their beverage room, 1962.

1961 was a banner year for Michael and Tena in many ways. They were completing the renovations to the hotel and ready for the official opening. George and Lessia were well on their way to completing their post secondary schooling and both were employed teaching with Alberta School Boards. To top things off, 1961 was the year of Michael and Tena's 25th wedding anniversary. This required a celebration, so Michael and Tena invited the entire Pohoreski clan to Krydor for a family get-together. As usual it was a crowded, noisy, jubilant Pohoreski—Tkaczyk get-together.

A typical Tkaczyk-Phoreski group photo with everyone talking and socializing and no one paying attention to the photographer. (1961)
Back row: Vesper Dobrowolsky, George Tkaczyk, Lessia Tkaczyk, Ted Panchuk, Jim Patrick, Michael Tkaczyk, Harry Dobrowolsky, Tena, Baba Pohoreski, Sylvia (Panchuk) Anderson, Royce Anderson.
Front Row: Mary Hupka, Dorothy Panchuk, Louis Pohoreski, Diana Pohoreski, Orest Panchuk, Valerie Patrick, Gail Patrick,
Kneeling: Dennis Dobrowolsky, Terry Patrick, Gordon Dobrowolsky.

GEORGE TKACHYK

Lessia and Mary pinning anniversary corsages on Michael and Tena prior to the 25th Anniversary festivities.

Michael and Tena, 25th Wedding Anniversary.

Left to Right: John Panchuk, Baba Pohoreski, Dido Pohoreski, Tena's Bridesmaid, Tena, Michael, Kay Pohoreski, Marie Dobrowolsky, Harry Dobrowolsky. Wedding cake made and decorated by Pauline Patrick.

Michael and Tena Tkaczyk. 1961.

George congratulating Michael and Tena on their 25th Wedding Anniversary.

DREAM TO REALITY

While Michael and Tena were planning their renovations to the hotel in 1961, they were also planning two weddings. Lessia was getting married to Gerald Slipchuk from Edmonton. The wedding took place on July 14, 1962 with the wedding ceremony taking place in the church of St. Peter and St. Paul in Krydor Saskatchewan with the reception taking place at the Narodny Deem or community hall. Following that, in 1963, George married Vera Nychyk on July 27, 1963 in the Ukrainian Orthodox Church of St. John the Baptist in North Battleford with the reception taking place in the North Battleford Civic Auditorium. Needless to say, Michael and Tena had their hands full with the regular hotel business, renovations, their 25th Wedding Anniversary and the two weddings. The two weddings were large affairs since Michael and Tena, the Slipchuk's/Derbowka's and the Nychyk's/Kowalsky's all had large families and many acquaintances. Wedding in the 1960's and 1970's were much larger than in the 1930's. As an example, 525 invitations were sent out for George and Vera's wedding. The immediate and extended families were large, but the Nychyk's and Tkaczyk's had numerous community acquaintances and business associates and connections to accommodate as well. Extended families and friends were invited from greater distances since there were better highways and better vehicles, thus making a trip of several hundred miles or more was a common occurrence. Trips from Edmonton to North Battleford and Krydor were quite usual for a weekend visit.

Mary and Alex had moved from Canora to Yorkton in 1959, where they were building a house with Alex opening up a television sales and repair shop which he operated until 1961. With a dire shortage of teachers in Saskatchewan at the time, Mary and Alex closed the television shop, rented their house in Yorkton and took up teaching positions in Tisdale, Saskatchewan where they taught until 1964. They returned to

Yorkton where a teaching position for Alex was going to open up in the electronics department at the new Yorkton Composite High School.

1962 saw George and Vera, and Lessia and Gerry settling into Edmonton where Lessia, George and Vera taught with the Edmonton Public School System. Gerry was in sales with Independent Food Wholesale, a food wholesale to grocery stores in Edmonton and rural Alberta.

With their children scattered from eastern Saskatchewan to Edmonton, the old 1954 ford was starting to show its age so Michael and Tena purchased a new 1963 Pontiac from Blaine Lake Motors in Blaine Lake. The auto dealership was owned and operated by long time friend Mike Ciona who was also a member of the Krydor St. Peter and St. Paul Ukrainian Orthodox Parish. Michael and Tena needed this car since the 1954 Ford was getting long in the tooth both age wise and mileage wise. They were putting on significant mileage making frequent trips to Saskatoon, Gronlid, Tisdale, Yorkton and Edmonton, visiting family and children. In November, 1963, Michael and Tena became grandparents. Dorianne Slipchuk was born to Lessia and Gerry on November 8, 1963. November 8 was also Michael's birthday, so this became a hallmark event. Since this was the first grandchild in the family, Michael and Tena increased the frequency of their trips to Edmonton.

Those trips to Edmonton again increased in frequency when the second grandchild Laurie, was born to Vera and George on March 13, 1965.

Michael and Tena's family continued to grow, when in September, 1965 Mary and Alex were blessed with a baby boy, George. Michael and Tena were grandparents for a third time, and now Yorkton was added to the more frequent trip calendar.

Meanwhile back in Krydor the school closure issue was still bubbling. Tena decided that she should get involved in politics and decided to run for school trustee, representing Krydor in the Blaine Lake School Unit. Tena took on the incumbent trustee and won the election with the Krydor townspeople solidly supporting her. She became the first woman to hold a school trustee's position in the Blaine Lake School Unit. Another male dominated office had succumbed. But, while Tena held her own in the position as school trustee, the valued Krydor School was destined for closure with consolidation becoming common among many rural school boards.

At the same time as the school closures were becoming imminent, Michael and Tena discovered that highway #40 was being rebuilt and that it would by-pass the village of Krydor on the north side of the elevators and railway track. This would further erode business since the old highway came right through town within feet of the hotel doors. Highway traffic had to slow down to 25 miles per hour as it passed through Krydor due to the sharp curves entering and leaving the village. Krydor was a convenient stopping place for travelers since they had to slow down travelling through the village and they were just steps away from accommodations, food and refreshments. With the new highway by-passing the village, the hotel business would definitely be affected in a negative manner.

It didn't take long for Michael and Tena to make the decision to sell the hotel. Michael was approaching retirement age, thus the highway issue just speeded up the process. The hotel was put up for sale in late 1964. There were many people who were interested in purchasing the hotel since business was good and the hotel was in very saleable shape with the new renovations. It didn't take long before the hotel was sold. It sold on December 15, 1964 with the possession date with the new owners set for January 1, 1965. The new owners lived in Prince Albert and offered their house as partial payment for the hotel. Michael and Tena were not planning to move to Prince Albert, especially with a new granddaughter in Edmonton and two more expected grandchildren, one in Edmonton and another in Yorkton. However, to facilitate the sale of the hotel with their asking price, they took the house in trade as a down payment on the hotel. In the short term Prince Albert wasn't their first choice of city in which to settle down, but it was a friendly city. Michael and Tena knew many people in Prince Albert, so they wouldn't be strangers there. In addition, the Panchuk's, the Dobrowolsky's and Tena's parents, Michael and Anna Pohoreski all moved to Prince Albert in the late 1950's and early 1960's. The Panchuk's sold their general store and bulk fuel business; the Dobrowolsky's lost their hotel to a fire and Michael Pohoreski retired as the postmaster in Lenvale in October of 1960. Michael and Tena moved to Prince Albert in January of 1965 and lived

Promotional Krydor Hotel calendar with notes written by Tena indicating the sale and possession dates of Krydor Hotel.

in their down payment house in Prince Albert for five months, January through to May of 1965. In the mean time, Michael and Tena had travelled to Saskatoon and Edmonton several times to check out the housing situation to see where they would actually like to settle down. They knew people in both cities, but Edmonton was selected due to two grandchildren already in that location. This still meant a lot of travel for Michael and Tena because now immediate and extended family was spread throughout Manitoba, Saskatchewan and Alberta. Tena had cousins, other relatives and acquaintances in the Garland (Zalicia) district in Manitoba where Tena grew up as a child. Then there was Yorkton, where Mary, Alex and new grandchild George lived, the Kotyk's in Regina and immediate and extended family in Gronlid, Prince Albert and Saskatoon. They sold their house in Prince Albert and bought an up and down duplex at 7005-101 Avenue in Edmonton. The big move took place in June of 1965. Michael and Tena moved into the upper portion of the duplex, approximately 1100 square feet of living space. They were like newly weds enjoying their first home. This was the first permanent home they owned since 1940 in Gronlid. After leaving Gronlid in 1941, they lived in C.P.R. bunk houses, foreman's section houses and finally the hotel, but the hotel was in fact a public place. Birthdays, Sviat Vechir (Christmas Eve), Christmases, family anniversaries, weddings and other family functions were all held in the hotel dining room. In Edmonton, all family gatherings could be held in their own home at any time, with no one coming in to request a room for the night, a meal, or access and service to the beverage room. This was a real treat. For the first time in 16 years Michael and Tena had privacy and space to celebrate with and entertain their family and friends.

Michael and Tena truly needed that space. In March of 1966, a second grandson was born; Michael Slipchuk was born to

Lessia and Gerry. Then on August 8, 1967, Daniel was born to George and Vera Tkachyk. Michael and Tena now had five grandchildren and were enjoying every bit of it, and to enjoy it they made the most of their new home. When they weren't hosting their immediate families with grandchildren from Yorkton and Edmonton, there were the travelling extended families from Gronlid, Prince Albert, Saskatoon and Manitoba that would make their way to Edmonton to pay Michael and Tena a visit. Reciprocally Michael and Tena often made their famous and unexpected 4-day tri-province tour through Alberta, Saskatchewan and Manitoba visiting their immediate, extended families and old friends.

The upper portion of the duplex at 7005-101 Avenue was a comfortable 3 bedroom, 1 bathroom home with a large kitchen and eating area, an L-shaped living/dining room: a typical 3 bedroom home with a detached single car garage of the late 1950's and early 1960's vintage. Tena immediately commandeered one bedroom as her sewing room, the second bedroom was a guest bedroom and of course Michael and Tena occupied the master bedroom. The lower portion of the duplex consisted of a self contained two bedroom home with approximately 950 square feet, an additional separate bedroom that was used by Michael and Tena for guests or storage, the furnace room and laundry area. Michael and Tena initially bought the duplex to house one of their three children should the need arise. Lessia and Gerry and Vera and George had already established themselves in apartments and would soon be purchasing their own homes. Mary, Alex and son George were settled in Yorkton where they were near to Alex's parents, and had other plans for the future. Michael and Tena rented the lower duplex out to other tenants which supplied them with some additional retirement income. Michael and Tena's home was close to where Lessia and Gerry were living so babysitting Dorianne and Michael and visiting was convenient. As well, the near-by St. Andrew's Ukrainian Orthodox Parish had become organized a few years earlier in 1959 with parish members just finishing the construction of a cultural complex; and the building of the church in their very near future. The situation just suited Michael and Tena just fine. They promptly became members at St. Andrew's and got involved in church volunteer work. With Lessia and Gerry and George and Vera already members at St. Andrew's, this was a natural fit. The religious and cultural roots that Michael pursued since coming to Canada in 1928 were again, immediately close at hand. Michael was pleased that the upbringing he provided for his children would be available for his grandchildren as well. Michael and Tena soon found out that several members at St. Andrew's parish had their family roots in many Saskatchewan and Manitoba communities in which they had lived or worked. Villages and towns such as Gronlid, Brooksby and the Yorkton, Melville and Canora areas, as well as the Garland, Dauphin and Winnipeg areas of Manitoba were the initial homes of many St. Andrew's parish members. Soon old acquaintances were revived and new friendships flourished. Michael and Tena loved being involved with the volunteer work, enjoyed the camaraderie with parish members and contact with their expanding immediate family. To say that they were kept busy would be an understatement.

St. Andrew's Ukrainian Orthodox Parish was a very young parish age-wise. Most of the adults were just starting their careers thus the majority of children were pre school and early elementary school age. With this young parish, Michael and Tena along with a few of the other older members were kept quite busy conducting classes and courses (formally and informally) in Ukrainian cuisine, customs and traditions, handi-crafts such as embroidery—regular and crossstitch,

GEORGE TKACHYK

weaving, pysanka drawing/dying, traditional dance costume design and sewing and church related activities.

Tena became active with the St. Andrew's Ladies Auxiliary. When she wasn't preparing for a family gathering or sitting at her sewing machine sewing for clients and grandchildren, she was working at the St. Andrew's kitchen preparing traditional Ukrainian breads and traditional Ukrainian cooking for tea and bake sales, or a catering. Michael was busy with his farm, gardening, maintaining his duplexes or assisting the parish priest, Rev. Father Kryschuk at St. Andrew's with church responsibilities such as Cantoring or serving as Palamar/altar server on Sundays and on special weekday church services or at funerals at St. Andrew's or at rural parishes surrounding Edmonton. After that first year of retirement when Michael seemed to have time on his hands and didn't have anything to do, he became a whirlwind of activity; always on the go and always pleased with his "productive time".

Michael greeting His Beatitude, Archbishop Andrew on St. Andrew's Day, with the traditional Ukrainian Greeting with Salt and Braided Bread. December, 1969.

While Mary, Alex and son George settled in Yorkton, George and Vera purchased a new home in Steele Heights since they were both teaching in North Edmonton. Lessia and Gerry bought a home in the Ottewell district not far from Michael and Tena's duplex.

In 1968 George graduated from the University of Alberta completing his Bachelor of Education degree. Michael was pleased that the third of his children had taken the opportunity to access the education that he was deprived of in his native Ukraine. Soon Lessia would add to her post secondary music degrees with her Bachelor of Education degree as well. This would complete Michael's "hat trick" of three post secondary educated children. Immigrant families were, and still are today, typically aggressive in attempting to achieve higher levels of learning or success in their endeavors. East European families who suffered due to the brutal social and political structures during the years leading up to the nineteenth and early twentieth centuries had something to prove to themselves and to the new world they were entering.

Michael and Tena at George's convocation at the University of Alberta. 1968

Son-in-law Alex, prior to 1968 had been re-evaluating his teaching career and had made a major decision to enter the Holy Priesthood of the Ukrainian Orthodox Church of Canada. This would mean a move to Winnipeg, where he would complete a two year course in ecclesiastical study at St. Andrew's College, the Ukrainian Orthodox Seminary at the University of Manitoba. Mary, along with the entire family was pleased with this decision. Mary, Alex and George moved to Winnipeg in 1968. In 1970, Rev. Father Alex Hupka was ordained as a priest of the Ukrainian Orthodox Church of Canada at Yorkton's Ukrainian Orthodox Church of the Holy Transfiguration, where Mary, Alex and son George along with Alex/'s parents had attended for many years. Alex's first parochial assignment was to Ituna, Saskatchewan, south east of Yorkton. The Ituna parish was large, serving several rural, village and town centered churches in the Ituna area.

9

EDMONTON~
THE RETIREMENT YEARS

During the first year in Edmonton, Michael kept busy with his vegetable garden in his back yard and looking after the tenants they had living in the lower portion of the duplex. To supplement his income Michael bought another house in the Beverly area of Edmonton and rented it out. He was kept quite busy initially with the upkeep and maintenance of the two properties.

Retirement had been talked about in the Tkaczyk household, but the planning for the time aspect never really took place. Tena kept very busy with her sewing, something she could never find enough time for while running the hotel. Word spread throughout the community that she was a talented seamstress, all be it self taught, for the most part. Tena had a knack for estimating the quantity of fabric without the use of a pattern and she would even sew a garment from a photo, sketch, or a verbal description. She would draw and cut her own pattern if necessary and sew up a garment tailored to fit any size, shape, or figure. She was taking on sewing projects large and small, from wedding dresses for brides and bridesmaids, to regular ladies fashions, to draperies, to Ukrainian and other Slavic dance and traditional costumes and later figure skating costumes for her grandchildren and skaters from the Royal Glenora Figure Skating Club. There was a constant flow of traffic through the Tkaczyk household and Tena's two sewing machines (one treadle and one electric) were kept humming from early morning to late into the night. With three grandchildren in Edmonton to sew for, Tena was very busy procuring fabrics and sewing dresses skirts and blouses for the girls and jeans, shirts and jackets for the boys. Tena was in all her glory with all that she had to do.

While Tena was extremely busy with her schedule of activities, Michael soon became bored without his usual daily hotel routine. He only had two properties to look after. His life had been one of work, work, work; first railroading and farm work as a laborer, then railroading and owning and running a farm operation, then being a proprietor of a hotel, renovating the hotel while being self sustainable in the food and hospitality operation of the hotel while farming at a distance and being involved in community activities. Michael's busy schedule suddenly slowed to a crawl. This retirement came as a complete and sudden reversal of activity for Michael. They hadn't had a travel away holiday for more than two days at a time in the 16 years that they owned the hotel in Krydor. The last holiday they took was a family holiday in 1949 when Michael still worked for the railroad, and that was the train trip to Toronto and Montreal. Michael with all this inactivity, lost his appetite and began to lose weight. He had time on his hands and didn't know how to handle it. George suggested that Michael and Tena buy an acreage where they could get involved in a large garden, plant some fruit trees and buy a small garden tractor to "tend to the land" so to speak. When Michael saw the prices that were being asked for acreages adjacent to the city of Edmonton and Sherwood Park, he exclaimed, "For $17,000.00 I can buy a whole farm, a quarter section of land, not just 3 acres." And he did!

In 1967 he found a quarter section of land in the Hilliard/Mundare area and bought it for $16,000.00. He went to farm auction sales in the area and bought a used Massey Harris 44 tractor, a seeder and harrows. At age 65 Michael started a farm operation. He drove 45 miles (70 kilometers) out to the farm daily to look after his land, his large garden and his machinery. He was content. He started gaining weight. Life was good. He was doing something productive and something that he loved. The old saying," You can take the boy from the farm, but you can't take the farm from the boy", held true. His upbringing in his native Ukraine was on the land and his roots were still there—on the land. The vast majority of Ukrainians that settled the prairies were agriculturalists and they were good at it. That was the reason Lord Sifton in the late 1800's reached out to Eastern Europe for potential settlers to settle the western Canadian prairies.

The family was concerned regarding the amount of driving and work that Michael had to do, but he was content and that was more important than all the details that bothered the family. He got neighboring farmers to help with the harvesting since he didn't have a combine, and he probably wasn't going to invest in the high cost machinery. With this help he took off several crops. He was making money and enjoying himself.

The farmers adjacent to his land were perplexed. They were a young generation of farmers expanding their farm operations and land holdings, while this 65 year old was just starting up a farm operation. Actually Michael's land was right in the middle of one of the young farmer's land holdings which interfered with the young farmer's, cultivating and harvesting because he had to go around Michael's land. After two years, the young farmer made Michael an offer for the land that Michael couldn't refuse. In the two years of farming Michael made money on the grain he grew and sold, raised two large gardens of vegetables and potatoes for the entire family, then sold the land to his neighbor for an $10,000.00 profit. He banked the $26,000.00, sold the machinery and shortly thereafter went out and bought another duplex for $27,000.00 in the Gold Bar area of Edmonton. Michael felt he overpaid for the duplex, but it was in an excellent location near the Ottewell Curling Club, was close to schools and shopping and was only a few years old.

Michael had become a whirlwind of activity at a time he was supposed to be slowing down in retirement. At age 67 Michael didn't know the meaning of the word retirement. He didn't have a fixed schedule as he did at the hotel. During the hotel years, other than Good Friday and Christmas Day, the hotel was open six days a week, 52 weeks a year as prescribed by the Saskatchewan Liquor Control Act of the 1950's and 1960's. Now he loved his freedom.

The shift to more sedentary lifestyle while enjoyable, was also very trying at the beginning of his retirement years. Michael was used to a lifetime of "productivity" and this retirement process was not productive in Michael's view. When one was employed or self employed there were definite goals and objectives to be achieved and one knew when he achieved them either through financial gain or the satisfaction of seeing a goal, objective or something tangible being achieved. This retirement process needed a few changes and Michael saw to

DREAM TO REALITY

it that he made those changes. He created situations that he was productive with the farm operation in the Hilliard area and with the city properties that he purchased, upgraded and rented. Michael was a contented person when he was busy, but it had to be "productive" busy. He made a distinction between busy work and productive work. He came to this country for that sole purpose; he wanted to be productive. He loved the freedom of movement, freedom of choice and the freedom of entrepreneurship, but that is another story that came soon on the heels of Michael and Tena's move to Edmonton.

The duplex in Goldbar needed some work. Michael with help from George assisting on weeknights and weekends re-painted the duplex inside and outside, repaired and painted the fence and soon Michael was renting out both sides of the duplex. The location of the duplex was ideal. Next door to it was the Ottewell Curling Club. Walking distance from the duplex was the Capilano Shopping Mall, schools and churches. Michael rented the duplex out within a week of refurbishing it and was quite content with the proceeds from his properties.

Within a year of purchasing the Goldbar duplex, a realtor came knocking on Michael's door at 101 Avenue and asked if he owned the Goldbar duplex and if it was for sale. Subsequently the realtor said he had clients that were interested in buying it and were willing to pay $35,000 for it. Michael told the realtor that he wasn't interested in selling the duplex since he was getting an adequate revenue for it. About a week later that same realtor came back and and raised the purchase offer to $40,000 then to $45,000 by the time he left, but Michael was not interested in selling the property since it was in good condition, he had just invested money in refurbishing it and was getting a good revenue from the rent of both sides of the duplex. A few weeks later the realtor came back with an offer of $60,000 for the duplex. By this time Michael was exasperated with this persistent realtor and told him that he wouldn't sell the duplex if the offer was at $75,000. Michael then phoned George and told him about the persistent realtor and his offers to buy the duplex. George couldn't believe his ears when he heard of the offer of $60,000 and that Micheal had pushed the ante up to $75,000; more than two times than what Michael had paid for it. George was down to Michael's in a flash and told Michael that if they should offer anything in the neighborhood of $65,000 to $70,000 Michael should take the offer. Michael called the realtor and told him that he was reconsidering the offer of $75,000 and that he might let the duplex go at that price. Michael was playing hardball with the realtor now but the realtor didn't counter the offer. He was down to Michael's home within an hour with a certified cheque for $75,000 and a signed purchase contract from the purchaser. Now why someone would pay that much for a duplex when the market value was approximately $35,000 to $38,000 was beyond Michael's and his family's comprehension, however Michael was not to question his good fortune. George and the rest of the family just shook their heads when they saw the signed contract and certified cheque. Michael just smiled all the way to the bank.

Michael's next venture into land acquisition was interesting to say the least. He noticed a legal notice in the Edmonton Journal referring to the judicial sale of property. A quarter section of land that was once a dairy farm on 82nd Street north of the Edmonton city limits was in the hands of the public trustee and was being offered for sale. The owner had passed away and the land was being disposed of by the courts. As usual with judicial sales, prospective buyers had to submit sealed bids on the property in question, with a 10% deposit that was refundable should the bid be unsuccessful. Michael sent in a bid with his deposit on this property, unbeknown to any family members. One day when George and his family were over visiting with Baba and Dido, Michael with an impish grin on his face disclosed to all that he had been dabbling in judicial sales and sent in a bid on this property on 82nd Street. Michael had not seen the property, in fact he didn't even know where it was, but a quarter section of farm land that was a dairy farm that had to be worth something. As soon as George heard of the location, he knew exactly where it was, since George and Vera had purchased a house and lived in the north end of the city for five years (1965-1970) at 13811—62 Street. The city was expanding northward in the direction of that dairy farm.

Michael displayed the returned deposit cheque in the amount of $3,000, with a letter from the public trustee indicating that Michael was an unsuccessful bidder for the said parcel of land. Michael then told everyone that the successful purchaser was some guy by the name of Buxton, and that he paid $250,000 for the land. This Mr. Buxton was the real estate firm of Buxton Real Estate, a major realtor in the Edmonton area during the 1970's. Michael with that impish grin, realized the fact that he had been in a financial skirmish with the "big boys" as he called them. That was the end of Michael's financial exploits in the 1970's. With interest rates in the high teens and low twenties, he was content to have his money securely invested in high interest bearing accounts in the bank with little risk involved.

- As a point of interest, the dairy farm that Michael had bid on, was located on the quarter section of land in north Edmonton that is part of the Mayliewan sub-division, Ozerna neighborhood, bordered by 153 Avenue on the South, 167 Avenue on the North, 82 Street on the West and 66 Street to the East. George and Vera built their new home in that area in 2005.

Michael and Tena had heard about a unique music program for pre-school age children. This program was the Suzuki School of Music which involved piano or violin instruction. They proceeded to go out and buy Suzuki violins (one fourth the size of a regular violin), for their granddaughters Laurie and Dorianne and urged George and Vera and Lessia and Gerry to enroll the girls in violin classes. This special course for pre-schoolers included enrolling the mothers as well, since they became the home tutors in this music endeavor. So, there were Lessia and Vera playing their adult size violins and Laurie and Dorianne playing their mini-violins along side them. Michael was extremely proud of his granddaughters Laurie and Dorianne as they played in recitals on the stage of Convocation Hall at the University of Alberta. Michael's quest for learning and pursuing educational challenges never left him even in retirement. Laurie and Dorianne continued with the violin lessons for several years but switched to piano when they started school. They both continued their piano into their high school years as well as pursuing other musical instruments throughout their high school years and beyond.

While Michael and Tena were pre-occupied with settling down in Edmonton in the late 1960's a note of sadness was interjected into the family when Harry Dobrowolsky suddenly passed away from a heart attack. Harry was married to Tena's sister Marie who is George's godmother. Harry and Marie's son Gordon was finishing high school and was planning to attend the University of Saskatchewan when this sudden passing occurred. With the family suddenly strapped for finances, Gordon was going to put his higher education on hold for a few years and help out with the family by finding a job to assist his mother Marie with bringing up the other two children at home. Michael, true to form being concerned that Gordon may not acquire the post secondary education he was planning, stepped forward, as he had done with previous family members and assisted with financing Gordon's post secondary education. Michael's continued quest for education and learning was never ending. He wanted everyone close to him to have the very best educational opportunity they could possibly have. With Michael's assistance, Gordon, being a very capable individual pursued his education and is successful in his business endeavors to this day.

The 1970's were as busy as ever for Michael and Tena.

Michael's dreams of success were coming to fruition. Michael had earned his retirement through hard work, self determination and perseverance. All of Michael's children had achieved a post secondary education with George and Lessia following Mary's lead when she achieved her Home Economics degree. George followed up with a Bachelor of Education and a post graduate diploma in curriculum development. Lessia completed her Bachelor of Education degree to complement her music degrees she achieved earlier in Saskatoon. The success of his children's education combined with the financial and moral assistance that Michael provided to some of Tena's siblings and nephew, Michael continued to encourage his grandchildren to strive for success, whether it was the Suzuki violin lessons, piano or band involvement or their elementary, junior high, senior high or post secondary schooling.

GEORGE TKACHYK

Retired life was anything but quiet and peaceful for Michael and Tena. Their life seemed to be a blur of activity, and that 1963 Pontiac of theirs was certainly getting a workout. Michael and Tena seemed to be a travelling road show in the late 1960's and on into the 1970's. They were constantly travelling through the three Prairie Provinces visiting friends and relatives with their usual visits to Krydor, Prince Albert, Gronlid, Yorkton and Garland, Manitoba. The highlight of these trips was visiting in Yorkton and being in attendance at son-in-law Alex's ordination into the Holy Priesthood of the Ukrainian Orthodox Church of Canada.

With Lessia and Gerry settled into their home in Ottewell and Gerry entering the insurance industry, Lessia decided to go back to university to complete her Bachelor of Education degree to complement her music degrees. Michael and Tena took on new roles as baby sitters for Michael Jr. and Dorianne. Baba and Dido took on the responsibility and enjoyed that role immensely.

Meanwhile, in 1970, George and Vera decided to build a new home in Sherwood Park. They sold their home in Steele Heights in North Edmonton during an upswing in the real estate market in May of 1970. Their new home completion date was set for July 15, 1970. Michael and Tena wouldn't hear of George and Vera renting a property for a few months while their new home was being completed, and insisted that George, Vera, Laurie and Dan move into their home for the months of May, June and July, and storing their furniture and appliances in their garage. Now Baba and Dido were in their glory. They had four of their five grandchildren present in their home most days. Baba was busy sewing for the grandchildren, baking her famous cinnamon buns and deep frying doughnuts every few days for her guests. Dido not to be outdone, was taking his turn at spoiling the four grandchildren. You would see

Michael daily with his entourage of grandchildren following him over to the Dairy Queen across the street, for their daily or twice daily treat of soft ice cream cones. George would come home from school to find Dido and the four grandchildren sitting on the front steps relishing the chocolate coated soft ice cream cones. This was great and the grandchildren enjoyed the attention and the treats, but when George and Vera would move into their new home in Sherwood Park, and when normalcy returned to the family unit, there

Michael on the front steps of 7005-101 Avenue enjoying his trademark Dairy Queen treats with four of his six grandchildren, Laurie, Robbie and Danny Tkachyk and Michael Slipchuk, 1975.

would be no day in and day out of a constant flow of treats for Laurie and Danny. That would however necessitate a trip or two to Baba's and Dido's every week to stock up on cinnamon buns and doughnuts and the famous trip to the Dairy Queen. Those baked treats continued for the grandchildren well into their teens.

In 1971, while Michael's and Tena's 1963 Pontiac was parked in front of their duplex, a passing motorist drove into their car causing enough damage to cause the insurance company to write off the car. With the insurance settlement Michael and Tena went out and purchased a new 1971 Pontiac two door coupe. This canary yellow coupe with a black interior was a sight to behold. This car had oversized tires and a powerful 350 cubic inch V-8, double overhead cam engine just a step below the legendary muscle car of the 1970's "The Judge". Michael and Tena's new 1971 Pontiac only lacked the hood scoop and the decals symbolizing flames emitting from the manifold air vents on the front fenders. This new vehicle made Michael's and Tena's "Tri-Province" tours more frequent and of course, much speedier.

During those early 1970's, Michael, Tena, their children and their grandchildren were very involved with the Ukrainian Orthodox Church and its associated cultural activities in Alberta and Saskatchewan. In Ituna, Saskatchewan, Father Alex was busy with his pastoral and parochial work, with Mary and son George accompanying and assisting Father Alex whenever possible. They were constantly travelling to the various parishes in the parochial district. Even at his young age George was learning to assist Fr. Alex with the liturgical readings and cantoring at the various church services and holy feast days.

In Edmonton, George and Vera along with Lessia and Gerry and their families had become members at St. Andrew's Ukrainian Orthodox Parish and participated fully. Vera became involved with "Sadochok" and taught the Ukrainian pre-school at St. Andrew's. George took on a Sunday School teaching position and later the directorship of the Sunday School program. He became involved in the St. Andrew's Men's Club and was its president for three years and in 1974 he took on the chairmanship of the Board of Management of St. Andrew's Ukrainian Orthodox Parish.

Lessia taught the children's choir at St. Andrew's and Gerry served on several committees and the men's club. Laurie, Danny, Michael and Dorianne were involved in Sadochok, Ukrainian Folk Dancing, Sunday School and attending the weekly church services with their parents and grandparents. Michael as a church elder, was busy with Palamar duties assisting the priest at the Altar,

Michael playing the role of St. Nicholas in classrooms that accommodated the Ukrainian Bi-lingual program at a school in the neighborhood of St. Andrew's Parish.

assisting with the cultural and Sunday School grams, often playing the role of St. Nicholas during the month of December in local schools and at the church itself. Tena was involved in the Ladies Auxiliary, the Altar Guild, cooking in the St. Andrew's kitchen, teaching the cooking and baking techniques of Ukrainian Cuisine and was constantly assisting and conducting workshops in the design and sewing of Ukrainian dance costumes.

GEORGE TKACHYK

In 1973, George and Vera welcomed their third child, Robbie into the world, a brother for Laurie and Dan. This made six grandchildren for Michael and Tena to enjoy and spoil. Family gatherings in Edmonton were frequent and to say the least, very active with all six grandchildren demanding and getting their attention from any and all adults.

Back in Saskatchewan, Tena's parents Michael and Anna Pohoreski retired from the blacksmith shop and post office operation in Lenvale and moved to Prince Albert in 1960. By the time that the 1970's approached they were having difficulty managing their yard and home due to their advancing ages and failing health. Michael and Tena opened their doors once again to assist family by offering Baba and Dido Pohoreski the opportunity to live in Edmonton with them in the duplex. Michael and Tena had two additional rooms that they could share plus the convenience of grandchildren and great grandchildren for Baba and Dido Pohoreski. Their daughter Pauline who lived in Edmonton and Pauline's children were also a positive factor. Then there was the church close by and a Ukrainian community into which they would readily fit. Baba and Dido Pohoreski sold their house, household goods, packed their belongings including Dido's anvil and hammer into their Vauxhall, and the entourage of vehicles forged their way on to Edmonton. Baba and Dido lived in Edmonton for several years before Baba Pohoreski took ill and passed away in 1972. Dido Pohoreski moved back to Prince Albert to live with one of his other daughters and passed away in 1973.

10

TO UKRAINE

Michael continued his correspondence with his brother John, sisters Zoya and Mary as well as with his brother-in-law George Kotyk and his wife Kateryna. The correspondence with George and Kateryna was broken off for a few years in the 1950's during their arrest and incarceration by the KGB and the communists. Michael was always second guessing himself as to whether he was the cause of their arrest and incarceration due to their correspondence and whether he had said anything in his letters to cause the communists to take such drastic action. During the post-war period and into the cold war period of the 1950's, 1960's and the 1970's the Soviets under the leadership of Josef Stalin and Nikita Khruschev and their successors exercised an iron grip over the travel and communication into and out of Soviet controlled territory or its satellite countries. Communication by mail was most common but it was censored by the Soviet government and mail was subject to being opened, screened and read. If there were offending or critical comments about the communist government, its policies, practices or people, the recipients of such communication in Ukraine were punished by arrest, interrogation and possible imprisonment.

GEORGE TKACHYK

When George and Kateryna were released in the mid-1950's correspondence continued as though nothing had happened. The Kotyk's and Michael in Canada did not want to cause them any hardship under the communist rule and did not pursue the issue, although it was a burning question just waiting to be asked. What happened? Why did the KGB remove George and Kateryna? Why were the children left alone without support and protection? It wasn't until Michael and Tena travelled to Ukraine in 1974, that they learned the true story of George's and Kateryna's arrest, incarceration and eventual release by the KGB.

The need for clothing, footwear and particularly winter outerwear was a necessity in post-war Europe, particularly in Ukraine where the Soviets were stripping the locals of everything they owned in the name of collectivization and the "common good". After the "Holodomor" of 1932-33, the devastation of the 1939-1944 Second World War, rebuilding Ukraine and all post-war Europe was a monumental task. The establishment of the "Iron Curtain" by Josef Stalin did not help this re-building process. Stalin essentially prevented any goods entering Soviet controlled territory unless it was intercepted and screened by the Soviets. Parcels to individuals and families, containing clothing and footwear were allowed to be sent from Canada to Ukraine, however the parcels were subject to more severe scrutiny than letters. Parcels had to have attached to them a label listing the items included. The parcels were opened by Soviet authorities to confirm what was being sent and items were then pilfered or stolen and the attached lists removed from the parcels. Sometimes the parcels never got to their destination, and the Soviets would simply claim that it was lost in transit by the inept capitalists. Sometimes the parcels got to their destination but half or more of the items were removed for the authorities personal use or for sale on the black market, which was illegal in Communist countries, but the Black Market continued as a thriving business in the corrupt Soviet structure. The receiving party never knew if they got what was intended for them from the sender. Michael would send letters well in advance telling his family what was being sent. The family would simply reply thanking Michael for the specific items received. In all the years that Michael sent goods to his family, the family never received the entire parcel. Michael's only wish was that whoever was stealing from him truly needed the articles for survival, since the items sent were usually boots, shoes, clothing, winter outerwear and head wear. Michael at times even sent sheets of leather so that the family could make shoes for themselves. By the late 1970's Michael stopped sending parcels since the families in Ukraine were getting their education and even though their salaries were substantially lower than elsewhere in Europe, families could afford to buy themselves staples such as clothing, food and some consumer goods.

The 1970's saw dramatic improvements in Ukraine. Travel out of the Soviet Union by Soviet citizens was not allowed except for high government officials, Communist Party members in good standing (rarely), artists (usually military members), The Bolshoi Ballet, Red Army Chorus Ensemble or athletes competing at world class levels. Travel was allowed into the Soviet Union but only under certain conditions. One could travel into the Soviet Union only on their national airline "Aeroflot". One could enter the Soviet Union through a bus tour booked only through their "Intourist Travel", or one could enter by car at his/her own risk, however there were limited roads, service stations, repair depots and one had to report every night at an "Intourist Hotel" where an "Intourist" guide would greet you and "debrief" you and your activities. These Intourist Travel guides were nothing more than KGB or under cover agents working for the Communiust Party. Travel to rural areas was not allowed, particularly to areas where the tourist had family. If a tourist wanted to meet family, the family came to meet the tourist at a specified location. Organized tours only were allowed, but only into recognized tourist attractions. Photo opportunities were limited to "Intourist Attractions". At border checkpoints and at customs in airports, your passports/ visas were checked along with the amount of money you were bringing into the country. On exit, the same procedure was used and your currency was checked to monitor how much you spent and where. All money and goods had to balance out or there were detentions and interrogations until a satisfactory balance in the minds of Soviet Officials, was achieved. Printed goods were carefully examined to prevent holy books or "western" propaganda to be brought in. Border checkpoints would allow one bible per person for personal use. Western travellers who were used to travelling throughout the world with ease found this tight control over travel difficult to deal with and to understand.

Michael was one such person. While the family was encouraging him to travel to Ukraine to visit his family, Michael was reticent to do so. His comment was, *"Why would I want to feed this corrupt and vicious communist regime through paying to use <u>their</u> airline, <u>their</u> Intourist and <u>their</u> hotels with <u>my</u> hard earned money so that <u>they</u> could further deprive <u>my</u> family of their basic needs and wants. And then I am not guaranteed that I will even get to see my family. They could divert the tour at the last minute."* That had been known to happen. Michael was very bitter about the treatment of his family by the Soviets. While he longed to see his brother, sisters, nieces and nephews he didn't trust the Soviets to actually come through with the travel plans. The Soviets were in total control of the tourist and his comings and goings. While Michael had the protection of the Canadian

DREAM TO REALITY

Government as a citizen of Canada, he did not trust the Soviets with his travel plans. He was willing to spend the money but he did not want the Soviets to benefit at the expense of his family. The Soviets had robbed him of enough through the years and he was not prepared to have them deceive him and take his money under false promises through their corrupt political, economic and social system.

Finally, in late 1973, Michael relented and agreed to go back to Ukraine to visit his family. Tena was excited about the trip and was instrumental in convincing Michael to change his mind and to plan on this trip back to visit his brother and sisters. She had never met any of Michael's family. She had corresponded by letter only, so Tena was looking forward to visiting them and meeting them personally for the first time. During the winter of 1973, Michael and Tena made the travel arrangements through East-West Travel in Edmonton, one of the few travel agencies permitted to arrange travel to, from and within the Soviet Union. In July of 1974, they boarded an "Aeroflot" airliner at Montreal's Mirabelle International Airport (later re-named Pierre Elliot Trudeau International Airport) bound for London and Moscow. All tourist travel into the Soviet Union was routed through Moscow. Once in Moscow and through customs and interrogation regarding the contents of their bulging suitcases, Michael and Tena were escorted to their Intourist hotel. Michael and Tena had loaded their suitcases with store bought clothes such as jeans which were in high demand in Ukraine, shirts and other clothing items, several bibles and Tena's home made dresses and blouses with false seams so that she could alter the dresses and blouses without difficulty once they got to visit family. The customs officials took a dim view of all these goods, questioned them at length about the bibles (which were officially banned in the Soviet Union), and Michael's large supply of jeans, but let them pass without incident. Michael didn't look like a member of the jeans generation, in fact he never owned or wore a pair of jeans in his life. Michael and Tena spent the next few days in Moscow "on tour" with other tourists visiting Lenin's tomb, Red Square, areas around the Kremlin, the GUM department store, parks, the subway, St. Basil's Russian Orthodox Cathedral and a few war memorials and museums. Michael and Tena, along with the other tourists put up with the tours. They had no choice. All the tourists had families to visit and were anxious to get on with the few days that they would have with their relatives.

Michael and Tena were then flown to Kiev (Kyiv) where they followed the Soviet Intourist itinerary of Soviet War Memorials, parks, Churches and Monasteries. In Kiev Michael and Tena could join a tour or venture out on their own within a limited area. They chose to go on tours, while others that wanted to visit with family did so on their own. One of the main points of interest that they visited was the "Caves Monastery" "Pechers'ka Lavra", the underground tombs of Bishops, Monks, Clergy and Saints of the Ukrainian Orthodox Church beneath the cathedral in Kiev. All of these sites were of immense interest to Michael and Tena since this was "their Ukrainian historical, religious and cultural history", the homeland of St.Vladimir the Great who converted Ukraine to Christianity in 988 AD, however the Soviet Intourist guides made everything Soviet history and Soviet centered and merely glossed over the religious aspects. This annoyed Michael but in his usual quiet manner he kept his cool and said nothing. He was not going to jeopardize this opportunity to see his family with a confrontation or an emotional outburst. The Soviets were known to either send tourists back to their country of origin on the next flight, or make things very difficult for them on their trip by diverting them to other areas where they would not see their families.

Several days later they were on a commuter aircraft on the way to way to Chernivtsi to meet up with family that Michael had not seen in 39 years. The commuter aircraft was comparable to 1940's bus transportation in Saskatchewan. Travelers sitting in their seats with baggage in the aisles and underfoot. There were no overhead bins with doors, just a shelf above the seat with stretchable cords to try to hold the packages from falling out. All that was missing was the produce, chickens and geese attached to each traveler. Air travel in the Soviet Union was primitive at best. The Soviets may have had a space program that challenged the United States during the 1960's and 1970's, however their commercial travel standards were decades behind the western world.

11

TO CHERNIVTSI, KITSMAN AND UZHENETZ

As soon as the plane touched down in Chernivtsi, Michael, Tena and the other tourists were herded onto busses and taken to their Intourist hotels. The city was still beautiful as Michael had remembered it. With its tree lined streets and old, some ancient, buildings dating back to the 7th, 8th and 9th centuries the city was a seat of Orthodox Christianity and with its Metropolitan's castle, now the University of Chernivtsi, it was still a hub of learning.

The tourists were instructed by the authorities (an official looking military type complete with shoulder bars) that they would be dispatched to the hotels and then they could contact their families to come to Chernivtsi to visit, or they could go on the scheduled tours that Intourist always provided in the larger cities. The tourists were told in no uncertain terms, that they were not allowed to go out to the villages. With those instructions the busses were allowed to leave the airport. The trip to the hotels was uneventful, except that Michael noticed some re-building had taken place since the war. Newer government buildings had sprung up, the austere look-alike apartment blocks lined the streets, but the downtown area with its tree lined streets by and large remained the same as Michael remembered it in 1935 when he had gone to pick up Mary.

The bus rolled up to the hotel and they disembarked, were checked in and taken to their rooms. The rooms were basic—a double bed, dresser, chest of drawers and a few chairs with a bathroom down the hall. Actually it wasn't much different than Krydor Hotel or any country hotel in Saskatchewan or Alberta during the 1940's, 1950's and the 1960's.

Michael and Tena couldn't contact Michael's family in Uzhenetz since they didn't have phone service in Uzhenetz at that time. The Intourist guide met everyone in the hotel dining room for dinner and gave them an overview of Chernivtsi and the sights to cover during the tourists' next three days that they would spend there.

Early the next morning Michael hailed a cab and asked to be driven to Uzhenetz. The cab driver refused, saying that he couldn't do that because it was illegal to take tourists to rural villages. Michael, being prepared, offered the cabbie a bottle of Vodka plus the fare to take them out to the village. Some haggling took place as to the quality of vodka, and Michael conceded to a high end vodka. If any request failed in the Soviet Union, a bribe, preferably in the currency of vodka or U.S. dollars was appropriate and expected. (The Black Market and bribery thrived in the U.S.S.R., but was "officially" frowned upon.) Soon Michael and Tena along with their suitcases were on their way to Uzhenetz. Out of the city they drove on paved roads to the city's edge then onto a major dirt road that connected Chernivtsi with Kitsman a larger town along the dirt road that led to the cities to the north, then from Kitsman onto a trail where horse carts once travelled, but only a footpath or bicycle path existed in 1974. There was evidence of the tracks of a few vehicles, probably trucks carrying farm produce, but in reality it was a footpath to the city. A few kilometres later of this grass overgrown trail and they were in the village of Uzhenetz, Michael's home town and birthplace.

Michaels' brother John, sisters Maria and Zoya and their families knew that Michael and Tena were coming but they did not know the exact date and time. As the cab pulled up to John's door, the families started pouring out of their houses. Automobiles were a rare site in the village and the arrival of a cab was cause for much excitement and curiosity. Neighbours were curious as to who the new comers were and were out in their doorways and yards. Word spread quickly since Westerners and Canadians in particular were a rare sight in the villages. Soon Maria's and Zoya's families joined the family gathering at John's house. Michael's and Tena's arrival was cause for much hugging, kissing, tears of joy and the hosting of guests was begun. The villagers in any part of Ukraine did not have much, but as soon as company came there was food and drink on the table to host them. Michael's family was prepared and were throwing out the welcome mat for them. Tena fit right in since she had been exchanging letters with John, Maria and Zoya for years. They knew each other in written communications but talking to each other was an entirely different and comforting experience. Of course the nieces and nephews were not to be left out either. They were all adults now, some married and with their own families. Michael and Tena started distributing their gifts of clothes and bibles. Tena started tailoring the dresses with the false seams to fit the individual ladies. The jeans were distributed to the males and toys to the small children.

As the day turned to late afternoon a pall fell over the festivities as a military jeep-like vehicle pulled into the yard. Two military officers got out of the jeep and started questioning Michael and Tena. They demanded travel documents, identification and started questioning the families. Michael and Tena were informed that they had violated Soviet law by coming out to the village and they were told to report to their hotel in two hours. The officers seemed to know a lot more about Michael and Tena than Michael expected. They knew where Michael and Tena were from, Michael's background and who they were visiting and what the relationships were. It made Michael feel a bit uneasy that they had so much information. The officers got into the jeep and left. The officers prior to coming out to Uzhenetz had summoned a cab, since it arrived shortly after the officers left. Michael and Tena told the family that they would meet again the next day, then bade their farewells, got into the cab and left for their hotel. As the cab pulled up to the hotel Michael and Tena were greeted by the two officers who had been out to the village. The officers noted the time, well under the two hours allotted to get back. Michael and Tena were told that they could host their family at the hotel, and that they were not allowed to go back to the village. Michael was livid. He spent all this money to get to see his family and was told by the authorities that he could not visit his family in their homes. He had to get back to the village one more time. The village had nothing to hide. It was not a military establishment that was top secret. In fact, as Michael recounted when he got back to Edmonton,

"Nothing had changed in the village since 1928 when I left the first time. The only positive change was that some straw thatched roofs

were covered in rusted tin from old bathtubs and that some houses had electricity — one pull switch light bulb per room and a hot plate on the counter that was used only when company arrived (they couldn't afford the electricity). The negative change was that the road was overgrown with weeds and only a footpath existed to Kitsman. There was no evidence of regular vehicular traffic."

After dinner and recounting their experiences with other tourists that experienced similar experiences, Michael and Tena turned in to plan their next day in Soviet Ukraine.

Bright and early the next day, Michael and Tena were again bribing the same cabbie with vodka to get out to Uzhenetz. The cabbie knew that he could risk taking them out because this time the tariff included two bottles of vodka, one for him and one presumably for the officers should they re-appear. The Soviet system survived on fraud, bribery and deceit and every one seemed to know it and thrived on it. Michael paid the bribe and the fare then the cabbie drove them out to Uzhenetz.

Michael and Tena visited with the families that second day making the most of this short three day visit. During late afternoon, Michael informed his hosts that he wanted to visit the cemetery where his parents were buried and set off on foot to the cemetery. While they were there, the military jeep drove up and the same two officers again questioned them, admonished them for going out to the village and ordered them back to the hotel. While Michael was extremely angry and upset at this intrusion by the officers, he calmly made this statement in Ukrainian:

"I'm a Canadian citizen who has returned to this land for personal reasons. Your government has dragged me through tours to see Lenin's body lying in state at Red Square in Moscow, your government has

forced me to visit your war memorials and other government sites. Because I wasn't here when my father passed away I just wanted to pay my last respects to my parents. Surely you can grant me that." The two officers seemed to be taken aback by this genuine and straight forward request. They replied, *"Kharasho!"* which means "Right!", "Agreeable!" or "Fine!" in Russian. They turned and drove away without uttering another word. Michael and Tena stayed on past late afternoon visiting. During this last visit to the village Michael and Tena arranged to have the family visit them at the hotel the following day. Michael and Tena left for the hotel in the evening. When Michael and Tena arrived at the hotel later in the evening, the two officers were in the hotel lobby waiting for them. They nodded, acknowledging Michael's and Tena's return and left without saying a word.

There was a positive and pleasant portion to the second day in Uzhenetz. Michael found out the full story behind his brother-in-law George's and sister-in-law Kateryna's incarceration during the 1950's. After 25 years of worrying and wondering if he was the cause of this injustice, he learned that he had not said anything damaging in his letters or contributed to their incarceration in any way. The Soviets had accused George and Kateryna of being "kulaks" or hoarders of wealth from the communist state and had investigated, interrogated and incarcerated them in Siberian work camps. After two years of investigation and incarceration George and Kateryna were allowed to return home. The Soviets could not find any hidden wealth that George and Kateryna were harbouring. They were still under surveillance but no further punishment was meted out.

During the 1940's and 1950's the Soviets rode roughshod over the people of Bukovina and Ukraine in general trying to get the population under their control and to eliminate any dissidents.

The Soviets attempt to Russify Bukovina and all of Ukraine took many forms of threats, torture, killing and relocation to other parts of Russia. The most popular destination for these potential dissidents, but mostly innocent people, was the "Siberian Gulag" (forced labour camps in Siberia), or as Solzhenitsyn referred to them—"the Gulag Archipelago".

During the third day in Chernivtsi, Michael's family arrived at the hotel in the morning. They visited for a short while then went out to visit the stores and parks in the city centre. Michael wanted to buy the relatives some items in the local stores, items of clothing or objects that they might need for their homes. The Soviet Union was not set up for the sale of consumer goods. First there was the problem of currency. Citizens of the Soviet Union did not have much money, nor was the communist system set up for consumerism. Their consumer products for the general population were of very low quality. In the stores, items on display were for Communist Party officials or tourists. If an ordinary person wanted to purchase a like item, say a sweater, the clerk would go into a stock room and bring one out and give it to him for the listed price. There was no regard for size, color or style—you took what was given to you. The general population accepted this since the government was all powerful, controlled all commercial establishments, and all goods that were sold. This was the only commerce they knew. This angered Michael. He and Tena meticulously picked out clothes and other items as though the items were for themselves, and paid for them, then blatantly presented the quality items to their family members in front of the shop managers. The shop managers just shrugged since they couldn't do anything about Michael's blatant but legal protest in front of passers by and other customers.

DREAM TO REALITY

The Soviet way of collective thinking and total control of the population was in its second generation and was in fact beginning a third generation of "automatons" as Michael called the subservient population. He wasn't criticizing the general population. He was commenting on how the Soviet political structure had curbed free thought, free enterprise and free speech in his once free homeland. He understood that they could not change the all-controlling Soviet Regime.

Upon their return to the hotel, Michael and Tena invited all of the family up to their room. Everyone was seated on the chairs, or on the bed or standing around talking. Soon there was a knock at the door and a hotel manager stepped in and started admonishing Michael's family for sitting on the bed. He stated that the furniture was for hotel guests and peasants should be sitting on the wooden chairs or the floor. At this point Michael blew his cool, opened the door and ordered the hotel manager out of the room, and ordered the hotel manager to stop harassing his family. The hotel manager left immediately and quietly.

The next day was Michael's and Tena's departure day from Chernivtsi. All of Michael's family came out to the hotel to say their goodbyes. Many of them knew that this would be the last time that Michael would be coming out to Ukraine under the present Soviet political system. Michael's family passed on gifts for everyone back in Canada—Michael and Tena, Mary and Alex, Lessia and Gerry, and Vera and George. While their money was scarce, they seemed to go overboard in hosting their guests from Canada. There were bandura's, volumes of Shevchenko's literary works, "korali" (traditional red coral bead necklaces) and embroidered shirts. There were many tears shed that morning as Michael and Tena boarded the bus for the ride to the airport to catch their flight to Lviv.

Arriving in Lviv, Michael and Tena were transferred to the usual "Intourist" hotel and were given the same set of options regarding guided tours or to be on their own. Tena had arranged to meet some of the Pohoreski relatives. They met with the families at the hotel and socialized, but this was not the same as meeting Michael's family. These cousins of Tena's knew of Dido Pohoreski but didn't know him personally since Dido Pohoreski came to Canada when he was 17 years old. Michael and Tena didn't travel out to the villages surrounding Lviv.

Two days later Michael and Tena were flying back to Moscow where, after an arduous and thorough search and interrogation from Soviet customs officials, they boarded an Aeroflot aircraft for the flight back to Montreal. Their suitcases were almost void of clothing since they left most of the clothing for the Michael's relatives. The suitcases were filled with mementos and gifts from Michael's family. Korali (coral bead necklaces, sopilka's or wooden flutes), Shevchenko's Kobzar, a four volume version of some his more famous literary works and wooden crafts of various types. The banduras were too large to fit into suitcases and Michael and Tena refused to send them as checked luggage because they were so fragile, so they convinced the Aeroflot officials to have them occupy a seat next to them. The two banduras occupied a separate seat all the way to Calgary, where Air Canada charged Michael a seat fare for the banduras on their last flight leg into Edmonton.

Michael and Tena arrived back in Edmonton tired but full of stories and events to relate to everyone. Travel to the Soviet Union from the West was becoming more common, thus everyone in the Ukrainian community was interested in hearing the stories of conditions in which the people lived and how the tourists were treated.

DREAM TO REALITY

Michael had tremendous difficulty talking about the experiences on his return visit to his family after 39 years. His most frequent comment was:

"Nothing has really changed since I left in 1928. There have been no real improvements in living conditions. Nothing compared to Canada. They have no means of transportation, what road there was for horse and cart, is now overgrown with grass and weeds, just a footpath. The houses still have thatched roofs, save for a few that that have had their roofs patched with rusted metal bathtubs that were dismantled. There was one corded light bulb per room for electricity. The people are run down, wasted through hard work, malnutrition and primitive health and medical care. The adults look fifteen to twenty years older than they really are. Most churches have been destroyed and where they do stand today (1974) they are museums or administrative buildings. The Soviets have tried to steal everything from the people—land, religion, language, history, self worth, health—everything for sake the state."

Michael was depressed due to the fact that while he and his family here in Canada prospered and were healthy, his family in Ukraine under the Soviets was suffering. Michael constantly worried about his family in Ukraine. He lost weight, and for the next few months was a mere shadow of his former self. He slowly came back to his normal self, but it took a great deal of support from the immediate family to help bring him about.

12

THE GOLDEN YEARS

A few months after Michael and Tena's return from Ukraine, life at 7005-101 Avenue slowly regained its normalcy. The church volunteer work, Tena's sewing, the grandchildren coming over for their Dairy Queen treats, the garden and yard work; everything was getting back to normal. Michael's older grandchildren were all in school. The older grandchildren were in elementary school with Robbie a pre-schooler. All of the children were progressing well in school and participating in Ukrainian cultural activities, music, sports and other community activities. Michael and Tena were hard pressed to attend all the school concerts, recitals and sporting events in which all the grandchildren were involved. Michael was pleased that all of the grandchildren were involved in music, be it choir, instrumental or Ukrainian folk dancing. Tena would handle the sewing and the embroidery of the costumes while Michael carved and stitched the leather for the Hutzul footwear.

Mary, Alex and son George had moved from Ituna to Saskatoon, where Father Alex was posted to All Saints Ukrainian Orthodox

Parish. All Saints was a new Ukrainian Orthodox parish in Saskatoon that was starting up just south of the University of Saskatchewan. For the Hupka's, this was a great move since George could then pursue his schooling in Saskatoon, and it was a few hours closer to Edmonton where the rest of Mary's family lived. Michael and Tena would make frequent trips to Saskatoon to visit Mary, Alex and George and Mary and Alex would visit Edmonton more frequently as well. Young George in high school, began volunteering his spare time with the Saskatoon cable television station and soon become proficient in running programs for distribution to the cable customers. This interest would lead him into post secondary studies and a future career in the Television Arts. His interest in electronic technology soon led him into photography and taping and producing some programs. George continued to cantor at church and joined church choir and youth choirs in the city. By the time George was graduating from high school in Saskatoon, he was looking at a film arts school for his university education and selected Ryerson University in Toronto. Alex applied for a parish in the Toronto area and was assigned to Scarborough, Ontario where he took over the Ukrainian Orthodox Parish of St. Anne. George enrolled at Ryerson and completed his degree in the Television Arts and was ready to venture out on his own. He applied for and received a position at CFQC-TV in Saskatoon. Mary and Alex then moved to Regina where Alex was the pastor of The Descent of the Holy Spirit Ukrainian Orthodox Parish. At least with the move back west to Regina, Michael and Tena could visit more often.

GEORGE TKACHYK

Michael's 74 birthday, Dorianne's 13th birthday, November 8,1976
Front Row: Robbie Tkachyk
Second Row: Michael Slipchuk, Danny Tkachyk, Laurie Tkachyk
Third Row: Dorianne Slipchuk, Michael, Tena.

The 1970's turned into the 1980's and the 1980's turned into the 1990's with Michael continuing his volunteer work at St. Andrew's Ukrainian Orthodox Parish where he assisted Father Meroslaw Kryschuk as Palamar (altar server) at the local church services and where he helped train younger church members as altar servers and the future "Palamari". Michael also assisted Father Kryschuk by accompanying him on to some of the rural church services as a Palamar and a cantor. One of these young "Palamari" that Michael trained was Gordon Ostapchuk, who became the head Palamar at St. Andrew's when Michael stepped down due to failing health in the 1980's. Gordon continues today as head Palamar with George following in his father's footsteps. Three other volunteers round out the current Palamar staff today sharing in the duties on various Sundays and weekday requirements.

Pictured in the ALTAR SERVICE 1981-82 photo above, is Michael, Father Kryschuk, Gordon Ostapchuk and three of Michael's grandsons, Robbie, Michael and Dan who were altar boys during those years.

Michael's grandchildren continued to do well in their respective schools, participated in community activities and all entered post secondary institutions and completed their post secondary education. This of course, was Michael's dream coming true — education for his children and grandchildren. It was something that eluded him throughout his lifetime due to the political and social conditions during his early life in Ukraine.

Dorianne Slipchuk was involved in figure skating, getting her figure skating teaching credentials, studied piano, was enrolled in dancing from an early age and then joined and studied Ukrainian Dance with the Shumka Ukrainian Dance Ensemble, completing a tour of Japan and Ukraine. After many years of active participation, she is still an active member of the Shumka alumnus. She was active in CYMK (the Ukrainian Orthodox youth group), singing in the All City Choir and enrolled in the Faculty of Education at the University of Alberta attaining her Bachelor of Education, and has completed her Masters degree in Music Education.

Michael Slipchuk was enrolled in Ukrainian dancing at an early age, was an altar boy at St. Andrew's, played hockey, switched to figure skating where he became a competitive figure skater at the Royal Glenora Club, went on to become the Candian Junior Figure Skating Champion, then won the Canadian Senior Men's Figure Skating Championship in 1992. He competed in the Olympic Games held in Albertville, France and was named as an executive to Canada's Winter Olympic Team at succeeding winter Olympic games. Today he is the Technical Director for the Canadian Figure Skating Association.

George Hupka was involved in Ukrainian Choral groups since his high school years and served as Cantor and Reader of the Epistle in the Ukrainian Orthodox Church since an early age. Besides his involvement in community television in his high school years and his church and choral commitments George graduated from Ryerson University and became a producer with CTV making several trips to Ukraine with University of Saskatchewan groups to film and to produce programs illustrating aspects of life in the Ukraine in the 1980's. Some of these trips occurred during "Perestroika" in 1988-89-90 when Ukraine was attempting to gain her freedom from the Soviet Union. His television productions were ground breaking coverage of the demonstrations in Lviv with the demonstrators toppling Lenin's statue in the public square. To this day, George is still singing with the choir and orchestral ensemble, Lastiwka in Saskatoon.

Tena, George Hupka, Mary Hupka, Rev. Fr. Alex Hupka, Michael. One of the frequent visits to Edmonton when Fr. Alex was posted to All Saints Ukrainian Orthodox Parish in Saskatoon. 1979

Laurie Tkachyk was enrolled in Ukrainian dancing from an early age, studied piano and flute, sang in the All City CYMK Choir, enrolled in the Faculty of Nursing at the University of Alberta and graduated with her Bachelor of Science in Nursing, and completed her Registered Nurse designation. She presently is a practicing nurse in the neo-natal unit at the Grey Nuns' Hospital in Edmonton.

Dan Tkachyk was enrolled in Ukrainian dancing from an early age, was an altar boy at St. Andrew's, participated in community sports excelling in soccer, entered the University of Alberta where he received several undergraduate degrees along with his Master of Arts Degree in Philosophy, studied at Tulane University on his doctorate, then completed his Juris

GEORGE TKACHYK

Doctor law degree at the University of Buffalo. Presently he is practicing law in Rochester, New York.

Robbie Tkachyk was enrolled in Ukrainian dancing at an early age and was an altar boy at St. Andrew's. He competed in community sports, took up electric guitar and drums, played in several high school bands and enrolled at Grant MacEwan University studying Theatre Arts. Presently he is the technical director at Festival Place, a live theatre and performing arts venue in Sherwood Park Alberta.

Michael was extremely proud of all the accomplishments of his grandchildren. Michael and Tena were very busy attending to church services, recitals, concerts, and competitions where their grandchildren participated. While the grandchildren were all very different individuals with a complete spectrum of interests and abilities they all achieved well in school and are successful in their endeavours to this day.

Michael's early years in Canada dating back to his first job with the Canadian Pacific Railway resurfaced in Edmonton just prior to 1988. Dorianne Slipchuk, the eldest grandchild was being courted by a young man by the name of Peter Martyniuk, a young man who belonged to CYMK, sang in the All City Choir, and was an engineering student at the University of Alberta. Dorianne and Peter were married in 1988. During Dorianne's and Peter's courtship, Peter's mother Victoria, and Peter's grandmother were invited over to Michael's and Tena's for dinner. Upon the introductions, it was disclosed that Peter's grandmother could only speak Romanian since she was of Romanian heritage. This was fine since Michael could converse with her since he had knowledge of the Romanian language even though he was a bit rusty at it since it had been 60 years since he left Romanian controlled Bukovina. Peter's grandmother's last name was Charuk. This name rang a bell in Michael's mind. That was the same name of the C.P.R. roadmaster from the Yorkton area, a Bukovinian by birth, that hired Michael when Michael first came to Canada. He asked her if the roadmaster was her husband. She confirmed that it was the same person. Michael's comment was "It is interesting that the wheel has come full circle in such a large country as this when the person that hired me to my first job in Canada was a grandfather to the young man that is marrying my granddaughter 60 years later." Dorianne Slipchuk and Peter Martyniuk were married on August 6, 1988.

Michael did not renew his driver's license during the late 1970's. He relied on the public transit system since the seniors in Edmonton were given a complimentary transit pass initially, then after the first year, they had to pay nominal fee of $25.00 per year thereafter. Michael made the utmost use of his transit pass travelling downtown to the Army and Navy Surplus Store to buy his grandchildren toques, mitts, socks and various sundry items. The Edmonton Transit bus drivers knew him well as he made his daily treks downtown, often referring to him by name.

However, in the 1980's, Michael called George and asked if any one of the family could drive him and Tena down town shopping, since public transit wouldn't do. Everyone in George's household was busy except Laurie and she was just too anxious to take Baba and Dido shopping. She dutifully picked them up and they proceeded to give her directions to a business block on 97 Street across from St. Josephat's Ukrainian Catholic Cathedral. Michael and Tena walked into the office and proceeded with their purchase. They were buying burial plots at St. Michael's Cemetery. Laurie who was in first year university at the time was taken aback by this type of shopping. She hadn't planned on spending an afternoon picking out cemetery plots. Their next stop was down the street at Edmonton Memorials where Michael and Tena were picking out their headstone and asking Laurie's opinion on the suitability of their purchases. Michael and Tena were quite excited about their pre-planning and purchases, but to an 18 year old this was a gruesome topic to be discussing, let alone purchasing. Laurie was most courteous and helpful as she could be during this process but really wished it would soon be over. Laurie reluctantly gave her approval to the headstone. When Laurie got home, she told the story to her immediate family that Baba and Dido were happy as clams that they got this task out of the way. The entire family laughed about this shopping adventure of Laurie's.

In 1984 Mary and Rev. Fr. Alex Hupka moved to Edmonton, where Fr. Alex assumed the position of pastor at St. Anthony's Ukrainian Orthodox Parish. Mary and Alex's son George remained in Saskatoon where he continued as one of the producers at CFQC—TV Saskatoon, the CTV affiliate. Michael was pleased that all his children and grandchildren were in close proximity of their home and visits were quite frequent with the usual family gatherings with all the children and grandchildren.

1986 was Michael's and Tena's 50th wedding anniversary. Michael and Tena informed the children that they wanted everyone to have a good time and forbade the children from organizing and paying for an anniversary get-together. Michael and Tena insisted on throwing a party for family and friends. They wouldn't hear of the children helping out with the expenses. They got the St. Andrew's ladies to cater, booked an orchestra and invited family and friends from Ontario, Manitoba, Saskatchewan, Alberta, British Columbia and especially their St. Andrew's friends to join in the celebrations.

Michael and Tena Tkachyk's 50th Wedding Anniversary August, 1986
Front Row: Robbie Tkachyk, Mary Hupka, Michael, Tena, Lessia Slipchuk
Second Row: George Tkachyk, Rev. Fr. Alex Hupka, Laurie Tkachyk, Dorianne Slipchuk, Gerry Slipchuk
Top Row: Vera Tkachyk, Danny Tkachyk, Michael Slipchuk, George Hupka

With Father Kryschuk, Father Alex and Archbishop John officiating, a special Moleben (Blessing) was held in the church and a banquet and party followed with approximately 150 people in attendance, including a few people from the original wedding party.

Michael and Tena Tkachyk toasting their 50th Wedding Anniversary Archbishop John on the left with Mary Hupka on the right. The traditional wedding bread consists of braided bread decorated with doves made of bread dough. Garlands of periwinkle decorate both bread and table.

The banquet Master of Ceremonies was their close friend Bill Dymianiw who did an exceptional job of entertaining guests and introducing guest speakers with Wedding Anniversary greetings. Of course the Pohoreski family orchestra consisting of Pauline Patrick on keyboard, Marie Oleksyn on guitar, Tony Pohoreski on banjo, Orest Pohoreski on saxophone and Lessia Slipchuk on piano, rendered a few old time polkas just for old time's sake and kept everyone dancing all night.

As Michael advanced into his late seventies, the yard work, snow shoveling and general maintenance of the duplex was becoming a greater and greater task. Michael for the first time in his life found the work around the yard difficult. He had developed late onset diabetes. Michael and Tena attended diabetic classes at the Royal Alexandra Hospital to learn how to cope with the diabetic condition. Later Tena would also develop the late onset diabetes as well. The diabetes was diet controlled plus Michael was placed on medication to help control it. In 1985 Michael was diagnosed with an arrhythmic heart condition and the doctors recommended that a pacemaker be installed to control his heart rate. The pacemaker was installed and a noticeable positive change could be seen in Michael. Although he often commented about that mechanical thing, "that timer" he called it, in there (pointing to his heart) being responsible for his well being and not his own heart. He was pleased to have the independence of doing what he wanted to do, but he knew that he was dependent on "the timer". These setbacks affected how much and what kind of physical activity Michael could perform. Yes, he had grandchildren and children that would come over and clear the snow and mow the lawn and trim hedges, however his independence was slowly waning.

In 1988 Michael and Tena decided to sell their duplex at 7005-101 Street and move into St. Andrew's Selo, a seniors apartment complex not far from where they lived and still close to St. Andrew's Parish. They did not have a problem selling the duplex since it was on a bus route and located close to all amenities. Clearing out all of their belongings was a task. There were half gallon, quart and pint jars from the 1940's, 1950's and earlier, when canning was the primary method of preserving foods. There were photos, documents, and various nostalgia that had to be dealt with. Thankfully Michael kept many of his documents and photos, since they form the basis of this written account of his life. A garage sale was held to dispose of all the surplus items that Michael and Tena would not require at the apartment. Much of the leftover goods from the garage sale ended up in George's and Lessia's garages and basements.

While there was sadness mixed with nostalgia on that last day at their duplex, there was also a feeling of relief that there would be no more maintenance concerns with the aging duplex. At the apartment they would have no yard maintenance or building maintenance. They would be in a Ukrainian speaking complex and have no responsibilities except to look after themselves. Their one bedroom apartment was certainly sufficient for their needs.

Michael and Tena enjoyed life at "Selo". It was a building with many of the seniors that they had worked and socialized with at St. Andrew's before they all became "seniors".

Michael often commented that he should have sold the house sooner. Life at "Selo" was good. He often joked that he was living the life of an aristocrat—no mundane daily chores, his grass was mown, the snow shoveled from his walks, the boiler of his heating system repaired and functioning at 100%, the flower garden groomed and the building maintained. St. Andrew's Men's Club provided complimentary taxi service to the seniors at "Selo" if they were attending church related functions at St. Andrew's parish or at any of the other Ukrainian Orthodox Parishes in Edmonton. Michael and Tena really didn't need that service often since they had three children and five grandchildren to ferry them about the city, plus the Edmonton Transit bus passes. As Michael said—"Life was Good."

In 1991 Michael and Tena celebrated their 55th wedding anniversary at "Selo". It was a low key affair compared their 50th wedding anniversary. Michael and Tena celebrated with the "Moleben" (Thanksgiving Prayers), a dinner and the usual family group photographs. The celebration involved only the immediate family of Mary and Alex, George and Vera, and Lessia and Gerry, and the grandchildren, the residents of "Selo" and Wally and Ann Tkach. Wally was the distant second cousin from the Edwand district of Alberta.

Michael and Tena celebrating their 55th Wedding Anniversary with grandchildren Michael Slipchuk, Dan Tkachyk, Robbie Tkachyk, Peter Martyniuk, Dorianne Slipchuk-Martyniuk, Laurie Tkachyk.

Ann and Wally Tkach, Michael's second cousin, his only relative on the Tkach side of the family living in Canada.

During these golden years Michael and Tena made the most of their time at Selo. They attended the Golden Age Club meetings at St. Andrew's Church on Tuesday mornings for fellowship and coffee. They sang in the Golden Age Choir, performing at Senior's Homes, at Nursing Homes, at Shopping Malls, for shut-ins, Caroling during the Christmas season and at various concerts. Michael and Tena went on various bus excursions with the Golden Age Club touring Alberta Tourist locations such as the Ukrainian Village, Kalyna Country, Fort MacMurray and Bar-V-Nok, the Ukrainian Orthodox Youth Church Camp. They were in attendance at Church at St. Andrew's every Sunday in their usual pew, with Michael checking and maintaining the

Michael and Tena celebrating their 55th Wedding Anniversary
Mary Hupka, Rev. Fr. Alex Hupka, Michael, Tena, George Tkachyk,
Vera Tkachyk, Gerry Slipchuk, Lessia Slipchuk. 1991

memorial candle stands, votive candle stands and assisting his Palamar protégé, Gordon Ostapchuk whenever needed. With the Golden Age Club, Church and Selo activities and family get-togethers they certainly didn't let any moss grow under their feet. They continued their busy schedule into the early 1990's.

DREAM TO REALITY

Michael and Tena with their Grandchildren. Christmas, January 7, 1991

Time, however was taking its toll on Michael's health.

On October 19, 1991, Michael succumbed to congenital heart failure and passed away 17 days shy of his 89th birthday.

Tena passed away on August 14, 2004 at age 92.

EPILOGUE

Michael's Tkaczyk's life was a life of dreams; a life of dreams that he worked at with purpose and dedication.

Michael was one of several hundred thousand Ukrainians who came to Canada with dreams of Freedom and Success in carving out a new life.

Michael found his freedom in Canada. He treasured it. He made use of it by supporting the country that gave him a chance at Freedom. He got his Canadian citizenship. He learned English. He worked hard, saved his money and made purchases of land to secure his future. Only then could he return to the Soviet Union to bring his daughter Mary to Canada so that she may benefit from, and enjoy the freedoms in Canada.

Michael's dreams of bringing the rest of his siblings and his father to Canada were dashed by the outbreak of World War II and the subsequent establishment of the "Iron Curtain".

As mentioned previously, Michael came to Canada and worked hard at menial jobs to make money. He saved his hard earned money.

GEORGE TKACHYK

He bought land, cleared it of trees and brush, cultivated it and produced crops of grain, vegetables and even some livestock.

He learned to read and write in the English language and worked his way up from a casual part time laborer to become a section foreman with the Canadian Pacific Railways.

Even with his limited education he made the best of his situation.

He bought farm land, then a business; and made it a successful financial venture so that he could educate his family and finance his future retirement.

In the meantime he provided all his children with the opportunity to get what he never did attain—a secondary education, a post secondary education—something that eluded him due to the chaotic and despotic milieu in which he grew up during his childhood, teen years and early adult years.

Michael never missed a Canadian election, be it municipal, provincial or federal. His opportunity to make a choice and vote was a treasured act. He never had the opportunity to have a say in politics in his Ukraine, thus this one freedom was one he would cherish above all. He imparted that treasure of voting on his children and subsequently on his grandchildren.

Michael like most everyone disliked paying taxes, but did so dutifully. His comment on taxes was philosophical:

"The taxes we pay are a small price for the freedoms we cherish. Where I came from there were no taxes, but we had no freedoms or choices either. Be thankful that you have the freedoms of religion, education, movement, speech and opportunities to work and further

yourself career-wise and financially, and for the greatest freedom of all—<u>to choose your government</u>. Paying taxes? They are but a minor inconvenience in our lives".

While Michael had little formal education he earned his achievements through hard work, self education, self determination and experience. He passed that attitude on to his children. He didn't have to say it. He led by example. All of Michael's children married into families of like minded, self-reliant and determined first generation Canadians, or immigrants from Ukraine. Those combined positive attitudes and determination continue on and will do so for generations to come.

Michael and many thousands of immigrants like him paid back to Canada with hard work, determination and a commitment to make a great country better. They have left a legacy of families that continues to contribute to the fabric of Canada, the United States and freedom loving democracies through Politics, Health Care, Science, the Arts, Education, Law, Religion, Sports and Athletics, Business and Finance and Communication. Could a country ask more?

Michael passed away in October of 1991.

Tena passed away in August of 2004.

Daughter Mary retired from teaching prior to their son George being born. Dobrodiyka Mary and Very Rev. Fr. Hupka served the Ukrainian Orthodox Church of Canada for many years and are presently retired and living in Saskatoon.

Grandson George Hupka left CTV and started his own video production company, Downstream Productions, producing feature length documentaries for television specialty channels, freelancing for television networks, doing special short features for the Vancouver Olympic Games and he worked the Vancouver Olympic Games (2010) for CTV, TSN and their related television outlets and national news and sports TV networks.

Daughter Lessia retired from teaching with Edmonton Public Schools as a teacher and a Bilingual Ukrainian Language Program Consultant. Her husband Gerry passed away in 1999. Lessia remarried in 2004 to Orest Mulka. Orest passed away in 2010. Lessia presently lives in Edmonton.

Granddaughter Dorianne Slipchuk-Martyniuk is married to Peter Martyniuk. They are the parents of two daughters Melia and Tianna. Dorianne is presently teaching for Edmonton Public Schools, completed her Masters Degree in Music Education in 2011 and choreographs figure skating at the Royal Glenora Figure Skating Club.

Grandson Michael Slipchuk, after winning the Canadian Senior Men's Figure Skating Championship (1992) and competing for Canada in the Albertville Winter Olympics (1992), turned professional and taught figure skating at the Glencoe Figure Skating Club in Calgary, represented Canada at International Figure Skating Judging revisions and is presently the director of the technical development component of Skate Canada.

DREAM TO REALITY

Son George retired from the Edmonton Public School Board in 1997 after 36 years of service as a teacher, consultant, principal and Supervisor of Consulting Services. After a 10 year hobby career in real estate, George actually retired. Today George and Vera are actively involved at St. Andrew's Ukrainian Orthodox Church continuing on where Michael and Tena left off with church related duties. George and Vera live in Edmonton.

Granddaughter Laurie Tkachyk is married to Jeff Landro. She presently continues her career as a Registered Nurse at the Grey Nun's Hospital in the neo natal unit.

Grandson Daniel Tkachyk is married to Ann Bianchi. After teaching philosophy at the Brockport campus of the State University of New York, Dan completed his law degree at Buffalo and is presently an attorney with the New York State Supreme Court in Rochester, New York.

Grandson Rob Tkachyk following high school, enrolled in Theatre Arts at Grant MacEwan University and is presently the Technical Director at Festival Place, a Live Theatre and concert venue in Sherwood Park, Alberta.

Unfortunately Michael did not live to see all his grandchildren complete their post secondary schooling, and take up their present careers. He would have approved of all their choices and successes.

Were Michael's dream's fulfilled? We believe they were.

GEORGE TKACHYK

While Michael, himself did not achieve his dreamed of education, he became a successful laborer, foreman, farmer and businessman. He nurtured, coached and ensured that his children and grandchildren had the opportunity to achieve their educational and career goals and to give back to a country that provided him and subsequently his family with the freedoms and opportunites to grow and succeed.

We owe a debt of gratitude to Michael and all those immigrants—the Hupka's, the Nychyk's, the Kowalski's, the Slipchuk's, the Pohoreski's, the Panchuk's, the Dobrowolski's, the Smetaniuk's, the Yuzik's and all the countless others who came to Canada in the 1890's, early 1900's, prior to the first world war, during the inter war period and prior to the second world war with the vision of finding their dreams and freedoms; and in doing so, helped instill those attitudes in their children to build this great country in which we live.

God Bless Them! Vichna Yeem Pamyat! Eternal Be Their Memories!

APPENDIX I

GEORGE TKACHYK

Romanian Certificate of Birth and Baptism,
Michael Tcaci, (Tkach) (Tkaczyk) 1926.

Romanian Registration form for a Marriage Certificate, Michael Tcaci (Tkach) (Tkaczyk) and Paraskeva/Paraska Kotyk 1926.

Romanian Marriage Certificate Michael Tkach (Tkaczyk) 1928

DREAM TO REALITY

Michael's Romanian Passport. 1928

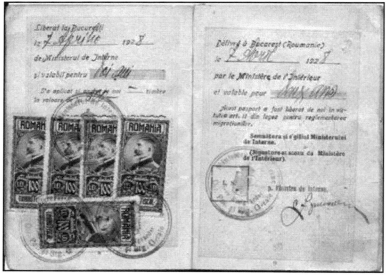

*Michael's Passport photo wearing his "kiptar",
a Ukrainian embroidered vest. 1928.*

DREAM TO REALITY

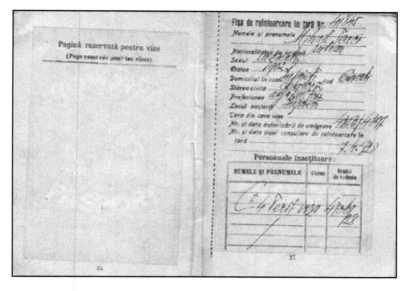

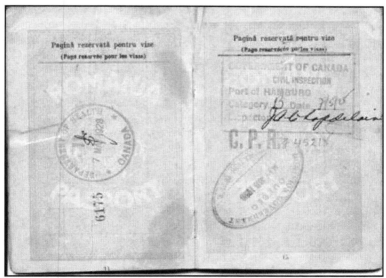

Michael's Romanian Passport with port and government stamps.

GEORGE TKACHYK

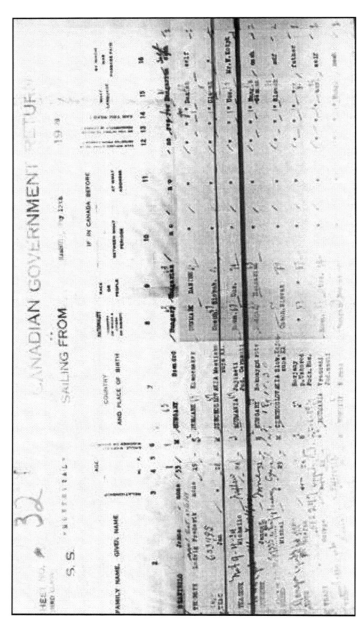

Ship Passenger Manifest from S.S. Montroyal, Hamburg to Quebec, arriving May 23, 1928. (see extension on opposite page) Michailo Tkaczuk highlighted—indicating country of Origin-Roumania, Passage Paid by Wm. Kotyk. Note spelling of name.

DREAM TO REALITY

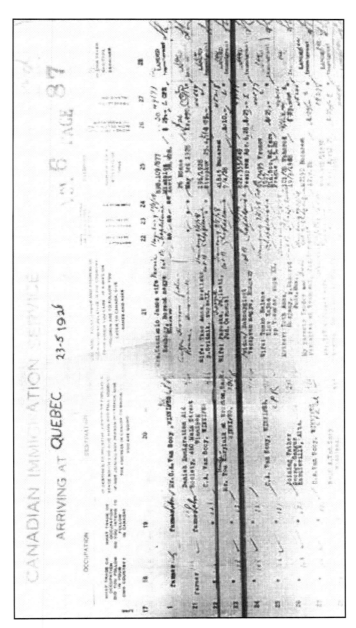

Extension of Montroyal Passenger manifest from previous page showing Sponsor—Tom Kuryluik. Second last column indicates the amount of money Michael brought into Canada—$10.00.

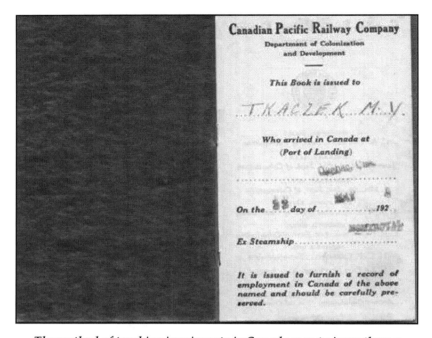

The method of tracking immigrants in Canada was to issue them a booklet that they had to carry with them and produce to authorities when requested. This record was required for the first six months to one year to ensure that the sponsoring individual (Tom Kuryliuk in this case) actually employed them or housed them. Once the immigrant attained a job, the records were then maintained by the employer. There were no government sponsored social safety nets. Family and sponsors were responsible for the immigrant and his where—abouts.

DREAM TO REALITY

NAME OF FARMER WITH WHOM PLACED	LOCATION	PLACED BY	DATE

NAME OF FARMER WITH WHOM PLACED	LOCATION	PLACED BY	DATE

APPENDIX II

Railway pass issued to Tena Tkaczyk as spouse of a C.P.R employee in 1949 when she had to travel to Rochester, Minnesota for her spinal fusion surgery. Railway companies allowed employee pass transfers anywhere in North America for sister railway companies.

GEORGE TKACHYK

BROTHERHOOD OF MAINTENANCE OF WAY EMPLOYES
OFFICIAL DUES RECEIPT
GRAND LODGE HEADQUARTERS: 61 PUTNAM AVE., DETROIT, MICH.

Date Paid: DEC 21st 1943

Y 20589

THIS IS TO CERTIFY that the bearer, Brother M. Thaczyk
Mem. No. L-75987, Employed as T.F. (Occupation)
on C.P. R.R., a member of Lodge No. 304
has paid dues on the date and in the amount shown hereon,
to April 1st 1944
and is entitled to all benefits and privileges of the Brotherhood, as provided in the Constitution and By-Laws, unless revoked.

Amount Paid:
- Initiation Fee $
- Grand Lodge Dues $ 2.50
- System Dues $ 1.50
- Subordinate Lodge Dues $ .50
- TOTAL $ 4.50

THIS RECEIPT IS NOT TRANSFERABLE AND IS VOID IF ALTERED IN ANY WAY

Grand Lodge Secretary-Treasurer

DREAM TO REALITY

Michael's Income Tax Notice of Assessment—1943. Note the mis-spelling of his name as referred to in the transliteration paragraph at the beginning of the biography.

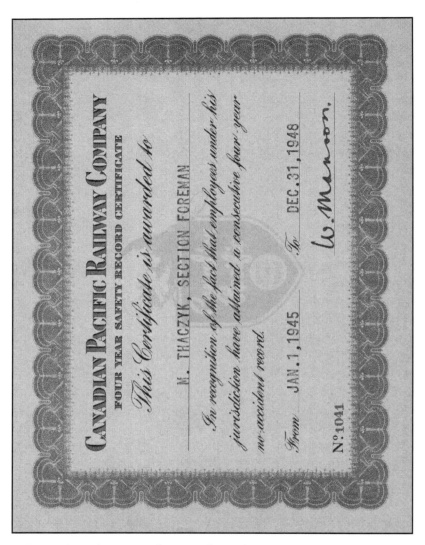

Recognition from Canadian Pacific Railway Company for Michael's safety record, prior to him leaving Canadian Pacific Railways in 1949.

BIBLIOGRAPHY

1. Garland History Book Committee, 1874-1985, In Memory Of Our Pioneers, Friesen Printers, D.W. Friesen & Sons Ltd., Altona, Manitoba, Canada.1989. First Printing.
2.-8. Simpson, G. W. Ukraine, An Atlas Of Its History and Geography, University of Saskatchewan, Oxford University Press, London, Toronto, New York. 1941
9. Pier 21 Historical Society, Halifax, Nova Scotia, 2006 Archives Canada, Ottawa, Ontario, 2006
10-12. Saskatchewan Wheat Pool, Calendar / Map of Rail Lines and Grain Elevator Locations, 1924, 1928, et al.
13. Pier 21 Historical Society, Halifax, Nova Scotia, 2006 Archives Canada, Ottawa, Ontario, 2006
14. The Ukrainian Historical Committee, Follow The Furrow, North Battleford and District, McIntosh Publishing Co. Ltd. North Battleford, Saskatchewan, Canada. 1985
15. Archives Canada, Archivianet.ca
16. Hall, Frank, Manitoba Historical Society, The Carleton Trail, The First Western Highway. 2002
17. Community Memories, A Line Through The Wilderness, Humboldt and District Museum, Humboldt, Saskatchewan. 2008

18. Blaine Lake District History Book Committee, <u>Bridging The Years: Era Of Blaine Lake And District, 1790-1980</u>. Freisen printers, Altona, Manitoba. 1984.
19. Marples, David, Professor of History, University of Alberta, <u>Formation Of Soviet Russia 90 Years Ago Changed Course Of History</u>, Edmonton Journal, Thursday, November 8, 2007.
20. Krawchenko, Bohdan, Canadian Institute of Ukrainian Studies, University of Alberta, Edmonton, AB, <u>The Great Famine Of 1932-33, Part I</u>, Visnyk / The Herald, No. 3. LXXXV, Winnipeg Manitoba, March 2008.
21. Krawchenko, Bohdan, <u>The Great Famine 1932-33, Part II</u>, Canadian Institute of Ukrainian Studies, University of Alberta, Edmonton, AB, Visnyk / The Herald, No. 4. LXXXV, Winnipeg, Manitoba, April, 2008.
22. Gronlid and District Historical Society, <u>Our Courageous Pioneers, History of Gronlid and Surrounding Districts</u>, Phillips Publishers Ltd., Melfort, Saskatchewan, 1991.
23. Ukrainian Association of Victims of Russian Communist Terror, <u>The Black Deeds Of The Kremlin, A White Book, Vol. I</u>, Basilian Press, Toronto, 1953.
24. The Democratic Organization Of Ukrainians Formerly Persecuted By The Soviet Regime in U.S.A., <u>The Black Deeds Of The Kremlin, A White Book, Vol. 2, The Great Famine In Ukraine in 1932-1933</u>, Globe Press, Detroit, U.S.A., 1955.
25. Kashuba, Steven, <u>Once Lived A Village</u> Trafford Publishing, Victoria, B.C. Canada, 2007
26. University of Regina and Canadian Plains Research Center, <u>Encyclopedia of Saskatchewan</u> University of Regina, Regina, Saskatchewan. 2007
27. Ostryzniuk, Natalie. 1999 "<u>Savella Stechishin, An Ethnocultural Feminist in Ukrainian Culture in Saskatchewan</u>", Saskatchewan History 51(2):12-28.

28. Ukrainian Canadian Weekly, July 14, 2002. No.28, Vol. LXX.
29. University of Saskatchewan Archives, <u>History, Honorary Degrees</u>. University of Saskatchewan, Saskatoon, Saskatchewan. 2007

Edwards Brothers Malloy
Oxnard, CA USA
November 18, 2013